ADVANCE PRAISE FOR

Power & Voice in Research with Children

"*Power and Voice in Research with Children* is exemplary of the new reconceptualist scholarship in early childhood education that rethinks the nature and process of doing research with children. Employing critical humanistic and decolonizing methodologies that respect what children have to say and that are attentive to and appreciative of their complex modalities of expression, the authors of *Power and Voice in Research with Children* refuse to reduce childrens' voices to sterile categorizations and passive articulations. The result is an important book that bravely challenges dominant theoretical approaches in early childhood education as well as dominant cultural formations and social relations within the wider capitalist societies."

Peter McLaren, Professor of Urban Schooling, Graduate School of Education and Information Studies, University of California, Los Angeles

"Throughout the world, children coming to the schooling enterprise from linguistic and cultural groups that differ from the mainstream confront a set of intellectual, social and cultural transitions that are too often a disadvantage to their educational well being. *Power and Voice in Research with Children* is simultaneously challenging and instructive to our research and practice colleagues about such circumstances and provides insights regarding research and practice that helps us to grasp the intricacies of diversity and early schooling. I congratulate the diversity of thinking among the editors and authors in their elegant and critical contribution."

Eugene E. Garcia, Dean, College of Education, Arizona State University, Tempe,

Power & Voice
in Research
with Children

Rethinking Childhood

Joe L. Kincheloe and Janice A. Jipson
General Editors

Vol. 33

PETER LANG
New York • Washington, D.C./Baltimore • Bern
Frankfurt am Main • Berlin • Brussels • Vienna • Oxford

Power & Voice
in Research
with Children

Lourdes Diaz Soto & Beth Blue Swadener
Editors

PETER LANG
New York • Washington, D.C./Baltimore • Bern
Frankfurt am Main • Berlin • Brussels • Vienna • Oxford

Library of Congress Cataloging-in-Publication Data

Power and voice in research with children / edited by Lourdes Diaz Soto, Beth Blue Swadener.
p. cm. — (Rethinking childhood ; v. 33)
Includes bibliographical references.
1. Early childhood education—Research—United States—Methodology.
2. Children of minorities—Education (Early childhood)—United States—Case studies.
3. Education, Bilingual—United States—Case studies.
4. Critical pedagogy—United States. I. Soto, Lourdes Diaz..
II. Swadener, Beth Blue. III. Series.
LB1139.225.P69   372.21072'073—dc22   2004010421
ISBN 0-8204-7414-2
ISSN 1086-7155

Bibliographic information published by **Die Deutsche Bibliothek.**
Die Deutsche Bibliothek lists this publication in the "Deutsche
Nationalbibliografie"; detailed bibliographic data is available
on the Internet at http://dnb.ddb.de/.

Cover design by Lisa Barfield
Cover art by Renée Krendell

© 2005 Peter Lang Publishing, Inc., New York
275 Seventh Avenue, 28th Floor, New York, NY 10001
www.peterlangusa.com

Printed in the United States of America

To our beloved children
Blue
Daniel
Deane
Kathy

► CONTENTS

PART I. ISSUES OF POWER AND VOICE

PART II. RACE/ETHNICITY, CLASS, AND GENDER IDENTITIES

PART III. LINGUISTIC AND CULTURAL IDENTITIES

► FIGURES

►FOREWORD

JOE L. KINCHELOE

It is my pleasure to write a foreword to Lourdes Diaz Soto and Beth Blue Swadener's book in our series. Over the last fifteen years Soto and Swadener have become powerful voices advocating for educational and social justice for children, especially marginalized young people in America. Dissatisfied with traditional shibboleths about children and the status quo of early childhood education and childhood studies, Soto has pushed the envelope of scholarship in the area as the context that shapes children's lives has changed over the last several decades. With the advent of socioeconomic changes, technological developments, globalization, and the perceived inadequacy of an old paradigm of early childhood education and childhood studies, Western societies and increasingly other parts of the world have witnessed the emergence a new type of childhood. This transitional phase of childhood has been accompanied by a paradigm shift led by Soto and others in the way many scholars study childhood and situate it in social, cultural, political, educational, and economic relations. Lourdes Diaz Soto's work is central to an understanding of this new way of conceptualizing childhood.

Swadener has also been dedicated to the reconceptualization of early childhood education and childhood studies. When Shirley Steinberg and I were writing *Kinderculture: The Corporate Construction of Childhood* in the mid-1990s, I quickly realized that Swadener was necessary reading to understand the state of the field of early childhood education. At a time when too many of her colleagues continued to operate in a Eurocentric, patriarchal, and class-insensitive modality, Swadener was pointing out the problems with traditional modes of viewing children, childhood, and childhood education. Since that time I have read her work carefully, gaining insight in the process into issues of justice for children in both a global spatial context and in the conceptual domain of research on children. Beth Blue Swadener is a key figure in the critical paradigm shift in childhood education.

This scholarly shift takes direct exception to the positivist view of childhood and its expression of a universal, uniformly developmentalist conception of the normal child. This positivist passive conception of children as receivers of adult input and socialization strategies has been replaced by a view of the child as an active agent capable of contributing to the construction of his or her own subjectivity. For those operating in the parameters of the new paradigm, the purpose of studying and working with children is not to remove the boundary between childhood and adulthood but to gain a thicker, more compelling picture of the complexity of the culture, politics, and psychology of childhood. With its penchant for decontextualization and inability to account for contemporary social, cultural, political, economic, and epistemological changes, the positivist paradigm is not adequate for this task.

Insisting that children existed outside of society and could only be brought in from the cold by adult socialization that led to development, the positivist view constructed research and childhood professional practices that routinely excluded children's voices. Advocates of the new paradigm have maintained time and again that such positivist silencing and general disempowerment is not in the best interests of children. In the name of child protection and family values, advocates of the new paradigm have argued, children are often rendered powerless and vulnerable in their everyday lives. As they construct their view of children as active constructors of their own worlds, proponents of the new paradigm work hard to emphasize the personhood of children. The children of the new paradigm both construct their worlds and are constructed by their worlds. Thus, in ethnographic and other forms of new paradigm childhood study, children, like adults, are positioned as co-participants in research—not as mere objects to be observed and categorized. Advocates of the new paradigm operating in the domain of social, political, and educational policy making for children contend that such activity must always take into account the perspectives of children to inform their understanding of particular situations.

Thus, central to the new paradigm is the effort to make sure children are intimately involved in shaping their social, psychological, and educational lives. In many ways such a new paradigmatic task is much easier said than done. In contemporary U.S. society in particular is to expose oneself to ridicule and dismissal by conservative child advocates in diverse social, political, cultural, and educational arenas. Such child-empowerment advocacy is represented by right-wing commentators as a permissive relinquishing of adult power over impudent and disrespectful children.

Undoubtedly, it will be a difficult struggle to reposition the child in twenty-first-century social relationships.

In rejecting the positivist paradigm of childhood passivity and innocence advocates of the new empowerment paradigm are *not* contending that there is no time that children need adult protection—that would be a silly assertion. Children, like human beings in general, too often find themselves victimized by abuse, neglect, racism, class bias, and sexism as Soto has argued in numerous books and articles. The salient point is that instead of further infantilizing children and rendering them more passive, the new paradigm attempts to employ their perspectives in solving their problems. In addition, such transformative researchers and child professionals work to help children develop a critical political consciousness as they protect their access to diverse knowledges and technologies. As is the nature of developing a critical consciousness in any context, we are arguing that children in social, cultural, psychological, and pedagogical contexts need help in developing the ability to analyze, critique, and change for the better their position in the world.

Another dimension of the new paradigm of child study involves the explicit rejection of positivism's universalist conception of childhood and child development. When advocates of the new paradigm enter diverse class cultures and racial/ethnic cultures they find childhoods that look quite different from the white, middle-/upper-middle-class, English speaking one presented by positivism. In these particularistic childhoods Soto and other researchers find great complexity and diversity within these specific categories. For example, the social, cultural, and political structures that shape these childhoods and the children who inhabit them are engaged in profoundly different ways by particular children in specific circumstances. Thus, such structures never *determine* who children are no matter how much consistency in macrostructures may exist. The particular and the general, the micro and the macro, agency and structure always interact in unpredictable ways to shape the everyday life of children. A central theme of the new paradigm reemerges—children shape and are shaped by the world around them.

Soto and Swadener's work represents the critical new paradigm in childhood studies and childhood education. The use of critical in this context signals the critical in critical theory and its concern with power structures and their influence in everyday life. In the case of contemporary children the sociopolitical and economic structures shaped by corporate power buoyed by the logic of capital as well as patriarchal structures with their oppressive positioning of women and children are central concerns of the critical paradigm. In this context the importance of Soto and Swadener's contribution to the new paradigm of elementary education and childhood studies emerges. Their work has sought out those domains of oppression so often overlooked by other researchers. Unfortunately, in the first decade of the twenty-first century the critical new paradigmatic work of Soto and Swadener has become even more important than before as new and more powerful oppressive forces have been unleashed. In the name of the free market, neoliberalism, privatization, and grotesque forms of trickle down economics the well-being of children is further undermined. I am thankful that Lourdes Diaz Soto and Beth Blue Swadener are here to raise questions about and propose solutions to these problems. When these two important scholars pool their intellectual resources, a synergy is created that explodes with new insights and creative modes of transgressive practice.

ACKNOWLEDGMENTS

Joe Kincheloe and Shirley Steinberg are powerful examples of mentors who support diverse scholars on a daily basis—our heartfelt thanks for their encouragement and friendship. We would also like to express our gratitude to Peter Lang Publishing for their support of our work. To our families and allies, we owe a long-standing debt for encouraging, nourishing, and sometimes "tolerating" our passion for social justice and equity.

Our work has also been greatly influenced by the scholarship and friendship of Gloria Anzaldua and Sally Lubeck. Their voices will be missed, but their legacies will live on in all of us.

INTRODUCTION

LOURDES DIAZ SOTO
BETH BLUE SWADENER

*Seeing with the eyes of compassion and understanding
we can offer the next century a beautiful garden and clear path.*
Thich Nhat Hanh (1991, p. 134)

This book problematizes the complexities and contradictions we face when conducting research with children/young people. Our goal is to critically examine and present possibilities for the roles that the often forgotten or misunderstood voices of children can play in research and deconstruct some of the power relations and colonizing discourses between adult researchers and the children we study. The main focus of this volume is on the nature of the relationship between the researcher and the child and how we might more adequately represent the complexities, multiple perspectives, and understandings that emerge when the research process includes, indeed foregrounds, children and youth.

Contributors explore issues of imposition and power so inherent in traditional research and how these are even more problematic with children, in their position as the "less powerful" and having "less voice." The volume documents and discusses how children's voices can better guide us in learning about multiple identities, including culture, social class, linguistic diversity, and gender. The authors represent critical, antiracist, feminist, ethnically diverse scholars intent on contributing to the process and construction of new knowledge by documenting the often-disregarded voices of children. Their work represents newly evolving possibilities for related fields by highlighting contemporary postmodern experiences reflected in children's voices and perspectives, as co-participants in the research process.

This book has been "on our minds" for many years. Several of us have presented on the topic of "children's voices in research" at annual meetings of the American Educational Research Association and other conferences. We are also long-standing colleagues and allies in the "reconceptualizing early childhood" tradition, as for so long many of our own voices have been marginalized as we call for decolonizing methodologies in the field (see, e.g., Cannella & Viruru, 2004; Soto & Swadener, 2002).

A growing number of international "reconceptualizing" scholars continue to critique dominant models of scholarship that have often privileged narrow areas of largely quantifiable research and have done little to enlighten the needs of learners in the democratic sphere. We have joined with these reconceptualist colleagues in the United States, New Zealand, Australia, Europe, and Africa (to name but a few: Sally Lubeck, Mimi Block, Gaile Cannella, Linda T. Smith, Jan Jipson, Shirley Kessler, Bill Ayers, Joe Tobin, Amos Hatch, Michael O'Loughlin, Sue Gieshaber, Rich Johnson, and many others) in both critiquing dominant theory in early childhood and engaging in work that attempts to open up new spaces of possibility. While we dream about social justice and equity, we join the contributors to this book in pushing the boundaries of research and scholarship that will open up new spaces of possibility in research with children and wish to trouble prevailing, often ageist and disempowering, assumptions about younger persons and what it means to learn from and with them.

The chapters in this book are concerned with issues of power while ascribing to decolonizing methodologies with children. Smith (1999), who inspires us to work with decolonizing methodologies, uses words like *claiming, testimonies, storytelling, celebrating survival, indigenizing, intervening, revitalizing, connecting, reading, writing, representing, gendering, envisioning, reframing, restoring, returning, democratizing, networking, naming, protecting, creating, negotiating, discovering,* and *sharing* (pp. 143–161).

Research "through imperial eyes" describes an approach that Western ideas about the most fundamental things are the only ideas possible to hold, certainly the only rational ideas, and the only ideas that can make sense of the world, reality, of social life, and of human beings. We argue that a similar decolonizing project is needed and is, in fact, under way in much of the research with children described within this volume.

ORGANIZATION OF THE BOOK

We have sought to include chapters that add to the complexities of deconstructing power and voice issues with young people and have encouraged contributors to present their work in ways that best mirror their concerns. We also asked all contributing authors to keep their chapters brief, allowing for more stories to be told and critical points to be emphasized, versus embedded in lengthy theoretical discourse. In organizing these diverse chapters, it became clear that many essays defied categorization but were texts that could be read in multiple ways. Our categories for organizing the book sought to emphasize some of the dynamics of power, voice, and multiple identities in doing research with children and youth.

In the foreword, Joe Kincheloe, distinguished professor and prolific scholar, sets the stage for us to consider the needed paradigm shifts in research and scholarship with children. Kincheloe reminds us of the effects of the positivist paradigms on childhood.

Part I, "Issues of Power and Voice," frames several overarching or contextual issues in doing research with children. Chapters in this section deconstruct the roles of "adults" and "children" in research. Lourdes Diaz Soto's opening piece (chapter 1), depicts children's drawings/voices in New York City during the World Trade Center tragedy. Soto, relying on narrative inquiry and the notion of mourning, asks us to "visualize voice" with children who may comprise the best source of theory. Janette Habashi's work (chapter 2) provides readers with a direct encounter with the narrative of a Palestinian girl, with whom the author seeks to be an ally and coresearcher. This chapter raises a number of paradoxes in doing research with children, as well as in the construction of "childhood" itself.

In their contribution to this section (chapter 3), Jennifer Jipson and Janice Jipson, a mother and daughter research team, critically examine relationships between researchers and subjects from transdisciplinary and intergenerational perspectives. Their journey is formative and continues to evolve, helping to guide each other's perspectives and scholarship. Elizabeth Graue and Margaret Hawkins (chapter 4) draw from their experiences as coresearchers and mothers, doing research in local schools and community contexts.

In the final chapter in this section (chapter 5), Brian Edmiston describes his "coming home to research" as he analyzes his play with his young son over a period of six years. His chapter, like others in this section, deconstructs assumptions about adult and child roles and viewpoints and argues that sharing authority while playing with children allows us to explore the meanings of events in imagined spaces.

Part II, "Race/Ethnicity, Class, and Gender Identities," includes chapters that draw from experiences of researchers in several national and local contexts, working with children and youth who are at the margins in many ways, yet powerfully self-expressive in others. Chapters in this section foreground children's own emerging, changing, and, at times, hybrid identities, as well as their views on which adults in their lives interact with them in meaningful ways. Other chapters explore the use of the arts and writing process in children's self-expression and identity development.

In chapter 6, Marguerite Vanden Wyngaard draws from her research on African-American high school students' perceptions of what constitutes culturally relevant pedagogy and how some teachers are "keepin' it real," including respecting their cultural and other identities. Yu-Chi Sun's contribution to this section (chapter 7) uses narrative analysis of her interviews with young Chinese girls who had immigrated to the United States in their elementary years. Respectful of cultural traditions that value listening over voice for young women, Sun sensitively facilitates their storytelling about life in ESL classrooms and other border-crossing experiences.

In (chapter 8), Mindy Blaise analyzes how femininity was performed and understood by young children in a kindergarten classroom by locating five gender discourses. Drawing from feminist poststructuralist understandings of knowledge, language, discourse, and power, Blaise demonstrates ways in which children took active part in the gendering process. In chapter 9, Susan Matoba Adler draws from her many years of research with children and her own family experiences to reflect on the diverse voices of Asian-American children. Her chapter contrasts self-expression in formal settings and with peers or other native first-language users and describes forms of "situational silencing" of voices often based on the degree of acculturation of these children.

Chapters 10 and 11 both address alternative schools or informal programs for children living in difficult circumstances and experiencing social exclusion, and include an analysis of the children's artwork and other forms of expression that reflect their identities, desires, and dreams. Aggelos Hatzinikolaou, with Soula Mitakidou, (chapter 10) describe the situation of Roma children and families in Greece and the many forms of social exclusion and oppression they have experienced. Working for many years in an alternative program for Roma students, Hatzinikolaou describes an extended activity in which children apply the United Nations Convention on the Rights of the Child to their own lives, in particular their concerns about housing.

In chapter 11, the last chapter in this section, Beth Blue Swadener reflects on her volunteer work with street children in Nairobi, Kenya, focusing on the use of expressive arts as a vehicle for entering the life worlds of the out-of-school children and youth with whom she worked.

Part III, "Linguistic and Cultural Identities," adds further complexities and layers to children's multiple identities by focusing more explicitly on language, literacies, and forms of expression in classroom and community contexts. The chapters in this section offer powerful stories of bilingual or multilingual children and youth and their forms of self-expression.

In chapter 12, Lourdes Diaz Soto and Juliana Lasta explore the art and narratives of young bilingual children who depict their bilingualism as a discourse of love and altruism. Min Hong and Celia Genishi (chapter 13) draw from discussions with young English language learners in Hong's first-grade classroom, and focus on how these experiences have challenged their own identities as teacher, teacher researcher, and collaborator with children. Carmen Martínez-Roldán (chapter 14) draws from children's discussions of literature in a second-grade bilingual classroom. Martínez-Roldán discusses the challenges and promises of a research paradigm that places children's voices at the center.

In chapter 15, Cathy Guitierrez-Gomez, in her investigation related to emergent literacy, describes the process of reanalyzing data on the literacy of 63 preschool children and their story retelling. Challenging herself to observe "more prudently" and listen "more intently," Guitierrez-Gomez was able to convey a more comprehensive interpretation of children's voices and how they expressed what they were learning and how they were making connections. In the final chapter in this section (chapter 16), Carmen Medina, Kelly Bradbury, and Susan Pearson continue to make connections among language, literacy, and culture, through an instrumental case study of a fifth-grade student from Mexico who had recently immigrated to the United States, focusing on his voice during a unit reading and writing bilingual narrative poetry. They evoke the notion of the "inner world of the immigrant child" and worked to avoid impositional and reductive research approaches, while facilitating this student's self-expression.

In the epilogue, Eric Malewski provides us with a theoretically rich essay that both ties the pieces together and calls for additional rigorous "precocious" work in our research with children/young people.

In conclusion, we would like to add that the scholars contributing to this book call for a humanization of research that includes participatory paradigms, decolonizing methodologies, and democratic processes thereby reflecting the daily lived realities of children and young people. Collectively, the authors call for interrogating and complicating issues of research with children and for better integrating children's perspectives and life experiences into theory and practice in childhood studies and related fields.

REFERENCES

Cannella, G., & Viruru, R. (2004). *Childhood and post-colonization: Power, education, and contemporary practice*. New York: RoutledgeFalmer.

Hanh, T. N. (1991). *Peace is every step.* New York: Bantam Books.

Smith, L. T. (1999). *Decolonizing methodologies: Research and indigenous peoples.* London: Zed Books.

Soto, L. D., & Swadener, B. B. (2002). Toward liberatory early childhood theory, research and praxis: Decolonizing a field. *Contemporary Issues in Early Childhood, 2*(1), 38–66.

PART ONE

ISSUES OF POWER
AND VOICE

CHILDREN MAKE
THE BEST THEORISTS

LOURDES DIAZ SOTO

"Where I come from
the words most highly valued
are those spoken from the heart."
Leslie Marmon Silko, 1996, p. 48

This narrative inquiry relies on the notion of "visualizing voice" by presenting children's drawings and words of the nine-eleven World Trade Center tragedy. This chapter is guided by Clandinin and Connelly's (2000) descriptions helping us to learn to describe the ways people experience the world and Britzman's (2003) notion of "mourning."

This piece focuses on the theoretical possibilities that can be garnered from our ability to "visualize voice" from children's drawings as the process pertains to research with children. hooks (2000) reminds us that, "Everything we do in life is rooted in theory" (p. 19). This inquiry relies on the notion of "visualizing voice" sharing children's drawings helping to describe children's "theories" of the 9/11 catastrophic rupture. In order to "visualize voice," I have interlaced the illustrations, understanding that visual representations have functioned as a form of communication since the earliest cave drawings of ancient peoples to the present. Robert Coles (1989) has relied on children's drawings for visual psychosocial interpretations. Coles came to narrative through life and through teaching and learning. "I was urged to let each patient be a teacher" (p. 22)." It is the intimacy of the inquirer that is the key for Coles' work. In this chapter the children's interpretations and wisdom serve as the discussion for theoretical possibilities.

Narrative inquiry has helped scholars to bring personal experience to bear on research and to validate and respect diverse voices (Carger, 1996; He, 2003; Phillion, 1999; Soto, 1997; Valdés, 1996). Narrative inquiry offers a contextualized experience developed as a means of understanding events and processes across linguistic, cultural, visual, historical, and social boundaries. The power of this line of inquiry lies in the potential to locate experiences within complex contexts to make sense of the daily-lived world reality. Narrative inquiry coupled with a critical/advocacy component thrives on the passionate involvement and commitment of the researchers/coresearchers helping to cultivate hope and possibility!

William Ayers (2003) notes how narrative inquiry affords us all the ability to demystify the research process as the data show their "rough edges" and become dialogical. In narrative inquiry, Ayers adds, the researcher is present, the work is humanizing (its dialogic nature changes you as you do it), you can "assume" since you are explicitly shown the data, you can cowrite the work-it talks back to us, it is engaged research (you work in solidarity and identify with it) and you never have to ask, "Why am I doing this work?"

Britzman (2003) in her essay relies on Freud to examine the process of mourning. Freud's essay (cited by Britzman) was written after World War I and examines the limits and proximity of knowledge that cannot answer the haunting question the child asks, "Why war?" War, Freud suggests "is the absolute breakdown of meaning and the most aggressive repetitive and evil return of a society's refusal to learn something from the failure of knowledge" (p. 94). The work of mourning includes the recognition of the loss to the world and to the self. Mourning for most of us usually represents the loss of a loved one but we can also mourn for constructs such as the loss of safety, the loss of freedom, or the loss of a signifier such as the World Trade Center.

The mourning, for the children whose drawings you will view, is for the (symbolic) violence to the famous World Trade Center buildings, for the horrific deaths that they viewed either personally or in the media, and for the ongoing displays of mourning in the community. These young (ages 4–8) New York City children's drawings include the original spellings, or as the children wrote them (e.g., "high jacked"). The first depiction included here is entitled, "The Twin Tower" (Figure 1). In this picture we see the "before" and the "now" with the children's words (typed by their teacher). These two young boys relay their ability to "read" emotions from themselves, from the "enemy" and by the community. These emotions are complex and layered based on the children's ways of knowing and ability to depict the world visually.

Figure 1. The Twin Tower

In Figure 2 the drawing of a set of "crying" Twin Towers evokes the loss of the buildings as the buildings themselves shed tears for the violence. "I drew the Twin Towers because I wish it was still there," this six-year-old kindergartner wrote. The third figure (Figure 3) drawn by two kindergartners ages 5 and 6, continues to mourn as the caption informs us, "We wish the day when the hijackers high jacked into the World Trade Center never happened." These young children growing up in a postmodern post-9/11-era world wrought with complexities, quickly embarked in the process of mourning. Britzman (2003) also observed that, "Why things matter when they are no longer present is part of what the work of mourning gives us to consider" (p. 92).

One child attending a child care center (4 year old, D.C.) near the Pentagon described how he was "trying to put on my Power Ranger Uniform. . . . I need to save the day!" His willingness to take action and stand alone is reminiscent of Audrey Lorde's (1984) advice about stand-alone survival for a common cause:

> Survival is not an academic skill. It is learning how to stand alone, unpopular and sometimes reviled, and how to make common cause with those others identified as outside the structures in order to define and seek a world in which we can all flourish. (p. 112)

Figure 2. The crying Twin Towers

Figure 3. The airplane

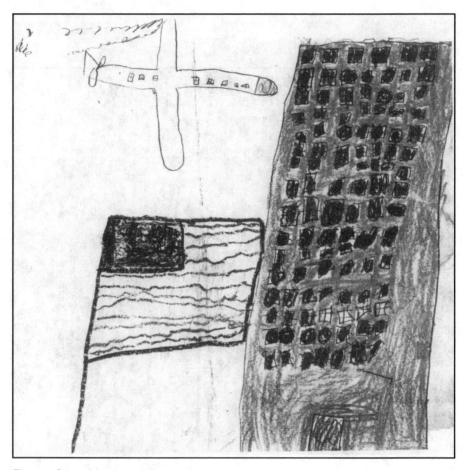

Figure 4. September 11

Figure 4 shows the first airplane on its way to the Twin Towers with an American flag next to the building. This eight-year-old asked us "Why do they hate us so much?" This important question was rarely debated by our nation yet this young child was able to perceive how "others" might feel about our nation. Freire (1985) noted that "Education of a liberating character is a process by which the *educator* invites learners to recognize and unveil reality critically" (p. 102).

This *educator* child was doing just that, asking for a critical analysis of the disastrous reality. In asking "Why do they hate us so much?" the child asks us to consider the "others" perspective. What are we doing that is causing such a violent reaction? With this question the critical analysis of the event is expanded pressing us to consider not only our reactions and feelings but also the nature of the complexity of this one event as it is related to other acts that *we* may have committed.

Figure 5. The crash blowy airplane

The responsibility is now shared and insists on self-examination and group (national) self-analysis.

In Figure 5 our young artist draws a sad stick figure jumping out of the attacked smoking building. The national media that captured couples and individuals jumping from the smoking smoldering windows documented this drawing.

Martin Luther King's (1981) words guided many of us during the tragedy and can help us to analyze the historical, current, and future needs of our community.

> This call for world-wide fellowship, that lifts neighborly concern beyond one's tribe, race, class, and nation is in reality a call for an all-embracing and unconditional love for all men [people]. This oft misunderstood concept—so readily dismissed by the Nietzsche of the world as a weak cowardly force—has now become and absolute necessity for the survival of man. (p. 48)

Figure 6. La Cruz Roja

The strength of the human spirit in New York City was demonstrated by thousands of volunteers. Figure 6 shows the HOSPITAL and the CRUZ ROJA (the Red Cross). Volunteers appeared from every direction asking to donate blood, waiting at the entrance of the hospitals, and willing to search the rubble for any survivors. These activities were reminiscent of the Sioux proverb, "With all things in all things, we are relatives."

The last depictions are two letters written to the firefighters by New York City children (original Spanish and English spellings).

13 de septiem

Queridos Bomberos:

quiro dales las grasias por todo lo que an echo por todas las personas eridas y gracias a las personas que ah donado sangre y lo ciento a los bomberos que an muerto

Sinceremente,
(nombre)

Dear Fire Fighters

I am sending this letter to thank you for tring to save other peoples live I feel sad fer all the people that died on the twin towers and for thr ores that are injured thank you for having Responsibility. You tried very hard to tried to rescue peoples live from the acident.

(name)

I was teaching in New York City that year and soon after the tragedy I was flying to a conference. Two young boys and their father were seated in front of me. The father was an attorney and was reading the *Sunday Times* with his boys. One child was able to read sentences while the younger child was looking for letters of the alphabet. The father was patient and answered the questions his sons posed to him. At this time the younger child was looking for the letter "T." He pointed to a letter "T" and asked his Dad to read the word. His Dad responded with "Tennessee." The young boy found a second "T" and again asked his Dad to read the word. The Dad responded with "Terrorist."

"Dad what is a terrorist?"
"A terrorist is someone who harms innocent people in order to get what they want," the father replied.

This child's question impacted me as I thought about the sadness of having to explain this concept to such a young child. The father hesitated and needed a few seconds to respond. The child was asking his father for a definition and the father in turn had to think about his personal definition and perhaps multiple elements while at the same time simplifying the complex question for his young son. The intricacy of terrorism places the topic within socio-historical contexts impacting many peoples of the world.
Steinberg (2003) asks,

How do we make sense of a world that has no sense?
We infuse social justice in the curriculum. . . . We teach peace and encourage the concept of peace. This will lead us to a pedagogy of hope.

The Hague Appeal for Peace, Global Campaign for Peace Education (May 1999) notes that a culture of peace will be attainable when "citizens of the world" understand global problems, issues of human rights, gender and racial equality, can resolve conflict, appreciate diversity, and respect the integrity of the earth. The children who shared their drawings and letters with us appear to demonstrate levels of awareness that are capable of guiding us with hope for the future.

CONCLUSION

Nicolas Rose (1989) in his book entitled, *Governing the Soul*, documents how childhood is "the most intensely governed sector of personal existence" (p. 123). Rose's historical treatment of childhood documents how children have been viewed as dangerous, maladjusted, deprived, abnormal, and in need of parent-teacher-social-governmental regulation. An article in the *New York Times* (Lisa Belkin, 2000) also shows recent resentment toward children by the "child-free movement" who view children as ankle biters, crib lizards, and sprogs.

This piece highlighting the struggle to mourn shows children in a very different light. Our ability to visualize children's voice, children's wisdom, and children's theory can be an integral part of participatory democracy. Children's representations, voices, and wisdom can guide our democratic dreams as we listen for what children intend to say. Even in the face of adversity there are spaces of hope as we listen to the voices of children in New York City.

Our role as narrative inquirers can help to guide knowledge about how children "experience the world" (Clandinin & Connelly, 2000), and how to afford voice, possibility, complexity, and theory in our research with children. "Necesitamos teorias that will rewrite history using race, class, gender and ethnicity as categories of analysis, theories that cross borders, that blur boundaries—new kinds of theories with new theorizing methods" (Anzaldua (1990, p. xxv).

Children's depictions and wisdom surrounding this life-changing event offer the possibility for us to continue to push the boundaries in narrative inquiry as we pursue the process of "visualizing voice" by child illustrators. The 9/11 tragedy serves as testimony to the strength of our children and their ability to theorize with "children's ways of knowing" about this catastrophic rupture thereby leading us to consider the possibility that "children make the best theorists" in light of Leslie Marmon Silko's (1996, p. 48) reminder that the "the words most highly valued are those spoken from the heart."

REFERENCES

Anzaldua, G. (1990). *Making face, making soul: Haciendo caras*. San Francisco: Aunt Lute Books.

Ayers, W. (2003). Discussant. Interactive Panel with Carger, He, and Soto: The art of narrative inquiry. American Educational Research Association. Chicago.

Belkin, L. (2000, July 21). The backlash against children. *New York Times*, pp. 30–35, 42, 56, 60–63.

Britzman, D. (2003) The death of the curriculum. In Doll, W.E. & Gough, N. (Eds), *Curricular Visions*. New York: Peter Lang Publishers.

Carger, C. (1996). *Of borders and dreams: Mexican-American experience of urban education*. New York: Teachers College Press.

Clandinin, D. J., & Connelly, F. M. (2000). *Narrative inquiry: Experience and story in qualitative research.* San Francisco: Jossey-Bass.

Coles, R. (1989). *The call of stories: Teaching and the moral imagination.* Boston: Houghton Mifflin.

Freire, P. (1985). *The politics of education: Culture, power and liberation.* Boston: Bergin & Garvey Publishers.

He, Ming Fang. (2003). *A river forever flowing between China and North America: A narrative inquiry into cross-cultural lives and cross-cultural identities in multicultural landscapes.* Greenwich, CT: Information Age Publishing.

hooks, b. (2000). *Feminism is for EVERYBODY: Passionate Politics.* Cambridge, MA: South End Press.

King, M. L., Jr. (1981). *Martin Luther King essay series.* New York: A. J. Muste Memorial Institute.

Lorde, A. (1984). *Sister outsider.* Freedom, CA: The Crossing Press.

Phillion, J. (1999). Narrative inquiry in a multicultural landscape: Multicultural teaching and learning. Unpublished doctoral dissertation. University of Toronto, Canada.

Rose, N. (1989). *Governing the soul.* New York: Free Association Books.

Silko, L. M. (1996). *Yellow woman and a beauty of spirit.* New York: Touchstone.

Soto, L. D. (1997). *Language, culture, and power: Bilingual families and the struggle for quality education.* Albany: State University of New York Press.

Steinberg, S. (2003, April). How do we make sense of a world that has no sense? Discussant remarks made at the annual meeting of the American Educational Research Association, Chicago.

Valdés, G. (1996). *Con respeto: Bridging the distances between culturally diverse families and schools.* New York: Teachers College Press.

CHAPTER TWO

FREEDOM SPEAKS

JANETTE HABASHI

This chapter invites readers to join the quest of beginning to understand and unpack the paradoxes of doing research with children and its limitations, using an interview with a Palestinian "child" as a prototype for the process. While this chapter foregrounds children and youth voice, some brief context will be helpful to the reader. This conversation took place during the second Intifada (Palestinian uprising) in the West Bank. For the last half century, the Palestinian people suffered from the Zionist ideology that has displaced generations from their villages, Israeli occupation, and collective punishment. This chapter is concerned with the deep intersection of research with children that is manifested in children's being and professionals'/adults' perspectives on children's ability to participate in society.

Interviewer: Why your parents called you *Hurriyah* (freedom)?

Hurriyah: My mom went for a doctor visit and he told her that in two weeks she would deliver. Next day my mom with my other two siblings went to the Jordan Bridge in Jericho to cross for Jordan. She wanted to finish some work for Palestine before she delivers me. They waited at the bridge from 7:00 A.M. to 11:00 P.M. and at that time my mom was also interrogated by the Israelis. After all of this, the Israeli soldiers told her to come back next day if she wishes to cross to Jordan. This happened three days in a row without any hope to cross to Jordan. On the third day, my mom gave up and went back home to Hebron (a city in the West Bank) with my two siblings. At night, my mom started bleeding and she thought that I am died inside her. She could not call for help, our neighbors were far, five minutes walking distance, and at that day the Israelis imposed curfew on the city. However, my mom was worried because she thought I was died. She walked to our first neighbors who were two Germanys females. The house was lit, but when my mom knocked at the door their thought that she was an Israeli soldiers and their immediately put the lights off. My mom yelled and yelled and they finally opened the door. They took my mom to Dijian Hospital, the closest one, but the doctor refused to check her in. The reason was that my mom did not have doctor visitations at this hospital. The German girls told the doctor, if you refuse to admit her to the hospital, you need to write it down on paper and if she dies you will be responsible. The doctor was fearful and my mom delivered me and they wanted to call me Nidiaa. But at that time my father was a fidai (freedom fighter), and the Israel government wanted him.

My mother passed the message that I was born through one of my father's friends. My father secretly came to the hospital; the nurse let him in to see me. He spent the night sleeping at the chair but when the shift changed, the new nurse on duty knew about his situation and she nicely took my father to her house for a rest. They wanted to call me Nidaa #1 but my mom said the land should be liberated (freed); that is why they called me Hurriyah (freedom).

Interviewer: Tell me something about Palestine.
Hurriyah: It is in the heart of the Arab world. It is a country that was first built by the Cananians. However, when we had the British Mandate in Palestine they gave the land to the Jewish people and they called it Israel.

Interviewer: Where are the West Bank and the Gaza Strip?
Hurriyah: Now Palestine has been divided but it is still occupied, the West Bank and the Gaza Strip is occupied by Israel and the rest of the land is now called Israel.

Interviewer: What does Palestine mean to you?
Hurriyah: It means everything, it means the country that I live for and in which I want to live in with peace, it is my homeland.

Interviewer: What makes someone a Palestinian?
Hurriyah: First any Palestinian person should have a commitment to Palestine, and Palestine should be in his mind and heart. If the person does not feel he belongs to Palestine, this means that he is a Palestinian in name.

Interviewer: How could one be a Palestinian?
Hurriyah: My family is Palestinian and my community is in Palestine and I belong to Palestine; I feel I have something in Palestine.

Interviewer: Anyone could be a Palestinian?
Hurriyah: No, not everyone; only on one condition that his grandfathers been born in Palestine and they built this land and worked hard for the homeland.

Interviewer: Who are now living in Palestine?
Hurriyah: Israelis, Palestinians, and visitors from abroad.

Interviewer: How do you decide that this guy is a good Palestinian and the other is a bad Palestinian?

Hurriyah: The bad Palestinians first of all are the collaborators [spies]. The one who spies against his homeland and give away his fellow brothers; this one is not a good Palestinian. The good Palestinian is the one who would not give away his homeland and he fights for his homeland, this is a good Palestinian.

Interviewer: How could you fight for your homeland?

Hurriyah: Through education, because when he grows up, he could do something for Palestine, he should fight for Palestine. Do anything for his people in Palestine.

Interviewer: Everyone could fight?

Hurriyah: Yes.

Interviewer: Are you fighting?

Hurriyah: Yes, I am fighting now; when I go to school every day and I get educated, I am fighting. This is one way but also when I want to buy candies, if I see Israeli product that is good and I see beside it the same product but it is Palestinian made that might not be as good as the Israeli one. I will buy the Palestinian product in order to support the Palestinians manufacturers; in this way I am fighting. In this way everyone could fight.

Interviewer: How should children know these things?

Hurriyah: From anyone, from their environment, families, from parents; if a child listens and he does not understand now, eventually he will.

Interviewer: Who taught these things?

Hurriyah: From school, news, and also when I see children dying. One starts thinking why the Israeli product is developing because Palestinian people are buying it and why the Palestinian product is not improving, because no one is supporting it. We need to help them improve their line of product.

Interviewer: What you mean by environment?

Hurriyah: I learn from the environment, when I walk every day I see people around me, imagine a small child trying to cross the street he tries to imitated the people around him, he is trying to learn in this way.

Interviewer: What do you learn from the streets in Palestine?

Hurriyah: A child who is walking in the street first learns the language. Imagine if I am in any neighborhood and they say this place is Israel I grow up knowing that this land is Israel, but if they say this is Palestine, I grow up knowing it is Palestine. This determines what you feel about your surrounding. Also what is written on the walls is a sign, if something is written in Hebrew, I know that this is not its place, this is a Palestinian country and it should be written in the Arabic language.

Interviewer: What does the street tell you about Palestine?

Hurriyah: If one looks around he sees trees, he will know that our grandfathers were farmers, if you look at the tools people used you will see the kind of civilization and what kind of economy they had.

Interviewer: Does the school teach you the same as at home and the streets?
Hurriyah: Every place teaches you different things.

Interviewer: Does the information conflict?
Hurriyah: No, every one complements the other, for example, at home you learn how to behave with your family in the street you learn how to behave with people around you and in school you learn science.
Interviewer: What does the home teach you about Palestine?

Hurriyah: In every house there are traditions, and these traditions express the Palestinian heritage and how in the old days the Palestinians lived and what kind of tools they had.

Interviewer: What is the meaning of Palestinian refugees?
Hurriyah: Palestinian refugees are people who were evacuated in 1948 from their home-land and homes. This happened because of killing and occupation. In 1948 Israel colonized us; some Palestinians fled but on the assumption of coming back and some people took their house keys with them. I am a refugee from a village called Faluja, near Gaza, even though I live in Rammallah [city in the West Bank] I am still a refugee.

Interviewer: Does your family talk about Faluja?
Hurriyah : They say it is a nice place and I also dream about it, and I want to see it. My father says it is a nice place and his wishes to live there.

Interviewer: What is your dream?
Hurriyah: I dream that Faluja is a cultivated land; it looks green and there are flowers everywhere and people are living together like brothers and sisters and there is no occupation. It is like a village all people are talking with each other and everyone knows everyone and no one is hurt.

Interviewer: Do you talk about Faluja a lot?
Hurriyah: In our house we talk a lot about these issues, we talk about life in the old days and how they were living and why the Palestinians were evacuated. It was against their will, we never had a free will.

Interviewer: Who also talks about Faluja in your family?
Hurriyah: My grandfathers passed away, but my parents were *fadaiyin* [freedom fighters], my mother was jailed for six months and my father was jailed for six years and he also was wanted by the Israelis.

Interviewer: You used an interesting word, *fidai* [freedom fighter], what you mean?
Hurriyah: *Fidai* is one who defends his homeland, and he is sacrificing himself in order to free the homeland. He thinks he could die for the homeland. He dies in order that someone will not die, he sacrifices his soul so that his homeland will be

free and he has his homeland back. If we continue in this way more people will die, now one or two are dying every day, but if occupation continues a lot of us will die.

Interviewer: What is the difference between *fidai* [freedom fighter] and a martyr? Which one do you prefer and which term should we use?

Hurriyah: I prefer the *fidai* because he defends his homeland he might die but he is defending his homeland, but if someone becomes a martyr, it might happen by accident and this person did not do anything for his homeland, but the fidai is fighting for the homeland.

Interviewer: What is the meaning of martyrdom?

Hurriyah: Someone who dies for his homeland.

Interviewer: What you think about someone dying for his homeland?

Hurriyah: I like it, but I do not like it at the same time. If they say that this guy is a martyr. It means that he died for his homeland. I hate the word martyr because it says that someone died. I hate for someone to die, however, to die for his homeland is much better than to die for something else.

Interviewer: Why did we change the term for *fidai* [freedom fighter] to martyrdom?

Hurriyah : Long time ago people used to be *fidai* but now they are thinking about death. They do not think in terms of sacrificing and resisting, they are thinking in terms of dying, they do not have hope. Although they have hope because they are fighting but it is not like the way they had before.

Interviewer: Give me an example.

Hurriyah: Long time ago the *fidai* who used to resist used to fight but not necessarily to be a martyr, but now there are a lot of death and martyrdom and they think about death, before they thought that one would resist but not necessarily to die. Now they are thinking about death and martyrdom.

Interviewer: What you think about the term martyrdom, is it associated with the religion?

Hurriyah: I think the freedom fighters could also go to heaven as well as the martyrs, because they are fighting for their homeland; I do not associate it with religion because both of them have the same goal.

Interviewer: Do you think both words [*fidai* and martyrdom] are the same?

Hurriyah : Maybe, but the term changed; I feel the term *fidai* is closer to my heart. The term *fidai* has hope; *fidai* is defending his homeland and hoping he will come back. The martyr he has no hope, because he is going to die. He does not think if he dies it might result badly on Palestine. Now we are in need for those people, we need them not to die. If we all die and we had the same way of thinking, when we grow up there will be no one, and therefore no Palestine, this time Israel will have it all.

Interviewer: Who taught you this?

Hurriyah: Life.

Interviewer: How?

Hurriyah: I thought about it, when someone dies and after him another one and so on how we will continue.

Interviewer: What is the main political problem for us?

Hurriyah: It started a long time ago, we are not living in peace we have occupation.

Interviewer: Do you talk a lot about political issues?

Hurriyah: No, but when the family comes together, even if they do not talk, I am witnessing what is going around me. I do not need anyone to tell me.

Interviewer: What you are witnessing?

Hurriyah :   People are dying, one is going to throw a stone and a bullet kills him. There is no compatibility between a stone and a bullet.

Interviewer: Do you know other villages that had the same experience as Faluja?

Hurriyah :   Haifa, Jeffa, Besian.

Interviewer: Did you ever visit Haifa?

Hurriyah :   Yes and it is nice.

Interviewer: Do you know in which form of colonization Israel came about?

Hurriyah: Through the British Mandate.

Interviewer: Do you know the name of the movement?

Hurriyah: Zionism.

Interviewer: Do you know anything about the Zionist movement?

Hurriyah: No.

Interviewer: What is the difference between Jew, Zionist, and Israeli?

Hurriyah: The Jewish people believe in Judaism, the Israeli are the people who are living in Israel. Zionists are the people who lived in our house or destroyed our homes and rebuild on it.

Interviewer: Which is the most difficult one for you and why?

Hurriyah: The Zionist is the worst one; however, not every Jew is a Zionist. A Zionist is one who colonizes the land.

Interviewer: What about the Israelis?

Hurriyah: He is the one who occupied the land.

Interviewer: According to your definition Judaism is a religion, but when we see an Israeli soldier we call him a Jewish soldier, why?

Hurriyah: Most of the Jewish people gathered from different countries and came and lived in Palestine, and long time they were killed. This why we call them Jewish, I think. We had the British Mandate because they wanted to get rid of the Jews and the solution was to put them in Palestine and the British could take advantage of the land through the Jewish people. The main important thing was to get rid of the Jewish people, they used to hate the Jewish people; they used to kill them. For example, look what happened in Germany. Putting them in Palestine was a way to get rid of them and use the land through them.

Interviewer: The Palestinians have a problem with the Israelis, Jews, or the Zionists?

Hurriyah: The Palestinian people have a problem with the Israelis and the Zionists not the Jewish people. We also have a problem with the Zionists as Arab people and we have a problem with the Israelis as Palestinians. We have a problem with the Israeli people and their government because if you do not approve of what the government is doing why are you complying. The Israeli people elected the Israeli government; the government is part of the people.

Interviewer: What is the political problem for the Palestinian people?

Hurriyah: Peace.

Interviewer: What is peace?

Hurriyah: Is to live in freedom, we could not move in freedom. We should have rights, and no one should attack our land and our homes, we should have jobs.

Interviewer: There are some Palestinians who are still living in Haifa and Jeffa what do you call them?

Hurriyah: I refuse to call them Arab-Israelis; they are Arab of 48 or Palestinian of 48.

Interviewer: What you think about the Palestinians who are living in Israel or Palestinian of 48?

Hurriyah : I have different feelings about them, sometimes I feel that they are better than us because they did not flee the land but sometimes I do not feel good about them, I do not know.

Interviewer: Could a Palestinian become an Israeli?

Hurriyah: No, as we said that the Palestinians of 48 have Israeli citizenship but they are not Israelis. Like we see now, there are some Palestinians from 48 who are defending their land and helping their Palestinians brothers in the West Bank. But if they were Israelis they will not defend us and they will not acknowledge that there is such thing as Palestinian people. They are a part of the Palestinian people and Palestinians of 48 are also defending Palestine.

Interviewer: How are the Palestinians of 48 living now?

Hurriyah: I do not think they are happy; however, if someone gives me an Israeli passport I would not be happy, and if they tell me you are Israeli I would not be happy.

Interviewer: What you mean by giving me an Israeli passport?

Hurriyah: If you do not have an Israeli ID or passport you would not be allowed to live in Israel and Palestinians do not want to leave and they want to stay in their homes, therefore they have to take it. If you do not take it you have to leave.

Interviewer: How are people in the West Bank living?

Hurriyah: First of all, we do not have rights, we are living in humiliation; when I say we do not have rights it expresses everything.

Interviewer: How are people in Gaza living?

Hurriyah: They are living in a difficult situation. It is not easy when your house is demolished and then after a second you die from by shelling attacks.

Interviewer: Do you know anyone from the 48?

Hurriyah: Yes, my sister's friends are from the 48 and friends of my grandfather; the grandfather who is living in Hebron.

Interviewer: What is the difference between living in the 48 and here in the West Bank?

Hurriyah: It is possible, they are living in their original place, they are in their land, but we could not go back. I do not know which one is better.

Interviewer: Do you think everyone should resist?

Hurriyah: Yes, all of us, everyone has a way.

Interviewer: How?

Hurriyah: I am getting my education, I am resisting, the ones who are committing martyr operations are resisting, the ones who are throwing stones are resisting, the ones who are boycotting Israeli products are resisting.

Interviewer: How are you resisting when you are boycotting Israeli products?

Hurriyah: Now there is Palestinian product and Israeli product, when we are not buying Israeli products and we buy Palestinian products we are supporting Palestinian manufacturers. When we buy Israeli product we give them good economy to buy weapons that they use to kill us.

Interviewer: What should people do in order to resist?

Hurriyah: Anything that could benefit their homeland.

Interviewer: Why should people resist?

Hurriyah: In order to liberate the homeland from occupation.

Interviewer: What is the political situation now?

Hurriyah: There is occupation.

Interviewer: Is there another problem?

Hurriyah: The economy.

Interviewer: What is the economy problem?

Hurriyah: There are some people who do not have shelter, and food for their families, this leads to some children working. There isn't enough income for the family.

Interviewer: Before, children were not working?

Hurriyah: Yes they were some, but now during the uprising there are more children working.

Interviewer: What should happen in order to solve our problems?

Hurriyah: First the people should unite, now everyone is saying something different. The Palestinian Authority is say something, the people are saying something else, and we are fighting each other. If we are fighting each other how we as people are going to stand up against Israel. Also we should help each other and resist and think which way is the best the way for resistance and what we can do.

Interviewer: What did you learn about Palestine?

Hurriyah: Borders, history of Palestine, cities.

Interviewer: What will happen after ten years?

Hurriyah: We will die or we will free Palestine.

Interviewer: Which one you think it will happen?

Hurriyah: We will liberate Palestine.

Interviewer: When we liberate Palestine we will fight each other?

Hurriyah: No, first we can liberate Palestine only if we are united and also to think about what we are doing and to plan the future. If we unite we will never fight each other. We need to correct a lot of things in us, in order to unite and liberate Palestine.

Interviewer: What do we need to correct?

Hurriyah: We need to be united, not like now we are killing each other. The people within the Palestinian Authority should have a discussion with each other. This discussion should lead us to a good conclusion.

Interviewer: Do you talk about these issues in your house?

Hurriyah: Yes, they call me the political analyst.

Interviewer: What you think is the perception of adults regarding children throwing stones?

Hurriyah: My mom objects to this idea; she said that there are other means for resistance rather than throwing stones and dying. Like I said before that we should think before dying, the Palestinian people need everyone, if he dies and other one dies, what will happen to our future?

Interviewer: What do you think about your mom's opinion?

Hurriyah: I agree with her, what is the point of children dying, but I also agree on the issue of resisting with stones; children do not see life yet. Sometimes I think it is OK to throw stones and sometimes not. Through throwing stones we show the world that we are standing tall, without the stone we will never have an uprising. We have no weapons the only thing we have is stones and we have to resist. Through stones we show them that we will never give up and we will continue resisting by any means, even though stones are not effective.

Interviewer: Do you think that when children go to throw stones they know why?

Hurriyah: Of course, because they want their land back. They do not want to continue living in this situation and they do not want their children living in the same situation, like this.

Interviewer: Do you think adults tell children to go and through stones?

Hurriyah: No, because no mother or father wants their children killed. There is no conscious parent who want his child to be killed.

Interviewer: What you think is the meaning of *jihad*?

Hurriyah: It is not important what the term is or the name, what is important is what one does. The *majihad* is defending his homeland, maybe the ones who are throwing stones are *majihad*, but it is not the right way. By education one act in *jihad*, think about solutions for the homeland is *jihad*. The physician is *majihad*, he is helping injured people, and he is helping his people. The one who is helping someone who could not find a piece of bread he is *majihad*. Anything you do for your homeland is *jihad*.

Interviewer: Is *jihad* associated with religion?

Hurriyah: No, one could say I will *jihad* through education, I am going to *jihad*, and there are lot of ways to do the same thing. I am going to *jihad*. Maybe also I want to do an operation. I do not think it is right when we kill them [Israelis].

Interviewer: Why?

Hurriyah: It is the same that we do not like it when they kill us. They do not like it when we kill them, maybe there is another way.

Interviewer: Like what?

Hurriyah: Like nonviolence policy, there is no need for violence, why kill? People should live; we did not create them therefore we should not kill them.

Interviewer: What makes you proud of being a Palestinian?

Hurriyah: We are people who do not lose hope, we are dying but we do not lose hope. The thing I like is hope. We are killed but we are still going on resisting and defending our homeland. If we were another nation and we did not have hope everyone would hide and no one could *jihad*. I am acting in *jihad* when I go to school and cross the Israeli checkpoints. It is very risky to cross these checkpoints. This is only to go to school and not to illiterate people.

Interviewer: What did you learn about Palestine at home?

Hurriyah: It is an occupied land and the Palestinian people are fighting for the land and they are dying and children work and how people could not find food because of occupation. And how children do not have rights and how occupation took their rights away, not only the children but also adults and everyone.

Interviewer: Now it is your turn to ask me.

Hurriyah: The Palestinians of 48 are they good people? Why is Israel killing us? How could a Palestinian be a collaborator? Why the Palestinian Authority do not provide for the poor people? Do you agree with what the Palestinian Authority, last week the Palestinian Authority came and arrested my father's friend, because a long time ago he was a member of the Palestinian Front Liberation for Palestine? Why is the Palestinian Authority trying to please the Western countries? Why does the Palestinian Authority not want us to resist? What do you think about the political position of the Arab world? Why do we have writings on the walls that are against the Palestinian Authority, how are we going to liberate Palestine if there are disagreements between the Palestinian Authority and the people? Did you ever hear about the Masonic Organization and the Freemasons? What are they? Do they have ties with Israel?

The aim of disclosing this particular interview is to provide an example of children's sophistication and their ability to reflect on the geopolitical surroundings; therefore to produce a paradoxical narrative. Hence, the objectives of sharing this interview are neither for its political statement nor to advocate a political position. As a result, I ask the readers not to draw assumptions or attempt to interpret the views of the interviewee. The significance of the interview is to guide us through the paper discussion; consequently, any postulations would not lead to an accurate conclusion. The chapter, nevertheless, is trying to challenge the inherent problem of the researcher role and the assumptions of child development across cultures. The dispute is in how we as scholars could be self-critical in the process while we conduct research, in anticipation of examining the power and imposition of adults' extent to the political empowerment of children's voices. These pages are presenting the journey of a research wherein children played a role in understanding the research questions and provided insight in the analysis process.

From the first reading of this transcript, I learned new perspectives on the issues that are in the line of personal, national identity, family role, and the political circumstances influencing the young individual in forming identity and national memory as articulated in Beck and Jennings (1991), Flanagan and Sherrod (1998), Hicks (2001), Jankowski (1992), Kansteiner (2002), Liebes and Ribak (1992), and Merelman (1980). Hurriyah in this context was sharing her reflections as being an active witness. She situates herself as part of the geopolitical spectrum in which she was able to reconstruct and position herself as a member of the community. The questions that Hurriyah raised to scholars are beyond the issue of identity and historical memory; they are concerned with her views and if they are communicated in research. If you notice, the transcript does not indicate the age of Hurriyah—one could speculate that the voice is that of a young adult or an adult, which has a different implication than if it was a child. The notion of the narrative changes in particular when realizing the age of Hurriyah. Hurriyah is twelve years old—I recommend reflecting on your reactions before proceeding to read: Are there nuances knowing Hurriyah's age? Would you think differently if her age were eighteen, older, or younger?

The challenge in researching children's issues, in my judgment, is that while children are contemplating life discrepancies such as regarding issues of poverty, racism, war, privileges, or adults' power, are the paradoxes of these issues conveyed in research from the perspective of children, or are they considered contradictions and lack of maturity? This leads to the question of whether the current research paradigms and methods mirror children's discernments, especially when the two, the child narrative and research tools, are not necessarily compatible. The diversity of children's perspectives is not inclusively integrated in the research of children, whether in social science or child psychology (Glass, 2001; Kennedy, 1998; Woodhead, 1999; Zimiles, 2000). In addition, accounting for children's perspectives does not necessarily evoke new research approaches. The cross-cultural research provided new situations and norms that altered the traditional human development theories; however, it did not intersect in challenging our deep assumption of children's voice. The apparent reason is due to the dominant supposition of children's definitions that continue to prevail in research and its unconscious guidance to interpret children's narratives particularly when children are revealing political views (Flanagan & Sherrod, 1998; Peterson & Somit, 1982). Children invoking political issues undermine adults and policy makers, which results in retreating to the traditional position of child definition. Within this position adults and professionals have created hegemony to limit children's articulations. Such hegemony is instrumental in the duplication of adults' imposition in child research as well as in developmental matters. The center of understanding child development, whether it is from the perspective of multi-truth or from child laboratory, is still within the assumption of adults knowing and children lacking experience. The beliefs that children lack sophistication and that any contradiction on the part of children is a lack of understanding are the foundations of echoing paradoxes.

The characteristics of a child definition lay the foundation to restrict the acceptance of children's geopolitical narratives. Therefore, the discourse of child chronological descriptions continues to direct and appropriate children's intellectual exchange, especially in political situation or when debating the right of children to vote (Harris, 1982). Although there are new attempts by the reconceptualists of childhood to include children's voices and allow more space as well as accept more child norms, it is missing the insight to develop a paradigm that is separate from the traditional thinking of children. The reconceptualizing theory stems from the criticism of the traditional understanding of children. The challenges of the traditional child theory are inherited in the reconceptualist notion because both theories are intertwined. In addition, the issue of child-adult power relation is not debated. The struggle of defining "child interest" and the interest of adults is in the core of inherited problems of the reconceptualizing theorists.

To present children voices as part of multi-truth assumptions does not necessarily provide an equal stand for a child's voice. To touch on the surface of the issue, one should ask how many books are written by children. Literature that is concerned with children's development, growth, and culture has found a place in libraries. However, there are no books written by children, but more books for children

(Cooper & Schwerdt, 2001). Even though the books written about children might include their voice, it is concluded by adults. Apparently the shortage is not in the amount of research paradigms or critiquing traditional child discourse or in finding research questions, but in the crisis of expectations that is assigned in the prepositions of chronicle development and maturity. Insofar, the quandary is in the deficiency in providing insight on the role of researcher and its power in "interpreting children's voice" or conveying children's perspectives. The dilemma is that researchers deny their role as adults and how much their statuses perpetuate the traditional role of adults. Hence, this might sound contradictory to the premises of this chapter—I did not want to include this discussion part and I thought Huyrriah is able to speak. On the other hand, I was much tempted to interpret the dialogue and its relation to children's sophistication in war zones, especially when I was worried about reader interpretations—I was thinking as a protector—but I refused to pursue this path.

The design of this chapter upholds some traditional views regarding children's voices, especially when adding the discussion part. However, this presents new challenges in this area. The scholar's struggles are within two domains: first, the child's classification and its effects on data as explained earlier. Second, the topics of research; traditionally we assume that children will grow to be adults and the focus is how to guide them to be so or children are not capable of presenting a complex argument or they should be sheltered. Therefore, there is little research done on children's political knowing, but more on children's citizenship education, which is hierarchal relation. Children are educated by adults/teachers. In addition, there are researches on political socialization but within a stable nation-state. It is drawn from the same assumption of hierarchal state doctrine. At one point, such themes deeply intersect but are not necessarily the same. The subject of political knowing is explicitly controversial and it touches on issues that the adult did not yet resolve. Scholars are reluctant to tap on these grounds; therefore, they reject the idea that children are political entities and politicians (Harris, 1982; Oldman, 1994), and the idea is more exclusively denied to children in a war zone.

To challenge the inherent problems in child research one should realize the traditional communications tools that inhibit us from understanding children. Buckingham (1997) states that children are not obstacles, rather tools of communication. Therefore, I learned to provide the opportunity for the interviewee to ask me questions, in which I perceive such questions as insight into children's abilities. I realized that while interviewing Palestinian children, some started questioning my attempt. I was asked many questions; this led me to reconstruct the approach by providing opportunity for the interviewees to question the attempt. Although participatory research encourages interviewees to be active in the research project, through reviewing the transcript, my approach was more allowing the children to critique the significance of the research in relation to their own lives. In theory, participatory research encourages children's reflection, but it still lacks child insight. If you noticed, Hurriyah asked me questions after the interview. When I introduced myself I made it clear that I welcomed her questions. In addition, I did not perceive the questions as contradictory to her answers, but it provided insight into children's paradoxical life.

In conclusion, our struggles are in the lack of reflections on adult's role, and its implications on restricting children voices, especially when their views challenge our status quo. The question, however, should be how we should start communicating children's views even if they challenge our scholarship.

REFERENCES

Beck, P. A., & Jennings, K.M. (1991). Family traditions, political periods and the development of partisan orientations. *Journal of Politics, 53,* 742–763.

Buckingham, D. (1997). News media, political socialization and popular citizenship: Towards a new agenda. *Critical Studies in Mass Communication, 14,* 344–366.

Cooper, C. A., & Schwerdt, M. (2001). Depictions of public service in children's literature: Revisiting an understudied aspect of political socialization. *Social Science Quarterly, 82*(3), 616–632.

Flanagan, C. A. & Sherrod, L. R. (1998). Youth political development: An introduction. *Journal of Social Issues, 54*(3), 447–456.

Glass, N. (2001). What works for children—the political issues. *Children and Society, 15,* 14–20.

Harris, J. (1982). The political status of children. In K. Graham (Ed.), *Contemporary political philosophy: Radical studies.* New York: Cambridge University Press.

Jankowski, M. S. (1992). Ethnic identity and political consciousness in different social orders. *New Direction for Child Development, 56,* 79–93.

Kansteiner, W. (2002). Finding meaning in memory: A methodological critique of collective memory studies. *History and Theory, 41,* 179–197.

Kennedy, D. (1998). Reconstructing childhood. *Thinking, 14*(1), 29–37.

Liebes, T. & Ribak, R. (1992). The contribution of family culture to political participation, political outlook, and it reproduction. *Communication Research, 19*(5), 618–641.

Merelman, R. (1972). The adolescence of political socialization. *Sociology of Education, 45,* 134–166.

Oldman, D. (1994). Childhood as a mode of production. In B. Mayall (Ed.), *Children's childhoods: Observed and experienced.* Washington, DC: Falmer.

Peterson, S. A. & Somit, A (1982). Cognitive development and childhood political socialization. *American Behavioral Scientist, 25*(1), 313–334.

Rosenberg, S. (1985). Sociology, psychology, and the study of political behavior: The case of the research on political socialization. *Journal of Politics, 47,* 715–731.

Woodhead, M. (1999). Reconstructing developmental psychology—Some first steps. *Children and Society, 13,* 3–19.

Zimiles, H. (2000). The vagaries of rigor. *Human Development, 43,* 289–294.

CHAPTER THREE

CONFIDENCE INTERVALS

Doing Research with Young Children

JENNIFER JIPSON AND JANICE JIPSON

Instant messages, iChat, cell phone calls while waiting for the train, and before that, e-mail across geographies, across disciplines, linking ideas, linking mother and daughter. This is the story of two university professors, who also happen to be mother and daughter, and their collaborative efforts to understand each other's work. By extension, it is also the story of psychologists and educators seeking to better understand the differences and similarities in how they think about doing research with young children.

It all began, we suppose, when Jan was finishing her Ph.D. in Education. A six-year-old Jennifer watched as her mom spent long hours transcribing audiotapes and analyzing data for her dissertation on parental teaching practices and young children's acquisition of household vocabulary. Two decades later, Jan offered support and advice as her daughter, Jennifer, worked her way through a doctoral program in Developmental Psychology and completed her dissertation on parent–child conversation and children's scientific thinking. We find it remarkable that, despite different academic backgrounds, we came to address very similar topics and issues in our graduate work. Our shared interest in how young children learn in informal environments allowed us to become part of each other's professional worlds—a seemingly inevitable extension of being part of each other's personal worlds.

Our collaborative academic relationship, however, required both of us to learn about each other's field and its assumptions. Jan, a reconceptualist early childhood educator, was an early critic of developmentally appropriate practice (Jipson, 1991, 2000). Jennifer, a developmental psychologist, is actively engaged in experimental research on the social context of cognitive development (Callanan & Jipson, 2001; Jipson & Callanan, 2003). Several of our discussions focused on doing research with young children who, because of their ages, may be limited in their abilities to understand and consent to the research processes we employ and who often cannot verbally report what they are thinking and feeling. Thinking about these issues led to many intense conversations. We agreed that conducting research with/on young children is important in helping us learn about their development, but that doing this research can be a complicated process, fraught with (mis)understandings and (mis)interpretations. We wondered whether and how well research in our fields reflected children's understandings. As we contemplated our own perspectives, we wondered what other developmental psychologists and early childhood researchers thought about these concerns. To pursue this question, we e-mailed the following query to several colleagues at other universities: "In doing research with young children how can we be confident that our understandings represent their thoughts/behaviors/experience?" As we awaited their replies, we continued to consider the question ourselves.

One topic that we explored in our conversations was the relationship between researchers and research participants. These relationships can take many forms, varying from the traditional, in which researchers position themselves as expert inquirers into the experiences of others, to research relationships in which the researcher and participants are seen as collaborators in the research process, coconstructing understanding. Variations on these models are used across child development research, with perspectives on this issue changing across time. For example, Jennifer noted that the guidelines provided in the 2001 Publication Manual for the American Psychological Association advise authors to use terms such as *participants, respondents,* and *children* in lieu of the previously accepted term, *subjects.* We wondered whether this change in accepted language use reflects a change in the social constructions of childhood that researchers in psychology hold, and whether these constructions are reflected in their research.

In the field of education, several scholars have written about social constructions of childhood (e.g., Cannella, 1997; James, Jenks, & Prout, 1998). Examples of ways that children are sometimes viewed include considering children to be objects of adult attention and care, such as may occur in childcare studies or teacher research examining pedagogical strategies. This perspective may lead to assumptions about children being unequally able to participate in rational problem solving or adult discourse and may therefore constrain researcher understanding of what children are actually able to do and of what meanings their activities have for them. Similar issues arise when one conceives of children as developmentally maturing organisms, such as is common in much developmental psychology research. Thus, the particular understanding of childhood by researchers from different academic disciplines may influence how research is conducted and interpreted.

The developmental perspective often leads to questions of identifying children's ways of thinking and acting at particular points in time (as evidenced by stage theories), linear assumptions of development as progressive and generalizable (but see Siegler, 1996), or both. In addition to similar concerns with the linear and temporal elements of "developmentally appropriate practice," early childhood perspectives frequently focus on looking at the effect of teacher behavior, the curriculum, and the environment on the child, often failing to examine the interactive nature of such encounters.

Both the educational and psychological perspectives described above impose limitations and expectations on children. Each also inscribes power and privilege in particular ways, thus creating particular social contexts and engendering particular possibilities. For instance, in each case, there is an imposition of adult authority on the child—through research activities themselves, through the "analysis and interpretation" of research data, and through researcher choices made in representing children's experience and understandings.

Notions about childhood that we bring from our own experiences as children can also project particular understandings onto our interpretations of children's experiences (Jipson, 2000). For example, for individuals growing up in a rural community where the entire family participated in "doing the chores" and the workday ended only when the barn and field work were completed, the intuitive belief is that everyone should inherently understand the importance of "pitching in" and persisting at a task until it is completed. But do people develop the same understanding if they grow up in cities and suburbs where much paid work takes place in high-rise buildings far from homes and where children may spend most of their days with other children in schools or childcare? As researchers, does where and how we were raised lead us to interpret, for example, a child's wandering from activity to activity as "developmentally appropriate," or as irresponsible, or as an "attention deficit"? And what about the young child who persists at a task for long periods of time— is he or she "focused," "obsessed," or the holder of good work habits?

Whether researchers' perspectives on childhood are based in personal experience and memories of their own childhoods or socially transmitted within academic disciplines as part of the cultural capital of their fields, the subsequent objectification of children and their experiences necessarily impacts understanding of the research.

As we clarified our own understandings, our colleagues at other universities began sending responses to our question of how confident we could be of our interpretations of children's thoughts, behaviors, and experiences. We had hoped this question would generate a thoughtful response about doing research with children—and it did. The responses from other researchers generated another layer in our ongoing dialogue about this issue.

Our first response was from a developmental psychologist who was concerned about the validity and ethics of doing research with children.

> Well, my immediate reaction to your question is—Uuuggh! This is one of those fundamental questions about philosophy of science and personal views on unresolved issues that we often put on the back shelves of our minds, maybe with issues involving nature-nurture, afterlife, and evolution. It strikes at the heart of one's belief in the validity of the data we gather from children. For people who were raised in an era of empirical inquiry that lauded rather than scrutinized scientific methods, it sounds like a postmodern challenge to the traditional beliefs. That may polarize folks into two camps: those who want to defend empirical methods with children and those who want to show the limitations and liabilities of those methods.

Personally, I try to see merits in both positions, but I retreat from the poles to some middle ground, perhaps mushy, perhaps dialectically unresolved, that says yes, researchers can study and collect information from young children (and infants) that can represent their thoughts, behaviors, and experience in reasonable ways. However, our confidence should be tempered with skepticism so that we look for weaknesses in the methods we use and the interpretations that we render about young children. Certainly, we are trained to be critical of the work of other researchers—we need to exercise the same balance of confidence and skepticism with our own work.

Jan was encouraged to realize that colleagues studying child development from a psychological perspective shared her concerns about the validity and ethics of how we do research with children. In response, Jennifer warned of the tendency to stereotype developmental psychology researchers as being only in the empirical camp when, in actual experience, many of them are struggling with issues of researcher imposition and representation.

To explain how he deals with these issues, the first respondent went on to say:

> Your question asks how can we be confident and not how confident are we, so I should say that we can increase our confidence in several traditional ways. First, use multiple methods to gather data. Second, look for converging evidence with your results and other research. Third, look for disconfirming evidence about the data and interpretations. Fourth, try to replicate or disconfirm your own work. Fifth, gauge reactions from peers to see if the data and claims make sense to others. This may be more politically and historically situated but seems to be as important as replication at times. None of these steps alone is adequate but together they can increase the confidence one has in the representations offered about young children.

A different reaction is that the question does not really get at "children's voices." The validity of the researchers' representation seems a different angle than how the data include and reflect the "voices" of children. The stock answer then is to include qualitative data, usually excerpts and transcripts (maybe even actual voices and video) of children to convey vignettes of what they actually said. Of course, these are elicited reactions and selected samples so the issue of validity or representation comes up again but the steps outlined above may apply as safeguards. This sequence of suggestions sounds like the current views of using both quantitative and qualitative data to reinforce the interpretations and represent the range of children's reactions. That is an advance over previous decades but the real hard-core postmodernists would probably snivel at such compromises and point out that the foundation is still cracked, even if the house looks fancy from the outside. They might argue about the political correctness of such compromises and the hegemony of the empiricists who throw in a few quotes from kids. They would also whine about the lack of respect they get and the idiosyncrasies of human experience that make all generalizations fallible. Yaddy, yaddy, à la Seinfeld is the reply of the other camp. (See how the middle ground invites schizophrenia?)

This response propelled our discussion in new directions. Jan expressed her concern with intersubjectivity—and examining the nature of the relationship between oneself as researcher and the individuals participating in one's research—regardless of the methods chosen. Jennifer agreed that it is important to recognize the relational issues inherent in doing research with children. In addition, she appreciated the concrete strategies the respondent shared, particularly the notion of using multiple methodologies to explore one's research questions.

Other respondents stressed the importance of inquiring into the social and cultural contexts in which people develop in order to understand how knowledge is constructed. A professor of Early Childhood Education involved in cross-cultural research offered the following perspective:

> About your question: There are two important aspects to my approach to researching children and their perspectives. First, I look to understand the social ecology of children's lives, with the goal of understanding how they construct or otherwise arrive at knowledge, insight, and understanding. Second, I look to establish a relationship in which some degree of trust develops—mutually. I find it necessary for children to know me, in some ways, if I want to know them in more than superficial ways. It requires risk taking, of sorts—and the sharing of vulnerability. What I ask, how I ask it, and later representations are all informed by a relationship that is at first, humane and caring—at least I hope so.

An Early Childhood Researcher from Taiwan similarly commented:

> I feel your topic is very critical in research with young children. While exploring my son's play, I often wonder if I really catch the themes, which he concerns from his point of view. To try to understand his thoughts/behaviors/experience during play, I usually need to refer to his daily life experience rather than only observe play behavior itself. I feel his play themes seem to be embedded in his life themes. We live together, play together, and inter-

act with each other intimately all day long. Involving in his life lets me be able to check repeatedly his play themes according to what he is acting, talking, laughing, eating, doing, and so on.

These early childhood educators echoed our concerns with researcher relationships with children who are subjects of their research and raised the issue of the importance of continued interaction. Their perspectives resonated with our shared theoretical belief that we must inquire into the social and cultural contexts in which people develop if we hope to understand how knowledge is constructed. Jennifer acknowledged that the "rapport building" she did with children participating in her own research often consists of brief visits to their childcare centers: "It makes them comfortable enough to cooperate but I wouldn't really call it a relationship and it doesn't help me interpret what I've seen, but then again, can you ever really know children with whom you have no ongoing relationship?"

One of the developmental psychologists also spoke to the issue of relationships with children:

> I've stared at your question a few times, intending to respond, but I have to admit I'm at a loss. I've never really considered the question of "how can we be confident that our understandings represent their thoughts/behaviors/experience?" Maybe that's the point you were trying to make? I guess if I had to answer I would say that it comes mostly from my own observations of my kids. Before I had kids I was not as good a developmental psychologist as I am now, because I didn't have a good stock of common-sense experience to compare abstract theoretical and experimental stuff to. Parents do a pretty good job figuring out the thoughts/behaviors/experiences of their own kids. If a finding corresponds to my experience as a parent, I tend to give it the benefit of the doubt. If not, I tend to be skeptical. I understand that my experience may or may not be representative, but I'm not sure there's a better way to go. By the way, this is not an answer to your question—it is the reason why I find answering your questions so hard! :^)

Like the previous early childhood educator, this respondent, in referring to his relationship with his own children, focuses on how having children helped him to better interpret developmental theory and understand his research. He goes on to acknowledge the limitations from his perspective of what he calls "the insight approach":

> But, on a completely serious note, I agree that the "I've got kids so I can have insight" approach is pretty flawed and doesn't seem much like a claim to knowledge in the scientific sense. But it strikes me as the same problem that a cross-cultural psychologist or anthropologist has—as an outsider it is difficult to know how to interpret stuff from within the framework of the subjects. The problem is compounded because most adults think they remember what it was like to be a kid. Especially in educational research, a researcher's recollections of their own childhood are often the knowledge base that is tapped first. There was a whole string of meetings in the museum world where people sat around and reminisced

on their favorite childhood memories involving museums—the resulting bunch of essays has become a favorite evidence base for what good museum practice should be.

Reflecting on his comments, Jan admitted that she frequently first looks at her research questions through the lens of her own life: "I hold no strong claim to knowledge in the scientific sense; I guess I believe that all knowledge is personal—that it needs to be personally meaningful for me to embrace or 'own' it." In contrast, Jennifer argued for the value of research knowledge as a platform on which to construct meaning: "I've never been a parent but I feel that I have a good understanding of children, one that comes from both experiential and academic sources. Personal insight leads to many interesting questions and understandings, however, there is important research that can help us understand children that may not come directly from our everyday experience."

Another developmental psychologist further elaborated on the idea that experimental research can yield valuable findings:

> I think that any developmental studies of cognition that are done well are designed to create situations that are real and meaningful to children. If not, then they don't tap into children's true understanding. The cleverness of studies, then, is a measure of their ability to create situations that tap into children's true thoughts on the matter, rather than some other uninteresting thing like demand characteristics, etc.

Jennifer noted that this was just what she had been talking about: "I'd like to believe that it's possible to create experiences that can provide opportunities for insight while still giving children the best possible chance to show what they know. While parents may be able to gain these insights across time with their children, researchers often must create settings that allow them to gain the same insights."

Jan responded,

> It is not unlike teachers creating curriculum and environments that allow children to discover answers to their own questions. None of us can ever escape the imposition of our adult perspectives, experiences, and needs on the children with whom we work, but I think it is important to remain aware of the impositional quality of what we do and to allow this awareness to engage us in critical reflection on what we think we know. The same concerns apply about the choices we make as researchers as to what we ask children to do and how we represent what we learn from them.

After considering the responses of other researchers, several issues were clarified for us. One of the difficulties we see in research with young children is the assumption that researchers make that they can actually capture a child's reality at any given moment in time. The problem is that this leads to other assumptions, such as that researchers can predict a child's thinking at other moments in time or that they can make assumptions about children's thinking at similar moments in time.

The deeper problem seems to be whether capturing a moment in time is capturing the child's reality or whether it is the researcher's representation of the child's reality, given his or her own filter and assumptions. We agreed, we can't help but impose our own social and historical context on what we observe.

Thinking about these comments and our own earlier discussion, the following questions occurred to us:

▶ How can we capture another's reality when it is continually changing and when the other is a child?

▶ How can we directly engage children in the process of meaning making and knowledge production?

▶ How might we do this, given the inherent positional power and status of the researcher, which can readily overwhelm and subvert the child's understanding of her/his own experience and agency?

Although we don't have answers to these questions, we recognize that it is important to identify how children's understanding and subjectivity are shaped through their interactions with us, as well as how these interactions shape our understandings of children. We must therefore consider the historical and the social situatedness of the discourses that frame and colonize our own experiences and position us as well as the children with whom we work. The challenge then is to ground our research in the interpretations of the children. We ask, with children as coparticipants in the inquiry: What counts as research? What matters as data? What procedures are considered legitimate and ethical for the production of knowledge? How can children, themselves, contribute to the making of meaning? And how can children's knowledge be faithfully represented?

Once again, we found ourselves reflecting on the response offered by our first developmental psychologist:

If we can step way back from the camps and look at the battleground in a broader landscape, we might see how small it is and ask more basic questions about the nature of the research, not about the accuracy or validity, but about the worth of it. Does it matter to children or improve their position? Does participation in research do more than advance personal agendas of researchers; does it help improve the lives and future of children, the participants directly and others more generally? That may be the voice that goes unspoken and unasked for in research from either camp.

So where does that leave us? Still e-mailing, calling, messaging, we continue to examine our own practice of research and teaching. We have once again learned what we already knew, that we can understand more in collaboration than ever when alone. And the dialogue, which grew to include colleagues in the field, has helped us more clearly articulate what we see as the real question about what we do, whether we are psychologists or educators. We continue to ask, in our efforts to improve the lives of children, how can we best act?

REFERENCES

Callanan, M. A., & Jipson, J. L. (2001). Explanatory conversations and young children's developing scientific literacy. In K. Crowley, C. D. Schunn, & T. Okada (Eds.), *Designing for science: Implications from professional, instructional, and everyday science,* 21–50. Mahwah, NJ: Lawrence Erlbaum.

Cannella, G. (1997). *Deconstructing early childhood education.* New York: Peter Lang.

James, A., Jenks, C., & Prout, A. (Eds.). (1998). *Theorizing childhood.* New York: Teachers College Press.

Jipson, J. (1991). Developmentally appropriate practice: Culture, curriculum, connections. *Early Education and Development, 2,* 120–136.

Jipson, J. (2000). The stealing of wonderful ideas: The politics of early childhood research. In L. Diaz Soto (Ed.), *The politics of early childhood education,* 167–177. New York: Peter Lang.

Jipson, J. L., & Callanan, M. (2003). Mother-child conversation and children's understanding of biological and non-biological changes in size. *Child Development, 74,* 629–644.

Siegler, R. S. (1996). *Emerging minds: The process of change in children's thinking.* New York: Oxford University Press.

CHAPTER FOUR

RELATIONS, REFRACTIONS, AND REFLECTIONS IN RESEARCH WITH CHILDREN

ELIZABETH GRAUE
AND MARGARET HAWKINS

How we define the object of inquiry in research shapes what we can know, how we plan research strategies, and what literatures we use to support our thinking. In the case of children, we can define a child physically, developmentally, socially, culturally, discursively, historically, linguistically, politically—and this definition serves as a template for all aspects of research and practice. In our chapter, we use Berry Mayall's (2002) concept of childhood as relational as a tool for analyzing our coming-to-know children's perspectives on home–school relations. For Mayall, childhood is "constituted in particular ways as a distinctive generational position— by contrast with adulthood" (p. 23). This perspective makes sense from a variety of theoretical positions—for example, for developmentalists, a child is a child in relation to his process of becoming an adult; for sociologists, childhood is a social category defined by the structural elements of society. Mayall (2002) helps us see that this is a dynamic rather than a static process. She suggests that we should think in terms of generationing:

> The relational processes whereby people come to be known as children, and whereby children and childhood acquire certain characteristics, linked to local contexts, and changing as the factors brought to bear change. (p. 27)

Key to this relational approach is recognition that (a) the relational nature of childhood is generated in part because of the power relations between adults and children, (b) each childhood is located historically in particular times and places, and (c) the identification and articulation of "characteristics" of children and childhood are virtually always produced by adults. For the purposes of this chapter, then, we are interested in how childhood is generated in the varied contexts of home and school through interactions between researchers and children. We address the following research question:

What can we know about ourselves as researchers in relation to children with whom we work, and how is what we can learn from children in the research process shaped by the relational roles in the situated interactions?

As we approached this topic, we found ourselves taken by the many ways that our understandings were relational. While the content of our project is not the specific focus of this chapter, our interest in home–school interactions is inherently relational in that it focuses on the roles, relationships, and interactions of educators and families with the child as an object. It is the child that brings the interaction of home and school into being. Further, we found that our understandings of these children's perspectives were located in several types of relations. Our understandings were situated within notions of identity and affiliation. Who we are as researchers is related to who we are as theorists; as mothers; as middle-class, middle-aged, white women. And who we are in all our complexity is constituted by the other—through our relationships and response to those in life. We examine children relationally, we construct our role as researchers relationally and the task of reporting our role vis-à-vis children relationally.

METHODS

This project began when Beth delved into the literature on home–school relations and found that children and youth typically were seen as outcomes rather than participants. At the same time, Maggie was working with a local kindergarten teacher to try to understand the connections made by diverse parents to the curriculum content. The two of us began talking about the possibility of working together to understand both student and parent perspectives on home–school relations, and we developed a project that involved interviews with pairs of parents and fourth graders who attended an integrated elementary school.

Several attributes are important in this sample. The school draws children from five very different neighborhoods. Three of the neighborhoods house diverse families living in modest homes and apartments (publicly subsidized and privately held), and the other two are populated by middle- and upper-income professionals. We selected a small sample of students to proportionately represent the demographic characteristics of the school. The initial sampling plan called for six white, middle-/upper-middle-class children (three boys and three girls) and two African Americans, two Hmong, and two Latino/as (evenly divided between working-class boys and girls). The fact that Beth is a parent in this community and Maggie has been doing research there made it impossible for us to suppose that we were detached observers. Our connections forced us to examine the ramifications of our research choices. Beth invited children whom she knew—friends of her son and their parents, to heighten the salience of "insider" knowledge, lessen the adult–child divide, and to attend to the issues of doing research in her own back-yard. Maggie worked through paraprofessionals connected to the school to identify families, ascertain their willingness to participate in the project, and obtain permission for interviews. Thus, Beth worked with children and parents with whom she had already established relationships, and from an assumption of shared cultural understandings, whereas Maggie worked with families she had never met, and from an assumption that culturally embedded viewpoints, beliefs, and communication strategies would require negotiation.

QUESTIONS THAT REFLECT, QUESTIONS THAT REFRACT

It's always about access. Our scholarly knowledge is always constrained by who is sampled. Our experience in this project was equally shaped by our participants. We found ourselves teetering as we crossed myriad borders—adult-child, gender, linguistic, cultural, friendship—and were frequently caught up short by the outcomes. We'll begin by talking about silence in this chapter as it provides some interesting lessons on generationing.

The initial sampling plan called for equal numbers of boys and girls across racial and ethnic groups. Beth's final group was composed of four boys and one girl. How did that happen? *Samples are not always defined by researchers.* She conducted interviews either at her house or at the participant's home, bringing a homemade treat to share. In most cases, she interviewed the parent and child at different times. For two girls who were classmates of her son, Beth interviewed in the child's home, talking at length with parents. In both cases, Andrea and Alyson disappeared during the interview and when it came to be their turn to speak, they quietly but adamantly refused. Multiple adaptations were offered, from giving them the interview protocol and a tape recorder so they could do the interview alone, to doing the interview with their parent(s) present or absent, to doing it later. They declined. Beth has worried about the ability of kids (and girls in particular) to opt out of research projects and was pleased that they were able to say no. The researcher side of her was disappointed, having just had really wonderful interviews with the parents and being curious about the daughters' views. The methodologist thinks it's fascinating. We've puzzled over how to understand it, stymied by an inability to ask because we take seriously the notion that no is not maybe later. What we have come to is a relational understanding, one that recognizes belatedly that at least for two middle-class girls in fourth grade, power relations between adults and children are permeable. That choosing not to speak is a way of making a very strong statement, and over time, perhaps we'll understand what that statement is. Further, our understandings of these children's voices, taken collectively, will require recognition absent voices.

Also absent from our group are children who are not school affiliated (i.e., have made strong connections with the school in terms of identity and activity). Regardless of the connections we had with participants, we found that all families placed high value on education, and while certainly not homogeneous in terms of their relationships with schools, all of the children saw themselves as students.

For Maggie, access to participants was mediated. Because she did not have direct personal relationships with families with fourth graders from these cultural groups, she relied on people who did. The people she knew to approach were paraprofessionals in the school. Thus, the relationships she could establish with participants were mediated through other relationships.

Additionally, for all four families, the father was the parent interviewed; thus, there are no mothers' voices represented. In one case this may have been because the father had enough English to converse freely, whereas the mother didn't. For the other three, however, we used the services of an interpreter. In these families, we hypothesize that this is a cultural phenomenon; we know, for example, that it is the fathers who attend conferences at school, and the children talk about their fathers checking to see that homework is done, and insisting on the children's focus on education.

There was only one African-American family. Because there is not an African-American paraprofessional in the schools, Maggie relied on teachers' suggestions to identify a member of the local African-American community who is a strong advocate for these families in school. And when Maggie explained the project, the woman simply stated, "You're asking for a favor. What are you offering them?" We were caught up short. What *were* we going to do for them? Unable to come up with a satisfactory response, our facilitator couldn't mediate access. The family who eventually participated was identified only through circumstance; they have another child in the kindergarten classroom in which Maggie conducts research, and through this she came to establish a relationship with the mother. It was the relationship itself that provided access.

Insider knowledge. Beth's location as a community member gave her insider knowledge that she could use to pick up references to local culture in interviews. Knowing the families and the school gave a common knowledge set to which she could refer—the names of important events and siblings could be used as currency. In the following example, Beth talks with Alex about school events his family might attend. She relies on her experience in the school community and her knowledge of Alex's family to build on his responses:

Beth: Now lots of times schools have different kinds of events to bring families into the school.

Alex: Right, the Roosevelt Carnival is coming up.

Beth: Well, tell me about the Roosevelt Carnival.

Alex: Well, um, I kind of forgot from last year. But there's games and a raffle that raises money for the PTO and, um—I don't know.

Beth: OK—can you think of other ones?

Alex: Um, the Lester Smith concert.

Beth: I didn't go to that concert but I saw you on TV.

Alex: We got it on tape.

Beth: Yeah—pretty cool!

Alex: Some of the strings events.

Beth: OK, so the ones that you went to, who went with you?

Alex: My parents.

Beth: Did Natasha go too?

Alex: Well for the strings, it's usually at 9:00, so she's in school. And the Lester Smith concert, Natasha went. For the Roosevelt Carnival, Natasha comes.

Beth: OK, what's it like for you when you go to those events? Is it fun, is it weird?

Alex: It's fun, I think.

Beth: What's fun about it?

Alex: Well, I don't know it's like, if it's like in the middle of school, if it's like a strings concert it's like a break from school, like a little recess. Where you get to do things with your friends and your classmates.

While the shared cultural knowledge provided connections, it also served to block productive questioning. Because both participants assumed certain shared understandings, the kind of unpacking of cultural knowledge that can be so productive in ethnographic interviews was sometimes slighted. Beth didn't follow up about the string program or work to get Alex to elaborate on many of his answers. In contrast, Maggie was able to question Shoua authentically about references to school events because she had general, but less specific, knowledge of activities:

Maggie: The school does different things to get the families together, and to get the families and the teachers together.

Shoua: Well, I don't really know.

Maggie: Like a school fair, or a carnival, or picnics, or different kinds of parties—anything like that does the school do?

Shoua: Well when I used to be in Mrs. Ansell's class . . . I think like first and second, well actually it's in first . . . and they do a supermarket in the school.

Maggie: Yeah—it's it's called something—it's called—I forget. But like the international—it's like a fair, you go around to different classes.

Shoua: Yeah.

Maggie: And buy stuff.

Shoua:	Yeah and they do it in the hallways and stuff.
Maggie:	Right.
Shoua:	And like they—the teachers give you fake money.
Maggie:	Cool—to spend?
Shoua	nods yes.
Maggie:	So did your family come to that?
Shoua:	No. There were no families at that.
Maggie:	Just the kids?
Shoua:	Yeah.

In some ways these interchanges could come right out of Spradley's *The Ethnographic Interview* (1979), illustrating how to elicit cultural knowledge (or not). But the issues are not just methodological. They are conceptual, illustrating the knowing that comes to be in scaffolding conversations versus giving an out. Interviews with children are often represented in the literature as examples of particular kinds of discourse, framed by the developmental understandings of the children and the pedagogical techniques of the interviewer. While we were aware that stylistic differences shape the nature of ethnographic interviews, we learned as much about ourselves through interview responses as we did about the children we interviewed. Identity and cultural models of interaction were key aspects of these interviews. Maggie came to the interviews assuming that she was crossing cultural borders, interviewing children who held quite different cultural models for schooling and family life than she had. This understanding was located within her work with English Language Learners, and traces of ESL pedagogy can be seen in her interview practice. Maggie uses multiple strategies to scaffold student responses, coming at questions a number of ways, restating responses, checking on understanding.

Maggie:	At home who's mostly in charge of your learning?
Pheng:	Ummm . . . myself.
Maggie:	You're mostly in charge of your learning?
Pheng:	Yeah.
Maggie:	Does anybody here help you with school stuff?
Pheng:	Yeah.
Maggie:	Who helps?
Pheng:	My brother.
Maggie:	Your brother—was that the one who just came in?
Pheng:	Yeah.
Maggie:	That brother helps you with school stuff. What does he do to help you learn? Your brother . . .
Pheng:	He tells me whatever I don't know.
Maggie:	So when you say you're in charge of your learning, what do you do? Like, what decisions do you make, and what do you do to take charge of your learning?
Pheng:	I just try to figure it out, and then, like, when I do all of them and I have like some left, I go ask my brother what they mean and stuff.

Maggie:	OK. So you have to say, "I'm gonna do my homework now." Or "I'm gonna work on this." But then if you get stuck and you ask him, he'll help you.
Pheng:	Yeah.
Maggie:	Is that right?
Pheng:	Yeah.

In contrast, Beth's interviewing occurred within presumed shared cultural models but across the adult–child developmental divide. She used humor, inside and historical knowledge to facilitate participation. The following examples provide a window on her thinking about interactions:

Beth:	At school, who is mostly in charge of your learning? [silence] The janitor?
Hannah:	The teacher.
Beth:	The teacher—OK. And what does the teacher do to help you learn?
Hannah:	She explains EVERYTHING practically.
Beth:	Oh—is that a good thing? [Hannah nods yes.] Can you give me an example of a time she explained things?
Hannah:	Ummmmm. [then silence]
Beth:	If you can't remember, that's fine too.
Hannah:	I can't remember.

Both interviewers used the same question framework and the same developmental expectations of interchange. Both restate responses to provide validation and to echo grammatical constructions. But each used cues given by the students in very different ways, which came out of their interpretations of how to facilitate interaction with particular children. For Maggie, hesitation was seen as a linguistic issue for which language scaffolding was the appropriate response, while Beth took hesitation as frustration or concern, and offered reassurance, or allowed students to opt out of answering. What does this mean? The first is that interview responses are not in and of themselves indicators of any particular knowledge on the part of participants. Interviews are conversations—interactions that ebb and flow and that represent opportunities given and taken by participants. And these interactions can be read in multiple ways. We were both clear that interview protocols are not blunt instruments that should be used in wholly standardized ways. But given the dialogic nature of interviews, how do we understand the respondents' words when they are so contingent on our invitations? Beth found herself puzzling over whether she was following her respondents leads or whether she had worked to silence them by skipping to the "next question." How had she shut down the conversation by not attempting to draw out further response, or redirecting? And Maggie wondered continually about whether the meanings constructed in the interactions in real time were shared between interviewer and interviewee, or if they were in fact discussing different things that she was not able to recognize. Then, too, because the questions themselves were constructed out of our understandings of children's worlds and linguistic abilities, were we providing the opportunities for them to tell us the things that mattered to them?

Another concern that this process brought to light was the contexts in which the interviews were conducted. Beth conducted hers either in her home or in the child's home. Her interviews, by and large, take on a less formal tone than Maggie's. When interviewing in her home, she often had to shift between roles of researcher and parent. During one interview there are a number of interruptions, including violin in the background drowning out responses (imagine a nine-year-old in his first month of school-based violin lessons, playing "Twinkle, Twinkle Little Star"—not something they discuss in methodological texts) and refereeing a wrestling match in the front yard. The interviews were a bizarre hybrid of research and playdate.

For Maggie, inviting the children to her home seemed both inappropriate and unfeasible. Although she was willing to go to the homes of the interviewees, the children and adults needed to be interviewed separately, and for some of the interviewees privacy was not available in their homes. All of the parents were interviewed at home. The first child interview, however, took place in school. Maggie took the child to the library and found a quiet table. The interview, although following the same formula as the others, felt stilted and stiff. On reflection, we tried to imagine how a child might feel when pulled out of her class at school by an adult stranger, told to sit at a table in the library (with the attendant formality and silence requirements of that environment), asked to participate in a form of structured interaction she had never experienced, and having a microphone placed in front of her. What must she have imagined we wanted of her?

Maggie moved to interview children and parents in their homes. For one child, this worked well; he had a rec room in the basement reserved for our use. For another, though, there were multiple siblings in a small space, and though the parents left the room, the children didn't. The interviewee was distracted as they prompted him, provided answers, giggled, and turned on the television. He, also, was not relaxed, and had difficulty focusing. For another child, the interview took place in a neighborhood bakery. The bakery was quiet, and the child enjoyed her snack, thus perhaps building some degree of ease and intimacy. Again, however, we found ourselves questioning relational aspects: how did the child perceive us? How did she perceive her task? What might she think we wanted and expected of her? She was taken by a white, middle-class stranger to a place outside her usual experiences, placed at a table with a microphone in front of her, and asked to engage in an unfamiliar pattern of communication. What we take this all to mean is that context is everything— it defines the meanings made of interaction. Too frequently, researchers gloss over these contextual frames in their reach for universal findings across universal children.

DISCUSSION

As we reflect on our interactions with children and our discussion of them here, we are reminded of the segment on David Letterman called, *Is this anything?* In this recurring piece, an individual presents something to the audience (a trick, an act, etc.) and Letterman asks, "Is it anything?" The gist is that something can be something but it isn't necessarily anything. Is the act that we are defining childhood relationally and illustrating the concept through our research exploits anything? We hope so—and for more than the reason that we are now nearing the end of the chapter. We hope that our case has helped to make more salient the ways in which knowledge in general and of children in particular is highly contextualized. Any entity, and our knowledge of it, is situated in particular times and places. What this project helped us to see is the dialogic relationships of our situatedness and our participants' situatedness. It brought to life Mayall's contention that

> [W]e can use the idea of generationing (analogously to gendering) as a concept that helps us understand processes through which social positions are constituted, reproduced and transformed through relational activity. Study of generationing is essential because childhood is essentially relational with adulthood, not least because the power to define it lies with adults, who define it as different from adulthood. (2002, p. 40)

This relational reading of the child and our methodological choices made to illustrate his/her sense of self can be theorized (be made into anything) in a number of different ways. We could, for example, use Bakhtinian theory to understand the self as a simultaneous composition of its uniqueness and its relation to the other (Bakhtin, 1990; Emerson, 1997). The particular situatedness of ourselves as researchers only takes on meaning within the location and relation to each other, to our varied communities (academic, professional, political, geographical), and to our participants. From a Bakhtinian perspective, the interview is a particular kind of speech act, with participants holding the dual roles of author and addressee. The conversation is framed by particular purposes that in Beth's case involved presumed knowledge but new roles, and in Maggie's case involved awareness of border crossing and the tenuous role of language in meaning making. Each of us and our participating children authored our interactions with particular knowledge, purposes, and intentions while simultaneously serving as an audience for the other. In this back and forth, we created intersubjective understandings that were both unique and shared. Further, these understandings were populated by the words of others—they reflected, refracted, and related to our histories, our needs, and the tools we brought to the interview. This Baktinian bricolage could be supplemented or substituted by other theoretical tools. It could be just as productive to read these experiences through cultural model theory (D'Andrade & Strauss, 1992), through identity theory (Holland, Lachiocotte, Skinner, & Cain, 1998), through symbolic interactionism (Goffman, 1959), among others. What it becomes is in relation to what we are making it, just as the children with whom we worked were something in relation to ourselves as adults. They were anything but passive in their conversations with us, enacting ways of thinking about the world and their relationship to us in a context of us thinking about the world and our relationship to them.

REFERENCES

Bakhtin, M. M. (1990). *Art and answerability: Early philosophical essays by M. M. Bakhtin.* Austin: University of Texas Press.

D'Andrade, R., & Strauss, C. (Eds.). (1992). *Human motives and cultural models.* Cambridge, UK: Cambridge University Press.

Emerson, C. (1997). *The first hundred years of Mikhail Bakhtin.* Princeton, NJ: Princeton University Press.

Goffman, E. (1959). *The presentation of self in everyday life.* Garden City, NJ: Doubleday.

Holland, D., Lachicotte, W., Skinner, D., & Cain, C. (1998). *Identity and agency in cultural worlds.* Cambridge, MA: Harvard University Press.

Mayall, B. (2002). *Towards a sociology for childhood. Thinking from children's lives.* Buckingham, UK: Open University Press.

Spradley, J. (1979). *The ethnographic interview.* New York: Houghton Mifflin.

COMING HOME
TO RESEARCH

BRIAN EDMISTON

Playing creates imagined spaces in fictional worlds that can be entered by people of all ages. Yet in early childhood research, play is almost exclusively regarded as the special province of childhood. Play is an activity to be observed by adults (Katch, 2001; Paley, 1988; Reynolds & Jones, 1997; Thorne, 1993) to understand children's perspectives (Graue & Walsh, 1998) rather than to be participated in with children (Cohen, 2001; Corsaro, 1985; Kelly-Byrne, 1989).

The potential benefit for adults, as well as for children, in playing together has been overlooked. The socially constructed categories of adult versus child reify hierarchies of authority and undermine "adult" participation in "children's" activities (James, Jenks, & Prout, 1998). Though we acknowledge that meaning is socially constructed (Vygotsky, 1978), as adults we are often wary of our participation in play events. We resist the introduction of our authority to structure and interpret play in "the child's world," as if that world were constructed exclusively by children in the first place (Dyson, 1993).

Looking outside-in at play as an early childhood activity, it is easy to forget not only that different adults can interpret the same events quite differently (Hauser & Jipson, 1998), but also that as adults we can misinterpret the reality of play for children. We can easily regard children's actions as abuses of power and ironically impose our authority as adults to control, ban, or limit play activities and interpretations that are actually significant for young people's meaning making (Carlsson-Paige & Levin, 1987; Katch, 2001; Paley, 1988).

Play creates imagined spaces in possible worlds (Bruner, 1986) that as adults we can enter with children to give us inside experiences and perspectives that are not possible if we remain on the outside looking in. If we play with a child we can productively use our power to share authority so that we may coexplore the meanings of events in imagined spaces.

Relying on the theories of Bakhtin (1981, 1984a, 1984b, 1986, 1990), I argue that when we share authority with children as we play our interactions will be "dialogic" so that children and adults can raise and explore questions of import that would otherwise not be possible (Edmiston, 1998; Edmiston & Enciso, 2002). Play is dialogic when different meanings of events are set in motion so that "all may be juxtaposed to one another, mutually supplement one another, contradict one another, and co-exist in the consciousness" (Bakhtin, 1981, p. 292). As children desire repetitions of play events, as was the case when I played with my son (aged two–seven), questions can be explored over time, the events can become more elaborated, and the dialogic meaning of the underlying ideas can become more complex.

I have often encountered the critique that playing with my son could have been interruptive for him, but rarely is the point made that, as a father, I necessarily cared about the development of my relationship with my son, Michael, or that our play could have been enriching for our lives, giving us both insights into humanity. Unlike other researchers who participate in child's play and then leave the research site (Corsaro, 1985; Kelly-Byrne, 1989), I knew that I would continue to live with the meaning of our play for myself and for my son. Instead of creating a voyeuristic or exploitative site for research, my inquiry into our play turned the research lens toward my actions, decisions, and understandings as much as it illuminated my son's explorations of human dilemmas.

My understanding of why and how we can share authority in adult-child research changed significantly through inquiry and play with Michael, who is now aged fourteen. In this chapter I show how adults could learn about some of the deepest aspects of themselves by researching their play with children. Over several years I examined some of my assumptions and beliefs about research, and life, and these understandings developed as Michael and I interacted as coauthors of action and meaning in the imagined spaces of play.

COMING HOME TO RESEARCH

I came home to research when I began playing with our young son. Playing was the primary mode of communication and relationship building with Michael in his early childhood. In the research, I focused on what I was learning about both play and myself as a researcher. I recorded play episodes over several years (1992–1997) and wrote narrative interpretations of the meaning of our play.

Our play and my inquiry created a "space of authoring" (Holland, Lachicotte, Skinner, & Cain, 1998) in which I could not only author actions but also author meaning about myself and the world that included my understanding of play and inquiry. Over time, a question that guided my analysis (and the one I used in writing this chapter) became: How did my understanding of myself as an adult-father-researcher change through playing with my son?

The lines of communication and analysis in inquiry are never straight but are rather bent, or "refracted," by people's perspectives and values as they select, use, and interpret words. Bakhtin uses the term *refraction* to highlight how in our use of spoken and written language we create meaning *indirectly* about ourselves and about our relationships with others. When we use words to write and when we interact with others, including when we play with someone else, language does not transfer meaning directly.

Bakhtin (1981) stresses that "Language is not a neutral medium" since it comes to us already "populated with the intentions [and values] of others" (p. 294). To understand anything using words we populate language with our own intentions and values. However, we never bend words to make individual meaning that is separated from other people's meanings and our own previous understandings. All ideas are located in intentions, assumptions, and beliefs that are to differing degrees shared with other people. Making meaning always requires effort that may become a struggle as we experience varying degrees of tension or conflict between and among prior and new understandings.

Part of coming to understand is becoming more aware of, and discriminating among, the competing ideological roots of our own and other people's ideas. In dialogic interactions not only a person's words, but also their values, are in degrees of competition with another person's words and values. Beliefs and values become more apparent in exchanges when our ideas are critiqued or challenged as my understandings of play and research were challenged when I played with Michael.

My research was interpretive (Erickson, 1986), reflective (Schön, 1983), and refractive (Bakhtin, 1981) inquiry. As an teacher–researcher I had engaged in reflective practitioner research into using drama and play with children for curricular purposes in my own third- and fourth-grade classroom and in other teachers' classrooms (Edmiston, 1993; Edmiston & Wilhelm, 1996; Taylor, 1998). I was comfortable both playing with school-aged children and using reflective analysis to guide my practice. Inquiry as a father–researcher was more seamlessly woven into the fabric of everyday life than it had been in the classroom.

Researching at home was more of a struggle and was less straightforward than I had expected. The meaning of our play was contested. I soon recognized that other parents and teachers had interpretations of the nature and value of play at home and in school that often differed from, and sometimes conflicted with, one another and with my own changing understandings.

The tensions among these views connected with and extended some of the questions in the field. When is play mostly imitation of external reality and important for the individual construction of understanding (Piaget, 1975) and when is it more significant as social interaction that plays with reality to lead development (Vygotsky, 1967)? How much are children manipulated by media and how much do they resist or transform intended meanings to actively construct their own understandings (Dines & Humez, 2003; Levin, 1998)? When is play more like a window into the existing reality of children's psyches and hidden desires (Freud, 1933), and when can play, like art, create a time-space in which social, cultural, and ideological reality can be examined (Bakhtin, 1990)? Are children being violent and/or might they become violent if they pretend to hurt and kill (Paley, 1988; Carlsson-Paige & Levin, 1987)? Why might boys learn to be aggressive and oppressive in gendered play (Thorne, 1993), especially in play with toys that are marketed for young males (Goldstein, 1994)? Does play only promote a stage in a child's moral development (Kohlberg, 1984) or through playing together might adults as well as children develop ethical understandings (Edmiston, 2000)?

Anyone who talks or writes about play, whether in an academic or family setting, is unavoidably using a term with ideological force that is populated with different people's assumptions and beliefs about the value of play in different situations and relationships. Everyone has a different understanding of play because of how the term is linked to various images, experiences, and other people's meanings, which often include ideas about what is wise parenting or good teaching.

As I inquired into my play with our son, I explored questions like those just listed. I also had opportunities to examine and change my understanding of myself as an adult-father-researcher. Ideas about play, parenting, and research that had previously seemed obvious and stable to me, looked less obvious and more open to question when they collided with and were refracted by other ideas.

PLAY

I had almost continual opportunities to play with my son because, like most young children, he had a playful attitude to almost any activity, transforming mundane events into imaginary possibilities. He focused much more on the possible fictional meanings of objects, actions, situations, and relationships than on their literal meaning (Bruner, Jolly, & Sylva, 1976; Garvey, 1977; Holland, Lachicotte, Skinner, & Cain, 1998; Pelligrini, 1991; Vygotsky, 1967). For example, though we had read and played with several of Beatrix Potter's stories, it was not until we had a walk in the woods one day that Michael, aged three, wanted to pretend to be inside the world of *The Tale of Jemima Puddle-Duck* (Potter, 1908/1984). Seeing a flapping crow, he transformed it into Jemima Puddle-Duck flying to the woods; one of the book's watercolor illustrations shows her gliding toward the trees. He scampered ahead of me on the path, took the map I was carrying, and sat on a log pretending to read the newspaper. He imagined that I was Jemima meeting him as the fox when he said, "Daddy, you're Jemima and you ask me where you can lay your eggs." A minute after we talked as goose and fox he had turned rocks into eggs. As in the original story, he pretended to be the fox, chased me away, and ate the eggs.

Playing with my son was extremely pleasurable (Huizinga, 1955), and was central to communication (Bateson, 1955; Schwartzman, 1978), conceptual development (Vygotsky, 1967), and building an intimate relationship (Kelly-Byrne, 1989). Our play was also carnivalesque when our individual or shared actions disrupted or inverted norms of hierarchical adult–child authority (Bakhtin, 1984b; Grace & Tobin, 1997). For example, I loved pretending to be the silly naïve goose meeting the clever but dangerous fox. Michael was learning about the dangers of trusting strangers at the same time as we were deepening the trust in our own relationship. It did not bother me that in play he was stronger and cleverer than I was, because we had created a carnivalesque space of pleasurable, shared authority. Our play was not a time where Michael overpowered me but was rather a time for dialogue.

DIALOGIC PLAY

Our play was dialogic when we each had the authority to shape and interpret play events and thus could encounter struggles for meaning. Though I usually followed my son's lead in terms of the focus of our play, I was not the object of his play but rather our play was most often "the meeting of two subjects and two authors" (Bakhtin, 1986, p. 107). We each improvised words and movement appropriate for imagined social situations. As Michael chose play events he was insistent about what should happen. However he did not dominate or silence me when I said or did something that was unexpected. Though he would use the medium of play to redirect my attention he most often listened and responded to what I said and did. His actions and responses might be loud and very animated but they were always possible ways of interacting I was the one who on occasions made interactions less dialogic when I curtailed or insisted on certain behaviors. Finally, if one of us wanted to stop playing the other did so, though often not without protest as far as Michael was concerned.

In improvisation we "piece together existing cultural resources opportunistically to address present conditions and problems" (Holland, Lachicotte, Skinner, & Cain, 1998, p. 277). We talk and move in response to imagined conditions and problems. To do so we selectively draw on cultural resources from our life experiences that include the fictional narratives we know.

Most of my improvised actions as I played with our son drew on fictional narratives that we had introduced to him since birth via literally hundreds of books and videos. When an encounter in a story captivated his imagination, for weeks or months he would ask one of us to pretend with him—to be the people or creatures in the story. When he was aged three we were imagining the events in Beatrix Potter's tales. Aged four we were battling as heroes and monsters from myths like *St. George and the Dragon* (Hodges, 1984). By the age of five we were pretending to be creatures like Frankenstein and the Wolfman from the Universal Studios movies of the 1940s and 1950s.

As we played I improvised actions that felt appropriate in response to Michael's actions within both the particular imagined social situation and the broader cultural milieu. Imagining that I was Mr. McGregor in Beatrix Potter's (1903/1984) *The Tale of Peter Rabbit,* I pretended not to find the hiding Peter Rabbit/Michael. Wanting Michael to learn more about sharing (and unlike the character in the tale), I mused aloud that if he was hungry and had asked I would have given him vegetables to eat.

Sharing authority in dialogic play was essential for each of us to be able to author actions and significant meaning. I used my authority as a parent to control his behavior when I was concerned that he might physically hurt himself; for example, by insisting that he not climb beyond my reach at the park. Most often I shared authority with him; for example, when we negotiated what and where we would play. As we played, it was not my words, but rather imagined spaces and contexts that provided the social controls for his (and my) actions (Vygotsky, 1967). For example, when he pretended to be Peter Rabbit sneaking into Mr. McGregor's garden, he quietly squeezed along the floor.

Authority was dispersed among the people and creatures we imagined within each of the fictional worlds that we explored in play. Michael took on the authority of whatever person (or creature) he pretended to be and he wanted me to do the same. We played with relating to one another in multiple ways beyond our everyday hierarchical father–son relationship. We authored meaning from related viewpoints that had very different degrees and forms of power. He loved pretending to be very strong and noisy, but he also wanted to imagine being weak and quiet. Pretending to be Mr. McGregor, Michael could yell, "Stop, thief!" as he chased me (pretending to be Peter Rabbit) and then pretend to lock Peter Rabbit/me up. Seconds later, he would switch to pretend to be Peter whimpering to McGregor/me as he apologized for taking carrots and then asking for some food to share with his family.

REFRACTIVE PLAY

As we interact with another person our views can range from being in close agreement to being in intense opposition depending on the "refractive angle" between them (Bakhtin 1981, p. 300). We cannot avoid dissonance when we play because play interactions, like all exchanges, are always to a degree refractive. Though much of the play with my son felt exuberant and unproblematic, our play was most refractive for me when I found myself improvising words and actions that felt at odds with how I believed I would have behaved in everyday situations. When I interacted with Michael, despite my discomfort, I became more aware of the values, assumptions, and beliefs embedded in my language and thought and more open to changes in my ideas.

Interactions are easy when there is already much agreement. The more divergent people's ideas, the more refraction there is between them, the more discomfort we are likely to feel. Usually when Michael wanted us to pretend to be elsewhere as if we were other people or creatures, I was aware of little refraction between Michael's ideas and mine. Most often there was fairly close agreement between what Michael asked me to do, and what I was comfortable doing. Occasionally I felt intense opposition.

One particularly refractive experience for me was the first time Michael wanted me to pretend to be a police officer shooting someone. As a pacifist and a Quaker I was fundamentally opposed to hurting and killing people. Having grown up in Northern Ireland living in a violent divided society, I believed that I would never use a gun in an aggressive act. I did not anticipate on that day, when I felt such antipathy, that our play and my subsequent inquiry would allow me to examine, clarify, and develop those and other beliefs.

PLAYING IN THE WORLD OF JEKYLL AND HYDE

From a set of stories of classic movie monsters that a librarian directed him to when he was four years five months old, Michael discovered Robert Louis Stevenson's story of *Dr. Jekyll and Mr. Hyde* (1886/1992). He was particularly captivated by the tale of the kind, respectable, and socially responsible physician Dr. Henry Jekyll, who turned into the monstrously egotistical Mr. Edward Hyde when Jekyll took a potion that he had made in his laboratory. As soon as he realized that we could rent the movies illustrated in the book, he begged to borrow them. Within days we had reread many of the stories several times and watched extracts from *Dr. Jekyll and Mr. Hyde* as well as *The Wolfman*, *Frankenstein*, and *Frankenstein Meets the Wolfman*. We had also pretended to be characters from the stories.

A central condition and problem of the story of Jekyll and Hyde that appealed to Michael, was how to react to the violent, and eventually deadly, deeds of Hyde. Play was integral to our dialogue as Michael responded to my questions and improvised his own responses from his images of the story and other narratives.

The following extracts are from a transcript of an audiotape of us playing in our living room.

Michael:	You're Mr. Hyde and I'm Dr. Jekyll. We're the same person.

[In quick succession he imagines he is a werewolf who tries to attack Mr. Hyde/me, a little boy asking me/Hyde for money, and an adult sitting in front of Hyde/me. Michael tells me/Hyde to push him out of the way. As the werewolf he tries to wrestle me. As the boy and the adult he falls over.]

Brian:	Get out of my way.
Michael:	Now I'm Mr. Hyde and you're a person.
Michael:	Get out of my way [pretending to push me and repeating the words I've just said as Hyde].
Brian:	Please help me.
Michael:	Get out of my way. I'm a monster.
Michael:	You're another person who helps him [i.e., the victim].
Brian:	Can you help me?

[He changes to imagine he is my wife and we talk about what to do. He tells me to phone the police. He imagines we are police officers and wants to write in a book what has happened. He wants us to look for Hyde and imagines that we go into a house. He looks up and points.]

Michael:	It's Mr. Hyde. Come on. Shoot. Shoot.
Brian:	Wait a minute. You have to be very careful it's the right person.
Michael:	Yea. Come on. Shoot.
Brian:	Wait a minute. You have to be very careful it's the right person.
Michael:	Oh dear. It's him his claws (inaudible).
Brian:	Shall we have it that he's up on the roof tops and you . . .
Michael:	and I (inaudible) yes.

[He changes to pretend to be Dr. Jekyll.]

As we began to play I felt little dissonance as we imagined that I was Hyde confronting my son who pretended in quick succession to be a werewolf, a child, and an adult. I was happy wrestling with my son, as I had enjoyed rough-and-tumble play since he was a toddler. In initiating our play he improvised from the narrative of *The Wolfman* as he imagined who might encounter Hyde. He had discovered this story at the same time as the tale of Jekyll and Hyde. Though I was not thinking about this as we played, as I enacted what Michael wanted to experience. By pretending to push the Wolfman/Michael, I confirmed by my actions that no child or adult, and not even a powerful werewolf, could stop Hyde from being violent.

REFRACTION IN INNER AND SOCIAL SPEECH

As we continued, our play became highly refractive as I experienced conflict between what Bakhtin (1984a) refers to as the "voices" of inner speech. My words "Wait a minute. You have to be careful it's the right person" suggest the hesitation I felt as part of an inner struggle between different voices. When Michael wanted us to pretend to be police officers, I found myself resisting using the imaginary police officer's gun. I heard different voices that I felt pulled me between pretending to shoot, and not shoot. In one ear I heard a voice insist that because I was pretending to be the police officer I should pull the trigger. This was a powerful voice that had developed since I had first played with Michael and that now urged me to enact whatever he earnestly wanted to experience if it was consistent with the fictional world of the narrative; it felt quite appropriate for an armed police officer to shoot Hyde in order to stop him from killing. In my other ear I heard the equally powerful Quaker pacifist voice developed over a lifetime that was adamantly opposed to killing people.

The words that I spoke, "Wait a minute. You have to be very careful it's the right person," along with my lack of movement, were, using Bakhtin's term, my "utterance." My utterance was an improvised response or "answer" to my son's utterance, as if he were a police officer, that he had "addressed" to me as he pointed and used commanding words: "It's Mr. Hyde. Come on. Shoot. Shoot." But my utterance at that moment was also in answer to the other voices by which I felt addressed.

As Bakhtin's collaborator Voloshinov (1986) noted, "the immediate social situation and the broader social milieu wholly determine—and determine from within, so to speak—the structure of an utterance" (p. 86). My hesitation was my conflicted answer to, on the one hand, my son's utterance in our social speech that resonated with an inner voice in the "immediate social situation," which addressed me with a demand that I shoot, and, on the other hand, an inner voice in my "broader social milieu" that demanded I not shoot.

At the same time our interactions were for me both inner speech and social speech. My utterance was "double-voiced" because in our improvised dialogue I was answering more than one voice. My discourse was directed both toward my son and toward inner voices that he did not hear. I experienced the voices "encounter one another and coexist in [my] consciousness" (Bakhtin, 1981, p. 291). As I struggled to pretend to be the police officer holding a gun that I pointed at an imagined Hyde, there was an intense interaction and struggle between the voices, which I felt as dissonance. As Bakhtin (1984a) notes, "What matters is the dialogic [or refractive] angle at which [the voices] are juxtaposed or counterposed" (p. 182). At this moment they felt oppositional.

EASING REFRACTION

The refractive angle of our play eased significantly as Michael shifted to pretend to be Jekyll. My utterances were still double-voiced, but I focused more on my inner speech than I did on the social speech with my son. It was only later as I returned to this moment and compared it with other similar moments that I was struck by the meaning that Michael was making.

Having announced that Mr. Hyde had changed back into Dr. Jekyll, Michael stood still looking puzzled.

Brian:	Henry. What are you doing?
Michael:	I can't remember.

[I pretend to read in a newspaper about the people who had been killed.]

Brian:	Who could have done this, Henry? Do you know?
Michael:	I changed into Mr. Hyde.
Brian:	Henry, you mean that was you?
Michael:	I don't want to do all this mean stuff.

[I pretend to read in the newspaper that the police say Mr. Hyde should be killed.]

Brian:	Henry, what do you think should happen? Should Mr. Hyde be killed?
Michael:	No, because if Mr. Hyde is killed that means me myself is going to be killed.
Brian:	But you're not Mr. Hyde, Henry.
Michael:	Well I change into him.
Brian:	Only when you drank this potion.
Michael:	Yea. I'm going to lock it up. Right now. Here.

[He pretends to lock it in a safe and I help him.] . . .

I was still thinking about the previous episode when the police officer/I was holding the gun. I was answering this voice when I improvised that there was an account in the newspaper that said the police thought that Hyde should be killed and I asked Michael if he agreed. When he said, "No, because if Mr. Hyde is killed that means me myself is going to be killed," he was restating the idea that he had articulated as we began to play "You're Mr. Hyde and I'm Dr. Jekyll. We're the same person."

It was only later as I reflected on our play that I realized Michael had captured a central understanding of the story that I did not carry with me as we imagined.

I was treating Jekyll and Hyde as separate people whereas he understood that they were two sides of the same person, a concept that he enacted by pretending, with no apparent preference, to be both of them.

RELATIVE POWER AND AUTHORITY IN PLAY

As we played, Michael effortlessly moved among multiple points of view on the narrative events as he took up the perspectives of different people along with their relative power and authority. Michael's utterances from these different positions examined the major theme of the story: How do you interpret and respond to Hyde's actions? In addition to pretending to be altruistic Dr. Jekyll and egotistic Mr. Hyde and other characters in the story, he also improvised by drawing on other narratives. He imagined that he had great physical strength (a werewolf); was someone with expertise and mechanical power (Dr. Frankenstein); was a person with social authority (a police officer); was someone like me (an adult), like his mother (a wife), and like himself (a little boy).

He explored different ways to use power to deal with Hyde's deeds. Immediately after pretending to be Jekyll locking up the potion and hiding the key in a hole, he pretended to be Dr. Frankenstein operating his machine. When I asked him, "Is there anything we could do so that maybe you [Dr. Jekyll] won't turn into the beast [the word he had used for Hyde]?" he improvised a response using images from the movie *Frankenstein Meets the Wolfman* (which we had just watched) in which Dr. Frankenstein uses his machine both to give and to remove the life force. He wanted Dr. Frankenstein/me to connect Jekyll/him to the machine to "break the power," which I did. After being disconnected, Jekyll/he tried taking the potion and it did not turn him into Hyde. When I asked, "What are we going to do about the people who got killed?" he replied, "Put them on Dr. Frankenstein's machine and I'll bring them back to life."

Through play, Michael would soon address me with the same question that he had raised earlier: Should a police officer shoot Hyde? Before that he intensified the dilemma by imagining that Hyde killed his victims. After pretending to restore Hyde's victims to life, I had expected that Michael would likely want to pretend that we were inside a different narrative world, as I felt a sense of resolution and order being restored. However, he turned his attention again to the relationship between Jekyll and Hyde and how to deal with Hyde. Toward the end of the movie that we had watched, Hyde's shadow is shown on a wall. Michael seemed to be thinking about this image when he said, "The Shadow of Mr. Hyde remains," and then, "the Shadow gets killed but not Dr. Jekyll." As he began to enact his thoughts he wanted me to pretend to be Jekyll.

Michael:	You're Dr. Jekyll finally dead at the end of his life.
Brian:	[I lie down and pretend to die.] Good-bye everybody. I had a good life.
Michael:	Now you're all the people that he's destroyed. I'm the Shadow.
Brian	[pretending to beg]: Please help me.
Michael:	But the people aren't beggar men. They're all young men.

[The Shadow/Michael pretends to kill three people/me in quick succession as he shouts "Get out of my way." I want to stop playing as I suddenly feel overwhelmed with all the killing.]

Brian:	Can we stop for a moment. I don't want to pretend we're killing.

[I hug him and he hugs me back.]

Michael:	Knock, knock.
Brian:	Who's there?
Michael:	Boo.
Brian:	Boo who?
Michael:	Don't cry it's only a joke.

[I laugh.]

My recognition of conflicting meanings and feelings intensified to the extent that I had to stop pretending. I felt Hyde's evil power so viscerally when I looked into my son's gruesome face, saw his violent movements, and imagined that he was killing me/three men. Having read the story many times, I was well aware that Hyde killed people, but seeing Michael for the first time show how Hyde used his physical power to kill, coupled with experiencing from the position of the victims, was overwhelming.

As soon as I asked to stop playing, Michael transformed into the sweet, concerned little boy who would "kiss boo-boos" and sing lullabies to his one-month-old baby sister. The grimaces disappeared as we hugged. In seconds he had me laughing as he told me a knock-knock joke that he had just learned.

As I chuckled, the understanding that we were just pretending became more prominent. Later, as I analyzed our play, I realized that I had heard his joke as a reminder that no one is ever actually hurt by imagined actions, even if they pretend to kill. Michael's utterance brought other voices to our exchange. I recalled, as Garvey (1977) noted, that though play activities may be deeply meaningful, they are "non-literal," so that whenever we pretend, we are "buffeted from consequences" (p. 7). We may resist pretending to hurt or kill, but we are not going to be hurt or die if we imagine death by shooting. My laughter and change in mood were part of my answer to his utterance and the voices he had amplified for me.

THE PAST AND PRESENT VOICES OF INNER SPEECH

Michael was eager to continue playing, and as I no longer felt a resistance to pretending, I was ready to reenter the world of Jekyll and Hyde. He took us almost full circle back to the encounter with which we had begun our play. Again I would pretend to be Hyde, with Michael pretending to have the authority of the police officer with the power of life and death in his gun.

Michael:	Now I'm the little boy. OK, Daddy?
Brian:	OK.
Michael:	Police. There's a monster who's killed some people.
Brian:	Yea we know. Have you seen him? Do you know where he is? We've been looking for him.
Michael:	Yea. He tried to kill me.
Brian:	Are you all right?
Michael:	Yea.

[He tells the police officer/me that Hyde is on the roof of a building.]

Michael:	Daddy, you be Mr. Hyde up on the rooftop.

[I climb halfway up the stairs.]

Michael:	Get down from that rooftop.
Brian:	No. Who are you?
Michael:	I'm a police.
Brian:	What do you want?
Michael:	Stop doing all those mean things.
Brian:	Why should I?
Michael:	Because they're all mean.
Brian:	Huh. What will you do to me if I do come down?
Michael:	Well if you don't come down I'll shoot you.
Brian:	And if I do? What will you do to me?
Michael:	I'll send you away to jail.
Brian:	Jail? Why should I go to jail?
Michael:	Because you know. Because you're mean that's why. Huh.

[We talk back and forth about rules until Michael refocuses us.]

Michael:	Just no talk about it. Now get down or I'll shoot you.
Brian:	How do you want it to end? Do you want to shoot him or do you want him to come down?
Michael:	I want to shoot you.
Brian:	No [laughing]. I can get away, I'm too clever for you.

[Michael shoots and I pretend to die]

Michael:	Now change back into the Shadow.

[I lie down and transform my body into Hyde's. Michael stands over me pretending to hold the gun. Pat enters the room.]

Pat:	Are you going to use that gun to shoot other people?
Michael:	I only use my gun to shoot monsters [said with a tone of this being obvious].

To understand some of the layers of complexity of our dialogic interactions, it is important to recognize that my utterances resonated with and answered many past utterances and voices in addition to the voice of Michael that I heard in the present moment. As Bakhtin (1986) noted, in extending his definition of utterance:

> Each utterance is filled with echoes and reverberations of other [past] utterances to which it is related by the communality of the sphere of speech communication. Every utterance must be primarily regarded as a response to preceding utterances of the given sphere (we understand the word "response" here in the broadest sense). Each utterance refutes, affirms, supplements, and relies on the others, presupposes them to be known, and somehow takes them into account. (p. 91)

As I imagined again the encounter between the police officer and Hyde, I experienced much more complex refraction between voices. Unlike when I imagined holding the gun, I no longer felt an oppositional resistance to killing Hyde. I felt a more complex inner speech Jekyll/Hyde was a human being but so were his victims. He was a human who was capable of monstrous actions that I had seen with gruesome intensity in imagination. His violent deeds refracted my view of him as a human being. If he was not stopped, I could see him killing again. As I stood on the stairs imagining that Hyde was on the rooftop, I heard multiple inner voices that had been uttered as we played. I could hear the cries of the victims of his heartless violence, including both those that he had killed and those that he would kill if he were not stopped. Jekyll was a kind physician, but I also saw Jekyll using the potion to change into Hyde because Jekyll knew where the key to the safe was. Jekyll might be reformed using Dr. Frankenstein's machine. But if Jekyll died and the shadow-of-Hyde remained, then it/he would have to be stopped. Killing Hyde was now an option. I knew this because as I climbed the stairs, I did not resist forming an image of the police officer shooting Hyde.

As the police officer, Michael took a different tack than I had expected. He threatened to shoot Hyde but at first wanted him to "stop doing all those mean things." He wanted to arrest Hyde and "send him away for jail." I began to explore his understandings of "jail" and "rules." However, as he wanted more action and less talk, I gave him the choice of what he wanted to do. He enacted shooting Hyde and then wanted me to show the Shadow remaining after Hyde had died.

Authoring Understanding

Our play on this occasion had been more refractive for me than ever before. But our refractive play meant that after about twenty minutes, I had authored a more complex understanding of the story of *Dr. Jekyll and Mr. Hyde* than my previous, somewhat dualistic view. I had also authored new understanding about my belief in nonviolence. My earlier feelings of intense discomfort as I imagined shooting a gun had been the product of extreme refraction between a principle of pacifism and a desire to play. As we played, additional views were given voice in situations that modified the idea of not killing; I recognized that killing someone who kills (in the context of an immediate struggle) had to be an option.

REFRACTIVE INQUIRY

My inquiry into our play has continued since I first started playing with Michael before he was two years old. My inquiry has been refractive when this process has led me to author new understanding of struggles and sometimes collisions among differing values, assumptions, concepts, beliefs, or other core ideas that create conflict among my own and others' interpretations of play and research.

INQUIRY AND THE LIVE EVENTS OF PLAY

Dialogue with Michael created refractive, or dialogic, angles between different voices that opened up an authorial space for the development of my ideas as well as his. As Bakhtin (1984) emphasized, living ideas are neither fixed nor experienced as moments of consciousness. Ideas develop in a dialogue between voices, or "consciousnesses," in "live events" that for me included the social and inner speech that occurred in our play and in my later analysis of those live events.

> The idea . . . is not a subjective individual-psychological formation with "permanent resident rights" in a person's head; no, the idea is inter-individual and inter-subjective—the realm of its existence is not individual consciousness but dialogic communion between consciousnesses. The idea is a live event, played out at the point of dialogic meeting between two or several consciousnesses. (p. 88)

Ideas cannot be separated from their sources in the narratives and other cultural resources from and with which I have improvised as I have made meaning about life. I have no space in this chapter to outline where my beliefs came from except to note that they have dialogically developed over a lifetime of interpreting events and narratives from my own life and those of other people that include fictional and well as factual stories. Ideas have developed through the live events of both inner and social speech.

Our play was always a live event that gave me, as well as my son, access to many fictional carriers of ideas with voices that could enter into the ongoing dialogic construction of understanding. Refractive play made me more aware of the process and more attentive to meaning making. Past utterances of mine, and those of my son, were joined by other voices that entered the dialogic meeting of voices from other sources such as books that I read and conversations I had with colleagues.

Developing Ideas

My language and ideas developed as I authored more "internally persuasive" and less "externally authoritative" discourse.

> The internally persuasive word—as opposed to one that is externally authoritative—is . . . half ours, half someone else's . . . it is not so much interpreted by us as it is further, that is freely, developed, applied to new material, new conditions; it enters into interanimating relationships with new contexts. More than that it enters into an intense interaction, a struggle with other internally persuasive discourses. . . . The semantic structure of an internally persuasive discourse is not finite, it is open; in each of the new contexts that dialogize it, this discourse is able to reveal ever newer ways to mean. (Bakhtin, 1981, pp. 345–346)

My belief that I would never kill someone had been much more externally authoritative than internally persuasive. The idea was much more someone else's than it was my own, coming from such sources as a rigid opposition to the tactics of paramilitary forces and a somewhat idealistic view of the lives of pacifists like Gandhi.

In the inner and social speech of refractive play and inquiry, I authored a more internally persuasive belief that was more open to other views than it had been previously. As I dialogued with voices that contextualized other views and as I visualized different scenarios in which I could see myself using violence, I answered those views and accommodated them into my understanding.

As I illustrated in the previous section, in my analysis of my language and action across different encounters and situations, some of my ideas became more flexible and open when they began to develop and "live" through play. "The idea begins to live, that is, to take shape, to develop, to find and renew its verbal expression, to give birth to new ideas, only when it enters into genuine dialogic relations with others ideas, with the ideas of others" (Bakhtin, 1984a, p. 88). My ideas began to develop when I recognized that some of my ideas were more rigid, closed, and less responsive to new situations than I had realized. For example, my belief that we can be nonviolent was more absolute and less inflected than I had realized.

As we entered other narrative worlds and my son interacted with me in more and more varied situations, which were sometimes increasingly extreme, I became more open to situations in which I could imagine and understand people's use of force to kill someone. At the same time I was more concerned with judging the rightness of actions through dialogue in each particular situation.

As I juxtaposed one play encounter or episode with another, I could recognize more of the layers of meaning beneath my words, feelings, and actions as we had played that were largely invisible at the time. The following are summaries of play encounters in mythic contexts that complicated my understanding of killing or violently stopping another's actions:

- ▶ The Wolfman asking to die
- ▶ An "unstoppable" vampire, like Dracula, being killed with a stake in the heart
- ▶ Frankenstein killing without intention
- ▶ Quazimodo pouring oil on his attackers in *The Hunchback of Notre Dame*
- ▶ Luke Skywalker exploding the Death Star in *Star Wars*
- ▶ Shooting "undead" zombies
- ▶ Freddy Kruger killing people and being killed inside a nightmare in *Nightmare on Elm Street*
- ▶ The Oklahoma City bomber about to blow up the federal building

As I dialogically connected our play around Jekyll and Hyde with thematically related interactions, I developed more dialogic and internally persuasive understanding about my belief in nonviolence. As Bakhtin (1981) stressed, meaning "is understood against the background of other concrete utterances on the same theme, a background made up of contradictory opinions, points of view, and value judgments . . . that complicates the path of any word toward its object" (p. 281). I did not abandon my antipathy toward killing people. Rather I have become more aware of circumstances, which I now carry with me as images and inner voices in an inner conversation, in which I could kill another. Any question related to contemplating another's death or understanding how someone else could kill is made more complex as I continue to dialogue with those inner voices.

TOWARD CONCLUSIONS

My understanding of myself as an adult-researcher changed considerably through researching play with my son. There were ongoing tensions between and among my own prior understandings, the views and actions of other parents and teachers, and the meaning I was making as I read professional literature. The understandings that I generated were not arrived at easily but were rather the product of ongoing struggles for meaning.

Researching and playing with a child can create spaces for authoring meaning. When play is dialogic, we can create meaning with children about the narratives that fascinate them and at the same time we can create meaning for ourselves about the issues that arise as we play. I've shown how in the privacy and intensity of a father-son relationship I developed understanding about a core belief.

To make play dialogic and to embrace its potential to refract meaning, I had to share authority with my son. He was never a disinterested bystander but always a person involved in making sense of the events in the narratives that had captivated him. I interacted with him when as a young child he pretended to chase, attack, escape, and kill. I also interacted with him as he imagined being a victim of violence and death but also as people who loved and tended others as caregivers.

Being a father–researcher with my son was often exhilarating and joyful. It was also, at times, harrowing and poignant. In my play with Michael, we authored meaning about matters of life and death as we raised and explored difficult questions about the human potential to do good and evil deeds. I followed Michael into narrative worlds, explored inner landscapes, and encountered people and creatures that I never expected to meet. I tried to be authentic in my relationship with him, listening to the questions he asked, talking from the heart in response, and at times asking my own searching questions.

Through inquiry and playing with Michael, as I shared authority with him, many research questions arose that have implications for other researchers but that I do not have space here to examine. However, I want to stress that as we played I struggled through refractive inquiry to explore these additional questions in a similar dialogic way as I considered the questions in this chapter. Pragmatically, I faced some questions daily. For example: When should I set or negotiate limits on the content of play? In imagination, should I follow him no matter where he leads? How should I try to teach him as we play? Other questions were regularly present though not so demanding of answers. For example: Why did our daughter want to play quite differently? How was my open-endedness in play different when I played with other children who were not my son? Further questions were ongoing concerns. For example: Can play be emotionally dangerous? How would Michael learn to control his actions in everyday life? Finally, some questions arose when I connected my professional life outside the home with our play. For example: How could I apply what I was learning to classroom contexts? How might early childhood educators apply my understandings?

I look forward to participating in the discussions and conversations that this chapter and book will provoke about the role of play in the lives of children and adults. Refractive inquiry has left me recognizing more clearly that there can never be a singular conclusion to research or to this chapter. We always move toward conclusions, and if we value vibrant living understandings, then answers, as well as questions, must always remain open to be reinterpreted and extended in dialogic interactions with other people in further situations.

> Life by its very nature is dialogic. To live means to participate in [open-ended] dialogue; to ask questions, to heed, to respond, to agree, and so forth. In this dialogue a person participates wholly and throughout his whole life: with his eyes, lips, hands, soul, spirit, with his whole body and deeds. He invests his entire self in discourse . . . When dialogue ends everything ends. (Bakhtin, 1981, pp. 252, 293)

REFERENCES

Bakhtin, M. M. (1981). *The dialogic imagination* (M. Holquist, Ed.; C. Emerson & M. Holquist, Trans.). Austin: University of Texas Press.

Bakhtin, M. M. (1984a). *Problems of Dostoevsky's poetics* (C. Emerson, Ed. & Trans.). Minneapolis: University of Minnesota Press.

Bakhtin, M. M. (1984b). *Rabelais and his world* (H. Iswolsky, Trans.). Bloomington: Indiana University Press.

Bakhtin, M. M. (1986). *Speech genres and other late essays* (V. W. McGee, Trans.). Austin: University of Texas Press.

Bakhtin, M. M. (1990). *Art and answerability: Early philosophical essays* (M. Holquist & V. Liapunov, Eds.; V. Liapunov, Trans.). Austin: University of Texas Press.

Bateson, G. (1955). *Steps to an ecology of mind.* London: Ballantine Books.

Bruner, J. S. (1986). *Actual minds, possible worlds.* Cambridge, MA: Harvard University Press.

Bruner, J. S., Jolly, A., & Sylva, K. (1976). *Play: Its role in development and evolution.* London: Penguin.

Carlsson-Paige, N., & Levin, D. (1987). *The war play dilemma: Children's needs and society's future.* New York: Teachers College Press.

Cohen, L. J. (2001). *Playful parenting.* New York: Balantine Books.

Corsaro, W. (1985). *Friendship and peer culture in the early years.* Norwood, NJ: Ablex.

Dines, G., & Humez, J. M. (Eds.). (2003). *Gender, race, and class in media: A text-reader.* Thousand Oaks, CA: Sage.

Dyson, A. H. (1993). *The social worlds of children learning to write in an urban primary classroom.* New York: Teachers College Press.

Edmiston, B. (1993). Structuring drama for reflection and learning: A teacher-researcher study. *Youth Theatre Journal, 7*(3), 3–11.

Edmiston, B. (1998). Drama as inquiry: Teachers and students as co-researchers. In J. Wilhelm & B. Edmiston, *Imagining to learn: Inquiry, ethics, and integration through drama,* 103–137. Portsmouth, NH: Heinemann.

Edmiston, B. (2000). Drama as ethical education. *Research in Drama Education, 5*(1), 63–84.

Edmiston, B., & Enciso, P. (2002). Reflections and refractions of meaning: Dialogic approaches to classroom drama and reading. In J. Flood, D. Lapp, J. Squire, & J. Jensen (Eds.), *The handbook of research on teaching and the English Language Arts,* 868–880. New York: Simon & Schuster Macmillan.

Edmiston, B., & Wilhelm, J. (1996). Playing in different keys: Research notes for action researchers and reflective drama practitioners. In P. Taylor (Ed.), *Researching drama and arts education: Paradigms and possibilities,* 85–96. London: Falmer Press.

Erickson, F. (1986). Qualitative methods in research on teaching. In M. C. Wittrock (Ed.), *Handbook of research on teaching* (3rd ed.) 119–161. New York: Macmillan.

Freud, S. (1933). *New introductory lectures on psycho-analysis* (W. J. H. Sprott, Trans.). New York: Norton & Company.

Garvey, C. (1977). *Play.* Cambridge, MA: Harvard University Press.

Goldstein, J. H. (Ed.). (1994). *Toys, play, and child development.* Cambridge, UK: Cambridge University Press.

Grace, D. J., & Tobin, J. (1997). Carnival in the classroom: Elementary students making videos. In J. Tobin (Ed.), *Making a place for pleasure in early childhood education.* New Haven, CT: Yale University Press.

Graue, M. E., & Walsh, D. J. (1998). *Studying children in context: Theories, methods, and ethics.* Thousand Oaks, CA: Sage.

Hauser, M. E., & Jipson, J. A. (1998). *Intersections: Feminisms/early childhoods.* New York: Peter Lang.

Hodges, M. (1984). *Saint George and the dragon: A golden legend* (T. S. Hyman, illus.). Boston: Little Brown.

Holland, D., Lachicotte, W., Skinner, D., & Cain, C. (1998). *Identity and agency in cultural worlds.* Cambridge, MA: Harvard University Press.

Huizinga, J. (1955). *Homo ludens: A study of the play-element in culture.* Boston: Beacon Press.

James, A., Jenks, C., & Prout, A. (1998). *Theorizing childhood.* New York: Teachers College Press.

Katch, J. (2001). *Under deadman's skin: Discovering the meaning of children's violent play.* Boston: Beacon Press.

Kelly-Byrne, D. (1989). *A child's play life: An ethnographic study.* New York: Teachers College Press.

Kohlberg, L. (1984). *The psychology of moral development: The nature and validity of moral stages.* San Francisco: Harper & Row.

Levin, D. (1998). *Remote control childhood?: Combating the hazards of media culture.* Washington, DC: National Association for the Education of Young Children.

Paley, V. G. (1988). *Bad guys don't have birthdays.* Chicago: University of Chicago Press.

Pelligrini, A. D. (1991). *Applied child study: A developmental approach.* Hillsdale, NJ: Lawrence Erlbaum.

Piaget, J. (1975). *The equilibration of cognitive structures: The central problem of intellectual development.* Chicago: University of Chicago Press.

Potter, B. (1984). *The tale of Peter Rabbit.* New York: Dover Publications. (Original work published 1903.)

Potter, B. (1984). *The tale of Jemima Puddle-Duck.* New York: Dover Publications. (Original work published 1908.)

Reynolds, G., & Jones, E. (1997). *Master players: Learning from children at play.* New York: Teachers College Press.

Schön, D. A. (1983). *The reflective practitioner: How professionals think in practice.* New York: Basic Books.

Schwartzman, H. D. (1978). *Transformations: The anthropology of children's play.* New York: Plenum.

Stevenson, R. L. (1992). *Dr. Jekyll and Mr. Hyde and other stories.* New York: Knopf. (Original work published 1886.)

Taylor, P. (1998). *Researching Drama and Arts Education: Paradigms and Possibilities.* London: Falmer Press. pp. 89–96.

Thorne, B. (1993). *Gender play: Girls and boys in school.* New Brunswick, NJ: Rutgers University Press.

Voloshinov, V. N. (1986). *Marxism and the philosophy of language.* Cambridge, MA: Harvard University Press.

Vygotsky, L. (1967). Play and its role in the mental development of the child. *Soviet Psychology, 5,* 6–18.

Vygotsky, L. (1978). *Mind in society* (M. Cole, V. John-Steiner, S. Scribner, & E. Souberman, Eds. and Trans.). Cambridge, MA: Harvard University Press.

PART TWO

RACE/ETHNICITY, CLASS, AND GENDER IDENTITIES

CHAPTER SIX

CULTURALLY RELEVANT PEDAGOGY

4 Rs = Bein' Real

MARGUERITE VANDEN WYNGAARD

"They reach out to the students and try to help them learn and look at them as an individual, not as just a number and or a seat in a classroom."

(LaShika, Grade 12)

In many high schools across the country, student "voice" rarely guides instruction or influences policies and procedures. There are individual teachers within those high schools who work steadily to honor student voice, experiences, and cultural knowledge to create dynamic learning communities that often influence the culture of the school. Al, a student at Angelou High School, where this study was created, was the strongest proponent of student voice and a school based on democratic principles. In describing his experience in the audience at a town hall meeting focused on race, Al believed that the students' voices should have been heard because "I feel like the people more my age or a little older than I am could have done much better because they woulda' spoken honestly without worryin' about tryin' to *impress* everybody else" (Al, Grade 11). Putting students' voices at the center of the education process is risky. It creates a tension and exposes the beliefs we hold as researchers and educators, if as activist–educators we are going to have work be led, guided, and constructed by students. Student-centered education as well as current politically influenced research "best practice" forces a researcher–educator to practice democratic principles within a system based fundamentally on control and management of students.

ABOUT THIS STUDY

The focus of this chapter is on what I learned from African-American high school students in my dissertation research, which focused on their perspectives of "culturally relevant" education. I continue to wrestle with many questions about this study and its implications for respecting the voice of young people, interrogating power issues in doing research with students, and creating moments in which transformative education may be possible. For instance, how can this research be a transformative act, versus an oppressor–oppressed, researcher–researched relationship, *if* I've already formulated the questions? Would their perspectives be honored and the students really be allowed to define culturally relevant pedagogy? Would the students even agree to participate . . . and why should they? If it "matters who tells the story and what social power they hold to enforce their meaning," as Lewis (1993, p. 115) has stated, how will voices of students be at the center and what role do I play in interpreting meaning and telling their story?

Scholarship that influenced this study included, but was not limited to, Paulo Freire (1970), African-American intellectuals such as hooks (1994) and West (1993), critical social theorists–educators such as McLaren (1997), Sleeter and Grant (1987), and Giroux (1992), and activist–educators such as Swadener (1995), Sapon-Shevin (1994), and Ayers and Ford (1996). All of these scholars discussed the issue of "voice" and who was not being heard, what societal barriers increased the likelihood of "silencing others," and what as educators we could do within our classrooms, schools, and communities to increase the likelihood that those "other" voices would be at the center of the conversation and our teaching practice. Following the lead of Ladson-Billings (1994) and Nieto (1996), I utilized case study methodology including student interviews and focus–work group, as well as strategies to support triangulation by interviewing the school administrator, educators, and parents. To ensure that interpretations were authentic and that student "voices" were captured, a focus–work group was formed. The purpose of the focus–work group was to have students of the study interact with each other, to respond and challenge my interpretations of their words. The second purpose was to create a safe environment where students could meet face-to-face with other participants, read each other's transcripts, offer feedback, and clarify for meaning. Leaders emerged from within the group, and after my initial facilitation, students led the discussion. As a result of this time together, students identified common themes and created the framework for the findings.

ENTRANCE INTO ANGELOU

Angelou High School was accessible to me through my supervising role for preservice secondary teachers. As such, I was introduced to a junior/senior social studies instructor, Tony. After describing the questions that would be asked, Tony offered access to any of his classes and introduced me to the students. I was able to attend the student forum held in the fall and listened intently for students who were creative and vocalized freely on a wide range of subjects involving school improvement; I also observed students who were interested but sat at the margins, and some who appeared to be totally disinterested. I asked the names of these students through other students seated around me. At the conclusion of the all-day forum, I was able to describe the study to the 200-plus students who were present and asked for volunteers. Twelve volunteers were identified, and I utilized network sampling, whereby the twelve volunteers recommended other students to participate in the study. Once this list was compiled, students who were in their first year of high school were eliminated, since a multiyear perspective was imperative to the study. The remaining students attended an orientation session to learn more about the study, sign permissions, and be given an early opportunity to withdraw. The five remaining students who completed the study were individually interviewed three times over a five-month period. Alumni, staff members, and parents were recommended by students in the study and were interviewed with questions created from the themes generated from the student focus–work group as a part of the triangulation process.

ANGELOU HIGH SCHOOL

The urban landscape driving off the highway to reach the school was full of life. Children walked the streets with adults in tow and there were many bustling shops as well as a grocery store, public library, and drugstore. Drawing nearer to the school, the street changed from business to residential, with several blocks of brick apartment dwellings. The entire area was well maintained, which made me chuckle as I remembered assumptions made by the preservice teachers I was supervising, which reflected the social construction of an "inner city" school—run-down, high crime, drugs, and violence.

Like other cities across the United States, Yeardley, the Midwestern city where Angelou High School is located, is a segregated city and has a minority population of 26 percent, a majority of whom are African Americans. It has been described as a working-class town, but with dreams of being more. Angelou High School, one of eight high schools in Yeardley, with its large, lush green lawn and several crabapple trees, is an imposing two-story brick building with a three-story middle section. The school, which was built in 1961 to hold over 3,000 students, has multiple additions jutting out at odd angles. "Because we are land locked," said the principal, Mr. Okey, "every time the school population outgrew a section, they added to the building with whatever property was left."

The student population was approximately 1,039 students, of which 99 percent are African American, with two or three Asian-American and European-American students, "so we can say we're multicultural," chuckled the principal. He was quick to resist essentializing the African-American community and stated "that assuming they were all the same" was not the case. The African-American community reflected the community of Yeardley in that it had a large socioeconomic range, from families on public assistance to low-income families, to a prominent middle class and a growing upper class. The faculty consisted of seventy teachers, 20 percent of whom were African American. The administrative staff, including the building principal, assistant principal, and guidance counselors, were European American or White.

STUDENTS IN THE STUDY

While all students had articulated some sort of religious affiliation, Aaron, a seventeen-year-old junior (Grade 11), was the only student who spoke of attending and participating fully in church activities. The church was the center of his world, and he believed that God protected him on a daily basis. He lived on a street where the economic stratification was visibly apparent. "We don't want to live here," he said as I drove him home, "but it's home." He waved continuously out the window as people instantly recognized him from their front porches. He hopes to study electrical engineering or architectural design.

Al, also a seventeen-year-old junior (Grade 11), was a passionate orator and committed to being a leader and "representing my male friends." Committed to becoming a teacher within an urban community and supported by his family and his Christian beliefs, Al has been a tutor throughout the summer for students in middle school. He admits, "Many students really test my nerves," but that has not diminished his drive to be a teacher someday.

India, an eighteen-year-old senior (Grade 12), gets her drive by watching her mother balance university course work and family. India admits that she believes her mother at any point in her young life could have "fallen off and gotten into drugs." Because her mother didn't, India has gained strength and a source of pride as she attempts to be as strong, persistent, and resilient as her mother. Both of them rely on their Christian church for their social and spiritual strength and guidance.

LaShika, also an eighteen-year-old senior (Grade 12), has excelled academically since first grade and has always taken courses ahead of her peers. In both her junior and senior year, she has taken courses at Yeardley University in conjunction with her high school courses. This will allow her to enter the university with twenty credits during her first year. She recognizes the opportunities that she has and acknowledges that most kids have not had the teachers she has had because she is on the accelerated track. She also acknowledges that because of academic success, she has not been a part of the Angelou community and has experienced firsthand student taunts of "actin' White."

> I always thought that I just talked educated so they were putting themselves down actually or putting Black people down because where is it written where is it said that Black people can't talk educated? I would just say don't worry about being Black or White. Worry about being yourself. You need to find out who you are and come into yourself. (LaShika, Grade 12)

Nickole Rice, a fifteen-year-old sophomore (Grade 10), was one of those students who attended the student forum and appeared interested but spoke only when she was directed to Shy around strangers, Nickole broke through some of that shyness when with her peers in the focus–work groups. She hopes to attend a local university and not move too far from home. At the same time, she is very interested in traveling and hopes that travel might be part of a career option. Bright and articulate, Nickole would like to be challenged more in school and was anxiously waiting for driver's training.

Tyreek, a twenty-year-old alumnus, was identified by students in the focus–work groups as someone who would "totally git what we're sayin'." Tyreek was an enormous man whose eyes disappeared in his face when he laughed, which was often. He had lived in Yeardley all of his life, and like he, two of his siblings graduated from Angelou. He was an honors student with a passion for math except for a "little spell in middle school where I think I was tryin' to con myself, you know." Extremely articulate, he was full of contradictions as he held Angelou in high esteem and in the same breath opined that it was "goin' downhill." The final contradiction, he hopes to be a teacher, but not at Angelou.

STUDENT VOICE FOR CULTURALLY RELEVANT PEDAGOGY = 4 Rs OR "BEIN' REAL"

Culturally relevant pedagogy, or as defined by students in this study as the 4 Rs Theory—Relationship, Respect, Responsibility, and Relevancy—transcended the classroom, not only influencing effective teaching practices, but also supporting the learning community as a whole. The findings of the students are supported in original premises of the research of Ladson-Billings (1994), while they more closely mirror the findings in the recent work of Ferguson (2003). At the same time, while all four components were necessary, these African-American high school students clearly identified relationships as the key foundational component to their theory.

> And everyday he [Mr. Okey, principal] and I would just sit there and he would talk to me, you know, get an understanding and a feel for me. I knew if he was to do somethin' to me, you know, or tell me to stop doin' somethin', he would be truly carin' about me as a person, you know what I'm sayin'? (Tyreek, alumnus, age twenty)

RELATIONSHIP

To establish a relationship, students expected the educator, whether the building administrator or teacher, to be personable, caring, trustworthy, and have an interest and understanding of the lives of their African-American students. Trust and caring were by far the most difficult terrain to traverse as teachers. For students, trust was demonstrated by the teacher, in not revealing any information given by the student to anyone else. Sometimes there were circumstances when the "trust" had to be broken. Caring is also a difficult line as LaShika described an African-American female teacher whose "intentions were good" but she was identified as a "real busy body."

> She feels that it's her responsibility to make sure that everybody is doing things the way she thinks they should be done. Her intentions are good, but she definitely goes about it the wrong way. She's always in everybody's business. She feels the need to tell people that when she doesn't think they look good enough or things along that line or when they need to lose weight or when they need to exercise more. Things like that. A little too personal. (LaShika)

Still, students in this study agreed that the relationship needs to be personal, a one-on-one opportunity to reflect and learn with an adult.

> Ms. E. who is African American was good, she was a real good teacher. She was a sweet person. She was like, I mean she can just talk to you. I could have a little conversation about anything. (Nickole, Grade 10)

> Mr. Okey [principal] really cares about the students, you know as people. He spent some time with me, you know, in his years there. He took some time just gettin' to know me. (Tyreek, alumnus, age twenty)

They also expected the teacher to reveal information and opinions about the lessons as well as issues outside of school. All participants in the study supported the students' notion about the significance of relationships between the students and educators.

> And so I lost her [his mother] in December of '95 to cancer—ten-year-long battle—which was devastating to me and I shared a lot of things with the kids. We talked about it through the years, and they've kind of been with me to see me through. Because they're kind of like a reality check. You can talk about anything with the kids. Hi, honey [to a student who entered the room]. (Tony, teacher)

I mean like Tony [social studies teacher], he know what we go through a lot more, and he's a White man. (India, Grade 12)

RESPECT AND RESPONSIBILITY

The students linked respect and responsibility together since they respected a teacher who was responsible for creating a safe learning environment and acted in a professional manner. Central to respect was the honoring and respecting of student "voice," and responsibility was acting in a professional manner. Combined, the students equated respect and responsibility with professionalism, which included high expectations for learning, and multiple ways in which to learn and demonstrate knowledge. Several key components of respect and responsibility were identified by the students. First, teachers they respected created an environment where the student "voice" permeated the classroom instruction and decisions for instruction were based on their needs. "They treated me with more respect. They, they broke things down for me" (Al, Grade 11). Nickole, Grade 10, struggled in some of her classes and also needed teachers to "break it down" so that she could understand. The term "break it down" did not mean "to simplify" or imply a lack of intellect. Rather it was a process by which students could understand components of the idea and through learning activities gain the understanding necessary to rebuild it for complete comprehension. The teachers' understanding of how to meet the needs of the students was a "signal" of respect and responsibility.

> M.: So its you determining what to study. Is that right?
> Nickole: Um hum.
> M.: Do you like that? How does that make you feel?
> Nickole: I'm in control of my learnin'.
> M.: Do you have that option in other classes?
> Nickole: No, not really.

A second key component of respect and responsibility was the expectations of the teacher for students' learning. Not surprisingly, most students in the study placed full responsibility for establishing high expectations within the learning environment on the teacher. Aaron and Al, both juniors, were the only students who specifically stated that the students had some responsibility in this relationship, but also put the burden on teachers to understand the needs and learning styles of each student.

> "So I think it's just, it's somewhat like a fifty-fifty exchange like." (Aaron, Grade 11)

> "Just sit down, do my job or you do your job, I do my job and everything will be straight." (Al, Grade 11)

A third component of respect and responsibility was in the teaching practice itself. The students were looking for a classroom that connected to the students' learning needs, had high expectations as stated previously, and had a teacher who provided multiple ways for students to learn and demonstrate their knowledge.

> Instead of the student up just sittin' at his desk workin' constantly, they get involved with each other as well as in the classroom. Like a majority of my classes, they let us work in groups and I think that group work benefits everyone whether you're a visual or well like me. I just learn by ear. Some teachers use it by combining methods. Some teachers may use like groups, writin' on the board and games with us. Some teachers allow students to go over in class up front so they see how they worked it out and let the other students see how they worked it out too. (Al, Grade 11)

> I expect to leave the class knowing more than I did going in at least. When a teacher can relate to you and teaches in a way, changes her teaching, his or her teaching style for each class, to respond to the, um, the dynamic of that class and how that class can learn. (LaShika, Grade 12)

> Lettin' you be able to work with other people 'cause you might know people that might be strong, you know, by theirself. (India, Grade 12)

Unfortunately, the students could readily identify problems within the school regarding professionalism. In fact, when the students reached consensus for the "4 Rs" and then were asked to identify those teachers who taught from that perspective, they only named four teachers out of a staff of seventy.

> It's borin' man, just borin'. (Aaron, Grade 11)

Nickole expressed a lot of frustration in not being challenged and in her inability to follow a teacher who lectured for ninety minutes.

> School is fun, but it could be more of a challenge sometimes. It's like the teachers just give you work instead of, it's like making work fun, they're just giving it to you. When I say challenging I mean like the work that we do. It's like even though we put effort into it, they just teachin' then you just s'posed to grab onto it. It seems like it should be more effort into what they teach. They talk for about ninety minutes, throw you a work sheet and you don't know what's goin' on. Sometimes then they sit and lecture so much, you'll fall asleep in the middle of it. I'd give 'em lectures, but I would just be more explanatory. I would explain more things with how they feel about the topic. See if they [the students] understand the topic, explain it more. (Nickole, Grade 10)

> Some teachers just go on and on and just go strictly by the book. And they may go strictly by the book, but the student's not getting anything out of it. (Al, Grade 11)

> Teachers that, uh, are consistently late to class. Teachers that leave in the middle of class, do their grocery shopping or to run errands and then when you ask them questions about

something or try to understand or if you understand and try to help other students, they then get defensive or if you try to, if you try to get help like by going to the principal or anything, then they begin to get defensive and have, and cause problems for you in class. (LaShika, Grade 12)

In the spring she was to graduate, by her second interview, India had still not taken the Scholastic Aptitude Test (SAT) needed for entrance to college. What should have been common knowledge for all students, India believed was withheld from her, with *intent* India linked the lack of access to information and opportunities as a "signal" of disrespect and lack of professionalism from the all-White counseling staff. For India, the counseling staff demonstrated disrespect by not knowing her and acted unprofessionally by basing their understanding of her on two underlying assumptions: she had a 2.0 grade point average and an eight-month-old son.

I believe that they [counselors] tell some people but I think they should pressure everybody even if they're not goin' to college to take it [SAT]. The counselor to me they didn't tell me and I didn't really know till my spring break this year. It was like last year that I even needed to take it when in my eleventh grade year, I didn't even know I had to take it though. (India, Grade 12)

RELEVANCY

They [teachers] need to help it [subject] be good for me today. If I can't use it, why teach it? (Aaron, Grade 11)

For the African-American high school students in this study, relevancy was the ability of the teacher to make a link between prior knowledge, the student's life outside of the classroom, and a glimpse into a possible future and provide a means for motivation. Tommy, one of 4 teachers students identified as teaching from a foundation of relevancy, was observed working on a recent project in his communication classes. He was dubbing a student-produced film, while using it to illustrate student voice, simultaneously giving students experience in real-world applications of communication technology.

Okay, this thing that we did that you saw me editing in the class was in a movie. They learned how to write dialogue from that. They didn't only learn editing. They went through the facets of what all they have to go through to put a movie together. For example they have to decide in this scene, what type of music do we wanna use, what's gonna be our dialogue. It had to be relevant. Does it pertain to the plot. And so you put them [the students] in the mix. And that's what I mean by the student going into the classroom. And I mean you saw them out there on the screen, you, you didn't see me anywhere. I'm not even in it. (Tommy, communication media teacher)

Reggie, teacher of government and also one of the four teachers identified, spoke of his American government class as discussing racism: "I illustrate, I teach a whole aspect in regards to government and racism in politics."

Both Nickole (Grade 10) and Tyreek (alumnus) spoke of specific programs and classtime devoted to future planning.

> In one class I be plannin' for the future. Like things we think we would be interested in. Like, um, read about it and do reports on it so we will know exactly what we want to do in the future. (Nickole, Grade 10)

> I was part of the "Jump-start" program ever since the sixth grade and they kept tellin' us "you gotta do it in school to get ready for college. This is what you do when you wanna get into college." I think that's what help make me, you know what I'm sayin'? (Tyreek, alumnus)

> But yet it may be the hardest class I have, but it's the funnest, too, because he makes it, he puts a, the lesson to where I can relate to it and some of the students too. But if you can put it to something like I can relate to or something or just break it down, I will learn things. (Al, Grade 11)

FINAL THOUGHTS

"Why do you want to write this book?" asked Al (Grade 11). What did Al's challenge mean for me as a researcher and activist educator? Al asked me this early in our interviews and as I read the transcript again, I realized that I gave him an "adult" answer that didn't come close to supporting student voice, which was the premise of the study. Was my answer even relevant or valuable? My answer was not relevant for the study except as a starting point in my transformation as an activist educator whose work is grounded in the lived experience of those students and adults I serve. The students challenged my position and my assumptions about teaching and learning. They continually challenged my beliefs and assumptions about students. Through their voices they made visible a framework for emancipatory praxis, which had up until that point been a philosophical and theoretical discussion, among adults. The 4 Rs Theory, created with African-American high school students, locates the student at the center and provides a place for students' voices to intercept racism, ageism, and classism and an instructional practice that is "real."

What the students provided in the creation of the 4 Rs Theory is a framework "adequate to the task of changing the world . . . open-ended, nondogmatic, speaking to and grounded in the circumstances of everyday life" (Lather, 1991, p. 51). They provided education with a challenge. I accept.

REFERENCES

Ayers, W., & Ford, P. (1996). *City kids, city teachers.* New York: The New Press.

Ferguson, R. (2003). Teachers' perceptions and expectations and the Black-White test score gap. *Urban Education, 38*(4), 460–507.

Freire, P. (1970). *Pedagogy of the oppressed.* New York: Continuum.

Giroux, H. A. (1992). *Border crossings: Cultural workers and the politics of education.* New York: Routledge.

hooks, b. (1994). *Teaching to transgress: Education as the practice of freedom.* Boston: South End Press.

Ladson-Billings, G. (1994). *The dreamkeepers: Successful teachers of African American children.* San Francisco: Jossey-Bass.

Lather, P. (1991). *Getting smart: Feminist research and pedagogy with/in the postmodern.* New York: Routledge.

Lewis, M. G. (1993). *Without a word: Teaching beyond women's silence.* New York: Routledge.

McLaren, P. L. (1997). *Revolutionary multiculturalism: Pedagogies of dissent for the new millennium.* Boulder, CO: Westview Press.

Nieto, S. (1996). *Affirming diversity* (2nd ed.). London: Longman Publishing.

Sapon-Shevin, M. (1994). *Playing favorites: Gifted education and the disruption of community.* Albany: State University of New York Press.

Sleeter, C. E., & Grant, C. (1987). An analysis of multicultural education in the United States. *Harvard Educational Review, 57*(4), 421–444.

Swadener, B.B., & Lubeck, S. (1995). *Children and families "at promise": Deconstructing the discourse of risk.* Albany: State University of New York Press.

West, C. (1993). *Prophetic reflections: Notes on race and power in America.* Monroe, ME: Common Courage Press.

LISTENING TO THE VOICES OF CHINESE IMMIGRANT GIRLS

YU-CHI SUN

Inviting three young Chinese immigrant girls to participate in my doctoral research was a way to give them voice and enable them to process their experiences and share their perceptions of what it was like to attend an American school for the first time as young children. Although they were expected to be quiet and respectful in their traditional Chinese schools, they were silenced in a different way in American schools. My qualitative research, using narrative inquiry (Clandinin & Connelly, 2000), not only gave them voice but also helped them begin to develop their own power through communicating and interpreting their own experience. They shared their stories with me as a researcher at a nearby American university and as a Taiwanese woman of Chinese descent who could understand their background and experience. I offer part of their stories here, using pseudonyms to protect their identity, along with my views of how narrative inquiry can give voice to other immigrant students who have much to teach us.

Two of the three girls I interviewed immigrated to the United States while in the elementary grades; the oldest was in the seventh grade. Lee Yuan, twelve, Liu Chen, twelve, and Wang Hui, seventeen, were born into professional families in China and currently attend mainstream secondary schools in Littletown (pseudonym), a university town located in the northeastern United States, where they now reside. I explore their experiences as newcomers to the American school system, as well as how they have interpreted and made sense of these experiences. In other words, as a researcher I have listened to and made meaning of these girls' personal stories, retelling and interpreting them to convey what it has meant to be an immigrant student in a mainstream American school. Besides having an influence on their personal lives, the American school is changing and moving forward under their influence and that of other culturally diverse students.

Lee Yuan was an only child until May 2002 when her mother gave birth to her baby sister. Born in the ancient capital city of Xian, in central China, Lee Yuan went to preschool there before leaving China at age 5. Her journey to the United States was somewhat circuitous. At age five, she and her mother joined her father in Germany, where he had worked for six months. Six months later, they moved to Puerto Rico, where Lee Yuan started school. They stayed there for a year and a half. In January 1998, halfway through the second grade, Lee Yuan moved with her parents to Littletown. She now attends middle school and is in the sixth grade.

Liu Chen, the only child in her family, had lived with her maternal grandparents from the age of five in her birthplace of Tainjin, a port city in northern China, while her parents were pursuing graduate studies at the university in Littletown. She completed the first grade while living with her grandparents in China. Unlike Lee Yuan, Liu Chen came straight to Littletown from Tainjin to join her parents in September 1997, as a second grader at age eight. She is now in the sixth grade in middle school.

Wang Hui is also an only child, as China has enforced its one-child policy since 1979 (Falbo, Poston, & Feng, 1996; Liljestrom, 1982). She spent her early childhood in Dalien, a port city in northeastern China, and moved with her parents to Beijing at age seven. She attended her Chinese school through the sixth grade. In the summer of 1997, Wang Hui and her mother came to the United States to join her father, who had emigrated to California a year earlier as a visiting scholar. Wang Hui began her schooling in the United States as a seventh grader in California. Six months later, she and her parents moved to Minnesota. They finally moved to Littletown in the summer of 2000. She is now in the eleventh grade.

I recruited my research participants through an acquaintance of mine at the local Christian church for ethnic Chinese. Before meeting and talking with the three girls themselves, I met their parents and a few other Chinese parents to discuss their daughters' possible participation in my research, because the girls were under the age of eighteen. A few weeks later, Lee Yuan, Liu Chen, and Wang Hui agreed to participate in my research. I then scheduled semistructured, two-hour interview sessions with each girl and audiotaped all of our interviews. To schedule the interviews, I met with the girls and their parents in person or talked with them on the telephone. After I asked the girls and their parents their preference of interview location, I had my first interview with Lee Yuan at a quiet corner of a study lounge in the local university library; we met in my apartment for another interview. I interviewed Liu

Chen and Wang Hui at their homes; each for three sessions. At their request, my interviews with Lee Yuan and Liu Chen were conducted in English; those with Wang Hui were in Chinese. I also conducted several short follow-up interviews and conversations with each girl over the telephone. Completion of all the interviews and conversations took approximately two and a half months.

Given their background, I thought it was important to help them understand their role in the interview. This was a new experience for them. Hsu (1981) asserted that, traditionally, Chinese children are taught to deemphasize self-expression, or as the Chinese saying goes, "children are said to 'have ears but no mouth'" (Chen & Starosta, 1998, p. 75). Since not only had the girls broken into a new school situation on their arrival, but they were now being asked to talk about it a few years later, so it was difficult for them to overcome their self-consciousness and be open in the interviews. Thus, to help these girls feel relaxed, comfortable, and free to express themselves during my in-depth interviews, I told them that the questions were not like school tests that required correct answers or a certain kind of answer. Instead, as I explained to them, I was just present to listen to their stories and to learn from their lived experiences. Especially, I assured them anonymity to put them at ease.

All three girls were very willing to share the stories of their experiences in the American schools, and I enjoyed listening to them as well. Gradually, we developed a mutual trust, and I could actually imagine and feel myself living their stories while listening to them. But, not everything went entirely smoothly during the course of our interviews. I had to overcome situations in which they were not as expressive as I had expected them to be. I constantly negotiated a relationship with each girl through our collaboration, which was built on our dialogues. I also showed my interest in their stories and frequently encouraged them to be more expressive by asking further questions, or by probing for the meanings of their experiences.

During my interviews with these girls, I sensed that they had begun to learn how to be active agents, although they probably weren't directly aware of it. Having to think hard to answer some of the challenging questions I raised during the interviews may have been the start of their exercise of agency. Certain comments like, "Umm, I never thought about this before," "I never thought there would be a relationship," and "I just thought the school would be like that" revealed their developing sense of agency. Though unaware of it, they were exercising human agency based on Freire's (1985, 1993) notions of conscientization, the process of becoming critically conscious about the sociopolitical world in which one lives, and subject, which refers to those who exercise agency.

The immigrant girls' storytelling about their school experiences was central to my research. Bateson (1989) noted that, "storytelling is fundamental to the human search for meaning" (p. 34). These girls engaged themselves in self-interpretation and self-understanding through their own storytelling, searching for the meaning of being an immigrant student in an American school. As the researcher who worked with these girls, I listened to and reinterpreted their individual stories, searching for what attending an American school has meant to them. Through these girls' telling of their own stories, and my retelling and writing them, we have woven the fluidity and complexity of their stories into the school system in both space and time.

STARTING A NEW SCHOOL IN A STRANGE LAND

Shortly after their arrival in this country, Lee Yuan and Liu Chen started school as second graders in a Littletown elementary school. Although Lee Yuan came to the United States when she was halfway through the second grade, Liu Chen arrived just a week after the fall semester had begun. Wang Hui began her American schooling in California as a seventh grader. However, these girls shared the common experience of encountering a language that they could hardly understand when they started school in this country. They all had learned some English at school in China or, in Lee Yuan's case, in Puerto Rico, but their formal English studies had not prepared them for real-life, conversational communication in an English-speaking environment. The English language difficulty was the first and primary hurdle they faced as they started life and school in this country (First, 1988; Fu, 1995). In Lee Yuan's words:

> At that time I had learned a little bit English in Puerto Rico, but when you say you learn a language, it keeps you vocabulary without learning "are" and "the" and "is," those kinds of words. You really can't say much. You can't stream the words together basically. It was just empty words floating around the place.

Being able to speak and understand the English language in a school context, therefore, became the first challenge that these girls had to deal with on a daily basis as new students in an American school. Lee Yuan, Liu Chen, and Wang Hui thus began their new school life by moving between their regular classes and an English as a second language (ESL) class.

WHAT HAPPENED IN THE REGULAR CLASSROOM

"I went to ESL class every school day, but most of the school day I was in regular class," said Lee Yuan about the start of her new school life, which mirrored that of Liu Chen, Wang Hui, and many other immigrant students in this country. In the regular class that was taught in English and targeted mainly for students fluent in English, the Chinese girls felt left out or like outsiders, who, sadly, perceived themselves as "invisible" to the English-speaking students and even to themselves. Due to the language barrier, lack of familiarity with the school culture, and lack of adequate support and guidance from their regular classroom teachers, these girls never felt as if they were full-fledged participants in the classroom. For instance, regarding reading and social studies, Wang Hui said, "When they [the other students] were reading novels, I was allowed to do my own stuff. They [the teachers] didn't ask me to take social studies either. So sometimes I would do my homework or play computer games in the back of the classroom." When these girls started school in this country, they went through a "sink or swim" experience (Del Valle, 1998; Olsen, 1988) in the regular classroom. They were not expected to participate in class and eventually their teachers developed lower expectations of them.

In our interview, Liu Chen revealed her frustration and anger about having sat alone and silent in the classroom without being able to participate in class activities with the other students when she started attending an American school. She said, "I probably felt bored. Sometimes I was annoyed 'cause I didn't understand and I couldn't do what other people were doing." Coming from the traditional, highly regimented school system in China in which each student keeps to the same structure as everyone else, attending every class and participating in class activities together, Liu Chen felt uncomfortable and frustrated by being unable to understand and do what the rest of the American class was doing. In addition to the language barrier, she had no idea how to participate in the activities of the school system, which was very different from the one she had been used to in China. She had been taught to keep quiet in her Chinese classroom, but students are generally expected to speak out and participate in the American classroom. Thus, initially Liu Chen needed to be taught by her teachers how to participate in her new classroom environment. Unfortunately, she, like Lee Yuan and Wang Hui, had to pick up things on her own, with little support and guidance from the regular classroom teacher.

Further, Lee Yuan indicated that she felt dumb in the regular classroom, especially when the teacher was talking to her. This was partly due to Lee Yuan's inability to communicate in English. She said, "It made you feel you were not at the same level as the teachers and they were superior over you when they were talking to you, and that made you feel dumb." Also, she suggested that her regular classroom teachers talked to her in a way that made her believe that they felt superior to her. Lee Yuan's feeling "dumb" or inferior was also related to the unequal power relations between herself as an ESL learner and her regular classroom teachers, who were native speakers of English (Norton, 2000). However, Lee Yuan had little control over the interactions between herself and her regular classroom teachers. She revealed the unequal power relations between language learners and target language speakers, in which language learners are often viewed as—to borrow Norton's (2000) words—"illegitimate speakers" of the target language.

Moreover, Lee Yuan, like Liu Chen, was eager to be heard and understood by her regular classroom teachers so that they could tell her how to participate in this new classroom setting. But in Lee Yuan's words:

> It was hard to get personal attention at all. So I just picked it up when it went along. . . . My second grade teacher he just treated me like most of them, and that made it hard for me to pick up stuff.

Apparently, Lee Yuan's second grade teacher failed to pay much attention to her, which led to his failure to develop an understanding of her prior learning experiences in China and Puerto Rico and of her needs in the new school. In fact, better understanding of the needs of those students with special backgrounds, such as immigrant children, has much to do with the teacher's willingness to listen to them, verbally and nonverbally.

None of the three immigrant girls in this research perceived their regular classroom teachers as paying much attention to them. As both an immigrant herself, coming to the United States from the Philippines at the age of thirteen, and as a teacher of immigrant children, Igoa (1995) asserted that listening to the children must be central to the work of the teachers of immigrant children. Utilizing her own classroom teaching practices as an example, she suggests that immigrant children's experiences and needs can be learned and understood through "their words, artwork, and behavior" (p. 63). She certainly models for other teachers of immigrant children that, through creative and subtle ways, they can better understand their students and help them learn.

WHAT HAPPENED IN THE ESL CLASSROOM

These girls also attended ESL class every school day for an hour or so when they first entered the American school. Lee Yuan went to ESL for a semester, while Liu Chen had one year and Wang Hui two years. If the regular classroom was a place in which they felt overwhelmed, insecure, frustrated, helpless, and unrecognized, then the ESL classroom provided a shelter where they could find some comfort after being exhausted by what happened as well as by the pace in the regular classroom. When talking about their ESL classes, Lee Yuan and Wang Hui both revealed the comfort and support that they found in ESL and from their ESL teachers.

Lee Yuan said of her ESL class:

> When you go to ESL, they are ready for a person who doesn't know English. It's different from regular class in expectation and everything. So I actually felt most comfortable in ESL and I really actually enjoyed it there. . . . It was fun. It wasn't boring like most of the classes. It was more relaxed. It was basically like conversations almost. . . . In ESL we had a lot

of Chinese people there. Some of them were more advanced and we translated and helped people pick up stuff from the advanced people.

Lee Yuan, on the one hand, was always encouraged to speak out and to participate in the ESL class, which made her feel like a real and active participant. She also felt more relaxed in the presence of "the advanced" Chinese students, who helped newcomers like herself adjust to the new school. She, too, felt more comfortable and secure practicing and speaking English because of her ESL teacher's "nice attitude" toward her. As she said of her ESL teacher, "She was nice and she like talked to us more [about] what we needed to know or [at] our level without making us feel we were really dumb or stuff. She had a really nice attitude and she was really patient." The ESL class became a safe and friendly place for Lee Yuan in which to learn on her own level and at her own pace.

Wang Hui also had better support from her ESL teacher. She said:

Because our ESL teacher was very nice, we were more like a group, and we got along with each other very well. . . . And when we ESL students had more and more time to get along with each other and with the ESL teacher, like we had lunch together, the ESL teacher would want to know more about our individual cultural backgrounds.

The sense of belonging to a group or a class is very important for Wang Hui, who had close relationships with her peers in China. Being able to share her cultural background with other ESL students as well as with the ESL teacher not only was a comfort for Wang Hui, but also made her feel that she was finally better recognized. As she explained, "In regular class the teachers seemed to ignore that you were from another country. They seemed not interested in letting you share something from your cultural background with the rest of the class." The comfort she received from both her ESL class and her ESL teacher helped ease some of Wang Hui's discomfort and sense of loss that she experienced in the regular classroom.

However, on a somewhat negative note, Wang Hui also said of the ESL class: "I think the function and purpose of ESL is helping you fit into American school and society as soon as possible rather than helping you preserve your native culture." Assimilating rather than integrating ESL students is still the primary goal of the ESL class. In fact, learning a new language should add to what one already knows and help one to be able to communicate in more than one way. Thus, learning a second language should not be done at the expense of the first or native language. I agree with Igoa (1995) that "understanding and respecting the immigrants' native cultural attitude [is] as important as helping them learn a second language" (p. 15). Immigrant children's native language and culture should be recognized and honored in the ESL classroom. ESL teachers' respect for their students' cultures, in fact, contributes to their students' respect for one another and reverence for differences as well.

Moreover, a different voice concerning the teaching of English as a second language has been emerging in recent years among ESL educators and researchers. It is a voice advocating that while teaching English to their ESL students, ESL teachers should also help them maintain their first or native language. Inspired by the conference theme of the 2002 TESOL Annual Convention—Language and the Human Spirit—Eggington (2002) responded to Richard Littlebear's personal reflections on losing one's own language: "If we teach English, let's make sure we do it in a way that protects and enhances the first language." I believe that he is right, and that all ESL teachers as well as the American educational system should adopt this policy.

ENCOUNTERING A DIFFERENT KIND OF LEARNING EXPERIENCE

After getting better adjusted to the American school system, Lee Yuan, Liu Chen, and Wang Hui have each found some thing(s) that they like at school. For instance, Lee Yuan and Wang Hui enjoy working on projects for homework and then presenting them to the rest of the class. Lee Yuan believes that the project assignment is not only a more creative way for her to learn, and through which she can learn on her own, but also serves as a tool for her to express herself and to reveal herself to her new world. She said:

> I like having projects actually because they are more free. They are more free activities and represent you. And there is no right answer thing. You can be good either way. It's more creative. It's not like those questions and you put one answer and if you don't get it right, that's sad.

But to be able to work on projects, Lee Yuan first had to learn "library skills," in order to do research in the library.

Wang Hui also described the value of her experiences of doing projects or research papers for homework assignments:

> When they give you projects or research papers for homework assignments, you have to go to the library and do some research by yourself. In this situation, of course, they ask you to think and learn by yourself. . . . Working on projects and research papers helps enhance my thinking skills.

Projects or research papers for homework assignments are something that Wang Hui had never heard of as a student in China, because the Chinese educational system emphasizes memorization and competitive examination (Biggs, 1996; Clark, 1986). It took time for her to understand and get used to the whole idea behind this kind of homework, but now she embraces the idea of learning on her own and of learning in a more creative way.

Moreover, Lee Yuan and Liu Chen enjoy the teaching style in many of their classes in which there are many discussions, whereas in China the teacher usually lectures. Lee Yuan spoke positively of the group discussion experience: "You get to speak out and get your opinion said. You have discussions on your ideas." Liu Chen also said, "I like two-way communication better 'cause it gives you more life skills, you know, more than just knowing facts or anything. . . . Also, it's more fun because you are actually participating." Class discussions or group discussions provide opportunities for these students to communicate in two or more ways, and to learn through communication and interaction. Proponents of current educational theories all agree that students learn through social interaction (Freire, 1985; Fu, 1995; Lave & Wenger, 1991; Savignon, 1997; Verplaetse, 1998; Vygotsky, 1978). By interacting with others in class, including both the teacher and fellow students, students get to think and exchange ideas, and therefore learn from one another. The idea that learning takes place through social interaction was previously unknown to the immigrant girls, who had been taught to deemphasize self-expression and to keep quiet in their Chinese classrooms. Therefore, through the teaching and learning styles in their American classrooms, these girls have started to learn and understand that, not only can knowledge be transmitted by others, but it can also be constructed by oneself.

POSITIONING THEMSELVES ON THE SOCIAL MAP OF THE SCHOOL

Lee Yuan, Liu Chen, and Wang Hui have also encountered things that make them unhappy in the American school, or that can be considered discrimination. Having been teased about her physical appearance by her American peers, Lee Yuan has been very angry and frustrated. She said of her encounters with both Puerto Rican and American students:

> In Puerto Rico, it was basically nice. They were curious and they were always around and that was actually annoying. And I was trying to get rid of them but they followed me everywhere. But here they are not quite so friendly. Some kids they go like this [put hands on her eyes] because their eyes open wider than ours. And they also go like this [put one hand on her nose] because our noses are not like as tall as theirs. That's really mean. But I have learned not to mind because if they want to tease you, that's because something is wrong with them, not me. And, well, I'm a Christian and as a Christian I know that God make you beautifully and wonderfully made and I am His creation and there's nothing to be ashamed of.

Although upset at first, Lee Yuan, with the support of her religious faith, has learned to face the discrimination of her American peers by having a positive attitude. Her defense is to ask them not to tease her again, while reminding herself that she must not be ashamed of herself, especially because of her physical characteristics. Apparently Lee Yuan has not been "silenced" by her American peers' discrimination. Although suffering from the effects of racism, she, nevertheless, is aware that fighting back in a racist way only confirms the prejudice of those who initiate it (Mathabane, 1992).

In addition, Lee Yuan derives her strength from her mother, with whom she has a close relationship. Watkins-Goffman (2001) wrote, "Many girls who have been at odds with American standards of beauty and who felt victimized by stereotyping . . . are more vulnerable and at risk, [and] they benefit from close relationships with their mothers or an older female mentor" (p. 50), and "immigrant girls, whose sense of self may already be fractured because of the move, particularly need strong feminine role models in the new culture" (p. 43). It is partly through her relationship with her mother, her major female role model, that Lee Yuan is better able to find her own voice and stay strong in who and what she is. She is also now better able to find security and learn how to question American standards of beauty that are often among the accepted norms of the mainstream culture. Through this experience, as well as through her strong ties with her mother, Lee Yuan may also be better able to question other accepted norms in everyday life in the United States.

These girls all have had difficulty fitting into the mainstream American classroom. Of the three, Wang Hui is particularly aware of her inability to socialize with her American peers. She said:

> It seems not easy for me to make friends in regular classes. I always feel I can't fit in maybe because I am isolated with others. And I won't force myself to fit in either. I always feel I am different, well, maybe not really different. I just don't feel I can fit in probably because I always feel I am not American and I am Chinese.

In this regard, Watkins-Goffman (2001) pointed out that "a member of the dominant culture needs to see something of himself or herself reflected in an individual from an immigrant group, in order for the former to accept the latter" (p. 4). In other words, to be accepted in the mainstream classroom, immigrant students constantly face the pressure of behaving, verbally and nonverbally, like their American peers. However, rather than copying her American peers' behaviors in order to fit in, Wang Hui has chosen to ignore or "forget" that she is an outsider. Her coping strategy is to pull back and detach herself from what is happening around her by focusing on her studies. It seems safe for her to be on the outside looking in at her new world where all seems so strange, and where it is so difficult for her to find a comfortable place. However, underneath her strategy of detachment, she longs for a close friendship with a peer just like the one she had in China—a friendship that has been an important part of her identity.

I have found some similarities between how Wang Hui and Eva Hoffman have responded to discrimination as immigrant girls. Wang Hui emigrated from Beijing to California at the age of twelve, and Eva Hoffman from Kracow, Poland, to Vancouver, Canada, at the age of thirteen. Since they have been marginalized in their new world, they both use the detachment strategy while romanticizing their earlier life in their country of origin. This mechanism, however, only veils their longing for something that has been missing from their childhood and identity since arriving in the new country. Hoffman (1989) wrote:

> My detachment would serve me better if it were entirely genuine. It isn't. Underneath my carefully trained serenity, there is a cauldron of seething lost loves and a rage at the loss. And there is—for all that—a longing for a less strenuous way to maintain my identity and my pride. (p. 139)

Hoffman's memories of her hometown of Kracow are woven into her childhood identity, as are Wang Hui's memories of her old neighborhood in Beijing where she spent time with her Chinese peers after school. While coping with their alienation, they both struggle to maintain their individual identity. And yet, both are driven to figure out where they each belong in their new world.

WHAT THE AMERICAN SCHOOL CAN TEACH CHILDREN ABOUT DIVERSITY

Lee Yuan revealed that she could do nothing to stop her American peers from discriminating against her because of her appearance, except to ask them to stop it. She sounded so frustrated and helpless in that she feels she is fighting racism on her own, without the help and support of the school. Similarly, Liu Chen expressed her frustration with being teased by her American peers. She spoke of the no bullying and no teasing program for all students that has been implemented in her school:

> We only have like a meeting once a month, and it seems pretty few, and I don't think people if they are going to bully, I don't think they are going to listen to the program. . . . Well, they say treat others as you would have others treat you. Besides that, I don't really see what other things students can learn from school.

Apparently this program has done little to prevent the bullying, teasing, and discrimination among students. In addition, it seems that Liu Chen's school has not yet done enough to talk with students about issues of discrimination and racism. In fact, for this program to work and for the American school to prepare its students for this rapidly changing, multicultural society, these issues cannot be absent from the program, the texts, and the classroom (Giroux, 1992). Igoa (1995) suggested that, to teach all students to be accepting of others, teachers should really spend time talking with students about why racism and discrimination take place and how to prevent them. They should first develop a better understanding of these issues themselves so that they are able to teach them to their students.

By affirming the diverse human experiences and voices found in this country and integrating them into the school curriculum to provide a more multicultural perspective, the American school could be the place where all students learn to equip themselves with the ability to be open to differences, and to respect and value those who are different. Addressing the issue of integrating diverse experiences and voices into the school curriculum, Connell (1993) took a more radical view: "Justice requires a counter-hegemonic curriculum . . . designed to embody the interests and perspectives of the least advantaged. . . . Social justice requires moving out from the starting-point to reconstruct the mainstream to embody the interests of the least advantaged" (p. 44). Social justice requires that the school curriculum be reconstructed to include the experiences and voices of the nonmainstream groups in this country.

Moreover, for social justice to be better achieved in the American school system, the school curriculum needs to be reconstructed to exclude the stereotypes of the nonmainstream groups. Nieto (2000), advocating a critical curriculum that teaches students about the discrimination that nonmainstream groups have faced, wrote, "Textbooks tend to . . . sustain stereotypes of groups outside the cultural and political mainstream" (p. 99). Immigrant experiences, for example, are generally romanticized in the textbooks as successful stories rather than as traumatic ones that so many immigrants have lived through and continue to endure. Social justice, finally, requires that all students be taught about the power of American hegemony as well as how it affects what they learn and how they learn it in school.

UNDERSTANDING THE POWER OF THE IMMIGRANT GIRLS' VOICES THROUGH NARRATIVE INQUIRY

Lee Yuan, Liu Chen, and Wang Hui have ultimately taught us, as researchers, the value of listening to immigrant children to help them adapt to the American school system. In addition, these three Chinese immigrant girls have proven to us that they are capable of being active agents who can empower themselves by speaking out about their lived experiences, when they are provided opportunities, and, most importantly, when they are respected and listened to. Letting them be my teachers helped shape our collaborative relationship by which we reached a shared understanding of their stories through our "continued communication" (Sarris, 1993, p. 6). It was through the process of this "continued communication" that I developed my understanding of them, and that I witnessed them beginning to learn to let their voices be heard. In this way, they shared in the research process with me, telling and making meaning of their own stories. I also showed Wang Hui the transcripts of her interviews because I translated them from Chinese to English, and I wanted to be sure that her words were not mistranslated.

We have learned from these girls that providing immigrant students like them with a caring and nurturing environment, as well as listening to them verbally and nonverbally, for example, through artwork and writing, are apparently more effective than simply leaving them alone and silent to fend for themselves in the regular classroom when they first enter American schools. The classroom should be a place where they feel safe and comfortable to learn to overcome the strangeness and difficulties that they encounter as immigrants, and to accept themselves as becoming a member of a multicultural society. These girls as well as other immigrant students need to be cared for and listened to initially with much more attention by their teachers.

Despite their inability to communicate in English when they were first adapting to the American classroom, each of the three immigrant girls was able to communicate fully in Chinese and, as Igoa (1995) asserted, had a rich inner world that the teachers could have reached if they had been willing to discover what these girls' experiences had been and what their specific needs were in the American classroom. The artwork, for instance, of these girls and other immigrant children, who are not fully able to speak and understand English when they first attend an American school, could serve as a means through which their English-speaking teachers can communicate with and better serve these students.

We have also learned from these girls' voices how they have been frustrated by the racial discrimination and alienation they have experienced trying to position themselves on the social map of the school context, as well as how they resist and deal with this. Educators in this country often hear about racism and discrimination, but they need to listen to what these children are saying about what happened to them, as well as how they resist and deal with it to understand what it is really like for these girls to be a marginalized person in a mainstream American school. Through a better understanding of what these girls experienced socially in school, educators will be better able to teach themselves as well as all students about the issues of racism and discrimination so that racism and discrimination can be reduced in the school setting and further in this multicultural society.

These girls' voices also revealed that they longed to be recognized and respected by their schools, teachers, and American peers. While adapting to the American school system, they need it to meet them halfway by first recognizing and respecting the cultural heritage that they have brought into the American classroom, and then by including their experiences and voices. These girls' and other culturally diverse students' cultures should be recognized and interpreted in a positive way in the classroom. Classroom teachers' respect for culturally diverse students' cultural backgrounds contributes to their students' respect for and acceptance of one another. Therefore, classroom teachers play an important role in reducing racism and discrimination in the classroom and in school as well.

Finally, Lee Yuan, Liu Chen, and Wang Hui have taught us that an important task for the American school is to teach all students to understand and accept their own cultural heritage, through which they learn to appreciate and respect one another's. This, in turn, helps them develop the ability to be open to differences, which is urgently needed for every member, old and new, of this society. The American school can contribute to the establishment of a more peaceful nation by providing a classroom environment where all students feel safe and accepted, and where they can be taught to understand and accept themselves as well as those who are different.

In conclusion, using narrative inquiry as a critical mode of inquiry in my study helped elicit "the 'emotive power'" (Soto, 2000, p. 14) of the stories of the three young Chinese immigrant girls whom I interviewed. This method enabled them to learn to exercise agency by critically reflecting on and speaking out about their lived experiences as newcomers to mainstream American schools. By using these girls' critical personal narratives, I also sought to decolonize the relationship between myself, as the researcher, and the girls (Burdell & Swadener, 1999). Their personal narratives allowed me to enter their worlds while better understanding my own. Finally, by offering part of these children's stories about being silenced in the American school system, I wanted to show that they were, in fact, capable of letting their voices be heard, which enables us, as educators, to better understand what it is like to attend an American school for the first time as young immigrant children. It is important that future research use narrative inquiry, incorporating the voices of immigrant children to reveal their needs for adapting to the American school system. Thus, by listening to young immigrant students' needs from their own experience, researchers can help give them power and voice, which would lead to a more equitable education for them in American schools.

REFERENCES

Bateson, M. C. (1989). *Composing a life*. New York: Grove.

Biggs, J. B. (1996). Learning, schooling, and socialization: A Chinese solution to a Western problem. In S. Lau (Ed.), *Growing up the Chinese way: Chinese child and adolescent development* (pp. 147–167). Hong Kong: Chinese University Press.

Burdell, P., & Swadener, B. B. (1999). Critical personal narrative and autoethnography in education: Reflections on a genre. *Educational Researcher, 28*(6), 21–26.

Chen, G. M., & Starosta, W. J. (1998). *Foundations of intercultural communication*. Boston: Allyn & Bacon.

Clandinin, D. J., & Connelly, F. M. (2000). *Narrative inquiry: Experience and story in qualitative research*. San Francisco: Jossey-Bass.

Clark, J. (1986). *Change and continuity in Chinese educational theory: A study of the persistence of Confucian educational ideas in the thought of Chinese republican and Maoist educators*. Unpublished doctoral dissertation, Rutgers, State University of New Jersey, New Brunswick.

Connell, R. W. (1993). *Schools and social justice*. Philadelphia: Temple University Press.

Del Valle, S. (1998). Bilingual education for Puerto Ricans in New York City: From hope to compromise. *Harvard Educational Review, 68,* 193–217.

Eggington, W. (2002). "When a language dies, it doesn't stink": Reflections on language loss lessons. *TESOL Matters, 12*(3). Retrieved December 1, 2003, from http://www.tesol.org/pubs/articles/2002/tm12-3-06.html

Falbo, T., Poston, D. L., & Feng, X. T. (1996). The academic, personality, and physical outcomes of Chinese only children: A review. In S. Lau (Ed.), *Growing up the Chinese way: Chinese child and adolescent development* (pp. 265–286). Hong Kong: Chinese University Press.

First, J. M. (1988). Immigrant students in U.S. public schools: Challenges with solutions. *Phi Delta Kappan, 70,* 205–210.

Freire, P. (1985). *The politics of education: Culture, power, and liberation*. South Hadley, MA: Bergin & Garvey.

Freire, P. (1993). *Pedagogy of the oppressed*. New York: Continuum.

Fu, D. (1995). *My trouble is my English: Asian students and the American dream*. Portsmouth, NH: Boynton/Cook.

Giroux, H. A. (1992). *Border crossings: Cultural workers and the politics of education*. New York: Routledge.

Hoffman, E. (1989). *Lost in translation: A life in a new language*. New York: Penguin Books.

Hsu, F. L. K. (1981). *Americans and Chinese: Passage to differences*. Honolulu: University of Hawaii Press.

Igoa, C. (1995). *The inner world of the immigrant child*. New York: St. Martin's Press.

Lave, J., & Wenger, E. (1991). *Situated learning: Legitimate peripheral participation*. Cambridge, UK: Cambridge University Press.

Liljestrom, R. (1982). The family in China yesterday and today. In T. Skuntnabb-Kangas & R. Phillipson (Trans.), *Young children in China* (pp. 1–43). Clevedon, UK: Multilingual Matters.

Mathabane, M. (1992). From the far inside. In S. Terkel (Ed.), *Race: How blacks and whites think and feel about the American obsession* (pp. 319–325). New York: The New Press.

Nieto, S. (2000). *Affirming diversity: The sociopolitical context of multicultural education* (3rd ed.). New York: Addison-Wesley Longman.

Norton, B. (2000). *Identity and language learning: Gender, ethnicity and educational change*. Harlow, UK: Pearson Education Limited.

Olsen, L. M. (1988). *Crossing the schoolhouse border: Immigrant students and the California public schools.* San Francisco: A California Tomorrow Policy Research Report.

Sarris, G. (1993). *Keeping slug woman alive: A holistic approach to American Indian texts.* Berkeley: University of California Press.

Savignon, S. (1997). *Communicative competence: Theory and classroom practice.* New York: McGraw-Hill.

Soto, L. D. (2000). Toward a critical postmodern narrative inquiry. *Contemporary Psychology, 45*(1), 14–16.

Verplaetse, L. S. (1998, Autumn). How content teachers interact with English language learners. *TESOL Journal, 7*(5), 24–28.

Vygotsky, L. S. (1978). *Mind in society: The development of higher psychological processes.* Cambridge, MA: Harvard University Press.

Watkins-Goffman, L. (2001). *Lives in two languages: An exploration of identity and culture.* Ann Arbor: University of Michigan Press.

CHAPTER EIGHT

PERFORMING FEMININITIES THROUGH GENDER DISCOURSES

MINDY BLAISE

This chapter briefly shows how femininity was performed and understood by young children in a kindergarten classroom by locating five gender discourses. Feminist poststructuralist understandings of knowledge, language, discourse, and power were used to make sense of how children were taking an active part in constructing gender. Moving away from biological and socialization understandings of gender, this study understood gender to be a cultural, historical, political, and social construction, and that children took an active part in the gendering process (Davies, 2003; MacNaughton, 2000; Walkerdine, 1990).

I spent six months collecting data with children as a participant observer, most often taking an active role with the children, which helped to create authentic collaborative relationships with them while spending time in their classroom. At times I took on a passive role, quietly observing from the sidelines when children were sitting on the rug for morning meeting or circle time, but the majority of the time I was more active as I talked with children individually, in small groups, and with the entire class. Data were collected through field notes, audiotaping informal discussions with children, and videotaping their play at the dramatic play center or during large group meetings. I would often share my findings with children, asking them for their opinions or "readings" about what I collected.

To do feminist research means not just taking a woman's perspective, but also engaging in the research process to provide understandings that enable girls and women to transform their own worlds and become conscious of oppression. In other words, theory, praxis, and method become inseparable from each other within feminist research (Fay, 1987; Nielson, 1990). By conducting a feminist poststructuralist study, I focused on the constructed worlds of knowledge, placing the social and political construction of gender at the center of the inquiry (Lather, 1992). As praxis-oriented work or an act of consciousness raising, I purposefully designed this study to turn critical thought into social action. That is, methods were utilized that influenced change on the part of everyone involved, including myself, the teacher, and the children. In doing so, I believed that this opened up the possibility of transforming patriarchy and improving the lives of girls and women (Cook & Fonow, 1990; Fine, 1994; Lather, 1991; Nielson, 1990).

Feminist researchers often use reciprocity as one way for creating a research design that is empowering to both the researcher and researched, as well as encouraging consciousness raising and transformation (Lather, 1991). I used reciprocity in a range of ways, particularly as I attempted to restructure the inequitable relationships that often exist between the researcher and the researched in many research projects (Alldred, 1998; Burman, 1992; Lather, 1991). Instead of a unidirectional process where I might go into the classroom extracting information from the children, I consciously attempted to encourage a more collaborative relationship between the children and myself (for a more thorough discussion see Ochsner, 2001). As a result, meanings about gender were negotiated with children through question posing, data collection, and analysis (Gitlin & Russell, 1994; Lather, 1991; Wilkinson, 1986). The examples that are provided throughout this chapter show my research relationships with children, including exciting and difficult moments that I encountered while researching.

Five gendered discourses were uncovered with the children and include *wearing femininity, body movements, makeup, beauty,* and *fashion talk.* They were discovered with the children through my observations, conversations with individuals and small groups of children, during large group meeting times, and by collecting student artifacts. Most of these conversations were audiotaped, and videotaping was used to document children's actions.

The term *discourse* refers to a grid of power and knowledge, in which knowledge and power are integrated with one another and impossible to separate (Foucault, 1977/1980). Discourse is a structuring principle in society and includes how we speak, write, think, and act, which incorporate particular things as given, unchallengeable truths. Dominant discourses appear "natural," supporting and perpetuating existing power relations, tending to constitute the subjectivity of most people (Foucault, 1977/1980; Gavey, 1997; Weedon, 1997). Subsequently, I was interested in the everyday lives of children and how they spoke and wrote about gender, as well as how they performed femininity and masculinity. How children used these five gender discourses to actively create what it means to be a girl or boy is the focus of this chapter, particularly how gender was performed through femininity.

WEARING FEMININITY

The most obvious and explicit way in which these children practiced gender and identified themselves as either female or male was how they presented themselves physically as gendered beings. Since girls have more clothing options than do boys, who wear only pants, shorts, and shirts to school, it was easier to notice and document the variety of clothes that the girls wore to school.

Although children take up femininity and masculinity in different ways, it appears that it is important for the majority of young children to get their gender "right" (Davies, 2003). Not only did the children in this classroom get their gender "right" through the clothing they wore (i.e., boys chose not to wear skirts), but girls' fashion choices portrayed a range of femininities. Two of the most observable forms of femininity displayed included what the children named as "girly girls" and "cool girls." Being a girly girl meant that you wore frilly, ruffled, and cute outfits, with matching shoes, tights, barrettes, and ribbons. Pink was a desirable color for this look. Maintaining this form of femininity was important and it seemed to take great effort. I often noticed girls checking their appearance in either the full-length mirror located near the dramatic play center or in the bathroom. Girls, not boys, were overheard discussing how hard it was to stay neat and clean throughout the school day. As a consequence, it did not surprise me when Holly, with both her hair and the front of her dress covered with glue, told Madison, "That center was gooey and messy. I got real messy. Don't go there, especially if you want your clothes to stay pretty."

Not only did skirts and dresses prohibit girls from climbing and swinging outside (because their panties would show), it also enforced certain ways that the girls sat on the rug during group times. For example, Sophie was seen frantically waving her hands, attempting to inform Laura, who was sitting across from her in the circle, that her panties were showing. Sophie showed Laura how to delicately pull her skirt over her legs and appropriately sit with her knees together so that no one could see her panties. Clothes enforced a different set of rules for the girls, since the boys did not seem to worry about how their clothing might prevent them from participating in activities or being a certain kind of boy.

The other form of femininity that was noticed in the classroom was sophisticated, mature, and cool. The cool girl look clashed with the innocent, sweet, and compliant girly girl. Cool girls achieved their look by wearing clothes considered to be the latest in fashion, such as bell-bottoms, Spice Girl logos, baseball caps turned backward, and the color black. Cool girls did not seem like they belonged in a kindergarten classroom, painting at the easel or building with blocks. Instead, they looked as if they should be out at a nightclub dancing. Valerie, a girl who worked hard at being a cool girl, always wore sophisticated and sexy outfits. Her clothes were never childish or frilly. One of her favorite outfits included tight fitting leopard-print stretch pants and a low-cut matching top, accented with black fake fur on the cuffs of her sleeves. Her outfit was complete with black Harley-Davidson–style boots, making her look more like an MTV star than a six-year-old girl.

Liza's book, *Things that I Like and Things that I Do*, brought me into the world of cool girls, specifically what cool girls are, what they like, and what they do.

FAGS TAT I LIC ABD FAGS TAT I DO	*Things that I Like and Things that I Do*
1. I SAWAM IN TA WIY	I swim in the Y.
2. I LIC TO WICH TAPS	I like to watch tapes.
3. I LIC TO BE LIC A BOY AND TASUP LIC A BOY	I like to be like a boy and dress-up like a boy
4. AND LIC A COL GRL	And like a cool girl.
5. I LIC TO GOW TO PRTEYS	I like to go to parties.
6. I LIC TO DO JMASTACS	I like to do gymnastics.
8. I LIC TO GOOY TO TA GAP	I like to go to the Gap.
9. I LIC TO GO TO COL PLASS	I like to go to cool places.
10. I LIC TO MAC DIGS	I like to make things.
11. TAS BAC IS DATACATD TO MIY FAMLE	This book is dedicated to my family.

According to Liza, cool girls like participating in a variety of activities such as swimming, watching videotapes, dressing up like a boy, going to parties, gymnastics, and shopping. When I sat down to talk with Liza about her book, she let me know that being a cool girl is hard work and takes a considerable amount of time and effort—"You aren't born this way. You have to work at it." Liza then went on to name the cool and uncool girls in her class, and I realized that the uncool girls, Charmaine, Anne, and Nancy, came from working-class backgrounds and are African American. For Liza, cool girls are white and middle-class.

Were Liza's attitudes and comments about Charmaine, Anne, and Nancy racist? At the time of our conversation, I did not quite know what to make of her comments, other than they made me feel uncomfortable. Was her honesty evidence of my ability to successfully create an authentic collaborative research relationship? If so, did my relationship maintain inequity? If I believed my role as a feminist researcher is about promoting equity, what should I have done? Why didn't I choose to confront and challenge Liza's understandings about cool girls? Was I afraid of ruining our collaborative research relationship?

Reflecting back on this moment allows me to see the missed opportunity I had for confronting and challenging Liza's understandings of cool girls. At the time of the study, I was hesitant of challenging these forms of racism and sexism. Now, as I continue to enact classroom-based studies of gender, I seem to notice when these moments occur and attempt to intervene by questioning children's assumptions and beliefs. Although I still find intervening difficult, I know that it is a necessary part of the work that I do with children.

BODY MOVEMENTS

How children moved their bodies and orchestrated how others see them through "posing," is the second gender discourse, and it was a strategy used by children to reinforce gendered ways of being a girl. After noticing the different femininities that girls portrayed through their fashion, it became easier to see the ways that girls physically moved their bodies and posed for others. Femininities were embodied most noticeably through twirling, sulking, slouching, and curtsying.

While sitting on the rug for morning meeting, read aloud, or show-and-tell, girls were observed unconsciously twirling strands of their hair. However, once they became conscious of being watched, the twirling became exaggerated, and the girls would boldly smile at whoever was watching them. I also noticed girls twirling their skirts while moving their hips in sexual ways. These body movements became more conspicuous when girls had an audience, such as sharing work or reading a story for the entire class. I remember when Sophie was asked to share the work she had done during center time, and I was shocked at how she seemed to transform from the quiet and compliant student to a sexy and provocative performer right in front of my eyes! While explaining to the class the patterns she created with the pattern blocks, Sophie began swinging her hips back and forth, twirling her hair, fluttering her eyelashes, and gazing up toward the ceiling. She started using a lot of "ums," "ya' knows," and "w::e::lls," in a singsong and raspy voice.

Sulking and slouching were two body movements that seemed to get girls noticed by others, enabling them to intentionally position themselves as weak, helpless, and in need of care and attention. Although sulking and slouching were not as "loud" as a twirl or a twist, they were equally as powerful. Being the last one to sit on the rug after cleanup, lagging behind in line, dragging your feet, slouching, and having a sad face were are all part of the sulk. These body movements encouraged friends to ask what was wrong or if they could help. In doing this, the idea of the helpless female was reinforced.

Curtsying was a popular way for girls to position their bodies after almost any type of public performance. Curtsying was first noticed when the class had completed a movement activity, and the leaders exclaimed, "Great job! Now, everybody take a bow!" Instead of taking a bow, Katy loudly resisted their request when she shouted, "Hey, what about a curtsy?" I soon started to see both Katy and Breanna curtsying after any kind of public performance. By refusing to take a bow, these girls chose to perform their understandings of a particular form of femininity.

Makeup

The third gender discourse, makeup, was found in several places in this classroom. Not only were children talking, writing, and drawing about makeup, but they were also bringing it to school. Entire books were being written by the girls about makeup, complete with detailed drawings about the kinds of makeup available, how it is correctly applied, and how it is used to attract boys and men (Ochsner, 1999).

Theresa, whose stories, drawings, and play centered on the Disney character Ariel, understood makeup as a powerful tool for determining and expressing femininity. Theresa explained her drawing of the mermaid Ariel:

> This is Ariel. See? [pointing to her mermaid drawing] She has lipstick and is showing off her stomach. She also has long hair, see? [pointing to hair] Oh, and Ariel also has fingernail polish on.

It was important that I notice Ariel's makeup (lipstick and nail polish), bare stomach, and long hair. For Theresa, Ariel is a beautiful object who uses her accentuated feminine qualities to attract Prince Eric. Later that week, Theresa told me that she likes wearing red lipstick, too, because it makes her pretty. She also added, "Well, Ariel also likes to, no she *needs* to wear lipstick because Prince Eric likes it . . . A lot."

Makeup also emerged in the classroom when some of the girls started bringing an assortment of real and pretend makeup for show-and-tell. Video data show how children were attempting to subvert one boy's interest in the lipstick, eye shadow, and nail polish that Liza brought to share, as they ignored his comments about the makeup being pretty, laughed when he commented on wanting to play with it, and then physically pushed him aside when he tried to ask questions about the makeup.

What was interesting about this classroom moment was how children were using the public space of show-and-tell to reinforce gender norms, illustrating the powerful ways in which children's talk and actions maintained the gendered social order of the classroom. That is, in this classroom it is not "normal" for boys to be interested in feminine items such as makeup. The discourse of makeup was talked and written about in this classroom and both the girls and boys actively used their knowledge of the politics of makeup to construct themselves as gendered beings.

BEAUTY

The fourth gender discourse that was discovered in the classroom includes concepts of beauty. This discourse was discovered while talking with children about make-up and shows how these discourses are interconnected and work together to support gender norms. When I asked a small group of girls about their interest in makeup and the makeup books that were being written, I was again told about the politics of makeup, particularly how it was used by girls and women to "be more beautiful" and "to get boyfriends."

In this classroom and for a small group of girls, being a beautiful princess means attending extravagant parties and balls, where dancing happens and a handsome prince is met. Dressing up in ball gowns and jewelry is a prerequisite for attending such social events. A variety of dress-up clothes such as party dresses, veils, high-heeled shoes, earrings, necklaces, bracelets, and handbags were available at the dramatic play center, and I would watch these girls use the dress-up clothes to transform themselves into beautiful, dancing princesses.

Getting ready seemed to be a ritual enacted in the dramatic play center as girls prepare themselves to look pretty and beautiful before attending social events. The following video data shows Nancy, Katy, and Theresa spending over half of their playtime getting ready for a date with an older boyfriend.

Katy and Theresa start packing for their dates. Nancy picks up a makeup compact and begins applying pretend powder to her face.

Nancy:	(Walking toward Katy.) M:o:m, do you want to look beautiful and in style? (She begins applying powder to Katy's face.) Here, it really does.
Katy:	(Stops packing and allows Nancy to apply powder to her face.) Oh, darling!
Nancy:	(When she is finished with Katy, she resumes powdering her own nose.)
Theresa:	(Looking at Katy.) Oh, you look beautiful! Are you wearing long hair tonight, on your date?
Katy:	Yea. (Takes her hand and strokes the scarf she has wrapped around her head as her long hair. She now takes off her dress and packs it.) Guys, we really have to look beautiful. You know, that is what our boyfriends want!

Being pretty and beautiful were not just characteristics important in the dramatic play area, both adults and children were seen recognizing and praising distinct forms of femininity. Adults were sometimes heard saying, "Oh, doesn't that dress look beautiful! You look so pretty today!" Children also took an active role in complimenting each other's outfits, especially how particular barrettes and bracelets made them look "Oh, so beautiful!" Interestingly, boys were never heard complimenting girls on their clothes or appearances.

These everyday and seemingly innocent comments become concerns if we think about the importance of children's talk and how it constructs gender. For example, praising particular gendered categories such as "pretty" and "beautiful" creates and sustains the gendered elements of the current social structure (Davies, 2003). These seemingly innocent compliments continue to establish and value certain ways of being a girl, while ignoring and marginalizing other ways of being gendered.

As the school year progressed and my understandings of the messages embedded within these comments deepened, I found myself cringing when adults made comments on girls' physical appearances. I was horrified the day I caught myself telling Nancy how pretty her new outfit looked! This moment also made me think critically about the times when the girls commented on my fashion, exclaiming, "Oh Mindy, those are beautiful earrings!" I noticed that I became conscious of my comments and interactions with children, questioning how I might be supporting gender norms.

FASHION TALK

Fashion talk was the fifth gender discourse and includes how children talked about gender. For these children, a desirable form of femininity was realized and embodied through "fashion girls," and masculinity was understood through their ideas of "fashion guys."

Fashion girls were defined, first, by how they dressed, and then, second, by their actions, particularly how they behaved toward others. Fashion guys, on the other hand, were determined almost exclusively by physical actions. I first heard the term *fashion girls* used by Alan while we were sorting Lego action figures by gender. When discussing with Alan which Lego action figures were girls and which ones were boys, he kept comparing the girl Lego action figures with the fashion girls in the classroom. Further conversations uncovered that fashion girls liked to wear cool girl clothes, makeup, and perfume; they liked sitting around being beautiful; and they had boyfriends.

One day, Alan initiated a conversation about fashion girls, telling me who was and was not a fashion girl in his class. Soon a small group of children joined the snack table, adding to our conversation.

Mindy: Charmaine, who do you think are the top three fashion girls?
Charmaine: Me, Kim, Liza, Debbie
Mindy: Oops that's more than three. Can you think of just the top three?

Charmaine: Me, Kim, Debbie.
Alan: ///Valerie. . . . Breanna. . . . .Katy. . . . .
Mindy: Who are the top three fashion boys?
Charmaine: Alan//
Alan: //I'm the king of boys.
Ian: I know [shrugging shoulders].
Charmaine: Alan, Liam, [having trouble naming a third]. . . . .Raoul//
Alan: //Me, Majindra, Ian
Mindy: Why are they fashion boys?
Alan: Because they always play.
Mindy: Oh, so it has nothing to do with what they wear?
Alan: But, I'm the king, I'm the king of boys, so I know who the fashion boys are.
Mindy: So, if you're the king of the boys, who's the queen of the girls?
Charmaine: Me.
Alan: No. Valerie. Valerie's the top fashion girl. But I'm the top boy of fashion. Number one, number one. [Making the number one with his finger.]

In this conversation, Charmaine considers herself to be a fashion girl. However, instead of letting Charmaine share her knowledge of fashion girls, Alan repeatedly interrupts her to be heard. The conversation gravitates to and focuses on Alan, and he informs the table that he considers Valerie to be the number one fashion girl in the class. We also learn that fashion boys are determined differently than fashion girls. That is, what boys wear or how they smell is not as important as what and how they play. What is interesting about this conversation is how Alan seems to take control of the conversation, and I did not do anything to make it more equitable for others. I did not use my power as the adult or the researcher to hear from the other children at the table, instead letting Alan mostly control the discussion. Not surprisingly, Alan continues dominating the fashion talk at the art table.

Mindy: Alan, what does it mean to be fashionable?
Alan: Fashion, it means . . . *sexy*. [Whispering while lowering his head and eyes.]
Mindy: It means what?
Alan: It means *very sexy*. [Looking at me with a sly smile on his face.]
Mindy: So there are some fashion girls in this classroom?
Alan: Uh hum [looks away].
Mindy: And who do you think is the number one fashion girl?
Alan: [Looking straight at me] Valerie.

According to Alan, "fashionable" means sexy! By whispering, lowering his head and eyes, and slyly smiling, Alan shows he is aware that this subject is taboo.

Throughout my time in the classroom, Valerie was repeatedly identified as a fashion girl. Children also distinguished the subtle differences between girls that were and were not fashion girls. Simply wearing a dress did not determine fashion girls, instead it also included being stylish and nice.

One way that masculinity was understood in this class was through children's understandings about fashion guys. When talking with Alan about fashion girls and fashion guys, I discovered that no one was actually a fashion guy in this classroom, because only grown-ups could be a "real" fashion guy. Alan went on to say that James Bond was an example of a fashion guy because " . . . he bungee jumps, breaks through glass, and shoots people." It was fascinating talking to groups of children about fashion guys and girls. These conversations illuminated the knowledge they held about gender norms. For example, when I asked if fashion boys could marry a girl not considered to be a fashion girl, Debbie and Breanna quickly told me that this would not happen, and if you wanted to get married, then you had to be a fashion girl.

Raoul and Alan clearly understood the power and politics of masculinity, especially when they showed how even slightly associating oneself with the feminine color pink is risky business. When we were sorting Lego action figures, I "mistakingly" matched a boy face on a pink body and when Alan noticed what I had done, he had a look of horror and disbelief on his face as he yelled, "Ahhhh!" Raoul looked and loudly said, "No." With a puzzled expression I asked them why this couldn't work and was told "If he walked down the street **for real,** all the people would laugh." Even when I asked them what they would do if all of their shirts were dirty and the only clean shirt to wear was pink, they told me that they would simply wait until the others were cleaned. Both Alan and Raoul said that they would never walk around in a pink, girly colored shirt, no matter what!

Conversations with children disclosed who they thought were fashion girls and fashion boys, and then the different ways that fashion girls and fashion guys were conceptualized. For example, fashion girls were defined first by the ways that they dressed and then by their actions, particularly how they behaved toward others. Fashion guys, on the other hand, were determined almost exclusively by their actions and play.

EXCITING AND DIFFICULT RESEARCH MOMENTS

Researching with children is both exciting and difficult. It was exciting to document children's gendered performances and their understandings of these five gender discourses because it showed them as powerful and active agents in the social and political construction of gender. I liked watching the girls perform femininities in the classroom and hearing what they had to say about being a fashion girl—they knew about gender. Children's feelings, thoughts, and actions exposed the hard and important work that they do constructing gender in their kindergarten classroom.

And yet, it was difficult acknowledging that children were also hard at work maintaining gender norms. I often found myself in relationships with children that made me feel powerless. For instance, I was uncomfortable when Alan and Raoul were making negative remarks about the color pink, writing in my field notes, "This doesn't feel right. Shouldn't I be standing up for the color pink? Or, telling them that wearing pink is not a bad thing?" Not only did their remarks make me feel inferior as a woman, but I was confused about my role as a researcher and what (if any) actions I should take. Observing and hearing the girls' excitement about makeup, being beautiful, and getting married forced me to question my beliefs about femininity and what I value as acceptable forms of femininity. They challenged me to reflect on my own gendered life and the ways in which I choose to embody femininities. When girls commented on my fashion, calling me a fashion girl (because my toenails were painted sparkly blue and I wore red dangly earrings), I did not know how to react.

Finally, I am beginning to recognize the significance of these research relationships, particularly the importance of intervening, even if it means disturbing the collaborative research relationships I have developed with children. Interventions can occur by questioning children's talk, actions, and writings and then engaging them in critical conversations about gender. In doing so, challenging gender discourses that help constitute gender norms becomes a possibility. It is important to remember that uncovering children's understandings of gender, through gender performances and gender discourses, is the first step towards creating new ways of being gendered.

SYMBOLS USED IN THE PRESENTATION OF TRANSCRIPTS

SYMBOL MEANING

Bold Words heavily emphasized by the speaker were written in bold.
?,! Exclamation points and question marks were used when they helped convey the question asked in an utterance or an exclamatory utterance.
/Indicates an interruption
. . . Indicates a pause, with the number of dots indicating the length of the pause
Do::n't Multiple colons indicates a more prolonged sound
quiet Talk that has a noticeably lower or higher volume than the surrounding talk.
[ ]Enclosed statements in parentheses describe the context of an utterance and any other information recorded in the field notes.

REFERENCES

Alldred, P. (1998). Ethnography and discourse analysis: Dilemmas in representing the voices of children. In J. Ribbens & R. Edwards (Eds.), *Feminist dilemmas in qualitative research: Public knowledge and private lives* (pp. 147–170). Thousand Oaks, CA: Sage.

Burman, E. (1992). Feminism and discourse in developmental psychology: Power, subjectivity, and interpretation. *Feminism & Psychology, 2*(1), 45–60.

Cook, J. A., & Fonow, M. M. (1990). Knowledge and women's interests: Issues of epistemology and methodology in feminist sociological research. In J. M. Nielson (Ed.), *Feminist research methods: Exemplary readings in the social sciences* (pp. 69–93). Boulder, CO: Westview.

Davies, B. (2003). *Frogs and snails and feminist tales: Preschool children and gender* (rev. ed.). Sydney: Allen & Unwin.

Fay, B. (1987). *Critical social science.* Ithaca, NY: Cornell University Press.

Fine, M. (1994). Dis-stance and other stances: Negotiations of power inside feminist research. In A. Gitlin (Ed.), *Power and method: Political activism and educational research* (pp. 13–35). New York: Routledge.

Foucault, M. (1980). Truth and power. In C. Gordon (Ed.), *Power/knowledge: Selected interviews and other writings 1972–1977* (pp. 111–133). New York: Pantheon. (Original work published 1977)

Gavey, N. (1997). Feminist poststructuralism and discourse analysis. In M. M. Gergen and S. N. Davis (Eds.), *Toward a new psychology of gender: A reader* (pp. 49–64). New York: Routledge.

Gitlin, A., & Russell, R. (1994). Alternative methodologies and the research context. In A. Gitlin (Ed.), *Power and method: Political activism and educational research* (pp. 181–202). New York: Routledge.

Lather, P. (1991). *Getting smart: Feminist research and pedagogy with/in the postmodern.* New York: Routledge.

Lather, P. (1992). Critical frames in educational research: Feminist and poststructural perspectives. *Theory into Practice, 31*(2), 87–99.

MacNaughton, G. (2000). *Rethinking gender in early childhood education.* London: Sage.

Nielson, J. M. (1990). Introduction. In J. M. Nielson (Ed.), *Feminist research methods: Exemplary readings in the social sciences* (pp. 1–34). Boulder, CO: Westview.

Ochsner, M. (1999). Gendered make-up. *Contemporary Issues in Early Childhood, 1*(2), 209–213.

Ochsner, M. B. (2001). Developing reciprocity in a multi-method small-scale research study. In G. MacNaughton, S. A. Rolfe, & I. Siraj-Blatchford (Eds.), *Doing early childhood research: International perspectives on theory and practice* (pp. 254–263). Sydney: Allen & Unwin.

Walkerdine, V. (1990). *Schoolgirl fictions.* London: Verso.

Weedon, C. (1997). *Feminist practice and poststructuralist theory.* Oxford: Blackwell.

Wilkinson, S. (1986). *Feminist social psychology: Developing theory and practice.* Philadelphia: Open University Press.

CHAPTER NINE

ASIAN-AMERICAN CHILDREN DEVELOPING VOICE

SUSAN MATOBA ADLER

As I observed a group of Hmong children on the playground at my research site in Minnesota, I noticed that they spoke Hmong quickly and with enthusiasm, but when it was time to return to the classroom, they became quiet and subdued. Their body language did not differ very much from setting to setting, but their response to the formal classroom was immediate and what their teachers described as "respectful." I think back to my interviews with Asian-American parents and their children in Detroit, and generally, the children were given suggestions, with unspoken expectations, to attend to something quiet while the parents spoke with me, the researcher. I do remember an exception, when a lively three-year-old Chinese boy kept jumping on his father's back while I was observing the parent–child interaction during a reading session of Asian-American picture books. The child's mother was on the phone with relatives in China for much of the interview. These research observations as well as my own experiences as a Japanese American growing up in the Midwest help us conceptualize diversity in the development of Asian-American children's voice.

Within the Asian-American community there is tremendous variation in ethnic group cultural patterns, history in America, degree of discrimination encountered, and generational change. Although there are similarities in phenotype and shared cultural values such as the importance of elders and extended family and the valuing of education, it is problematic to stereotype them into one category called the "Model Minority" (Lee, 1996; Takaki, 1993; Zia, 2000). Parental socialization of Asian Americans could be considered bicultural or multicultural because they prepare their children to both "make it" in mainstream society and maintain their ethnic identity (Adler, 2001). This chapter focuses on how the "voices" of Asian-American children are developed to both incorporate Western assertiveness and to learn a more Eastern nonconfrontational interaction style. It examines ways in which researchers give voice to Asian-American children. First, I share some personal experiences and reflections of my Midwestern upbringing. Second, I discuss identity formation and perceptions of others in the development of Asian-American children's voice. And third, I critique the model-minority myth in relation to ascribed silencing of Asian-American children. I also make suggestions for teachers and researchers who are attempting to assess acculturation and situational silencing and foreground the authentic voices of their Asian-American students.

A JAPANESE-AMERICAN EDUCATOR AND RESEARCHER

I grew up as a number two daughter in a Midwestern postwar Japanese-American family. My parents both worked (mother was a secretary; father a teacher/professor), and my grandmother lived with us. She spoke "broken" English and I learned to understand but not to speak Japanese. When we were young, my older sister would translate for her if we were in public. I had much less responsibility and "voice" as a second daughter. It was assumed by my father that I would marry and have children, and thus have control of *uchi*, the inside or home domain rather than *soto*, the outside public domain, which traditionally was the role of a male (Tobin, 1991). And when my brother was born thirteen years later, he was being groomed to lead and speak for the family. All of this was done through modeling and subtle hints of encouragement and dissuasion. Gender differences were rarely communicated in a direct manner, but expectations were clear to us. Of course, these expectations were Japanese (from the Meiji Era of my grandparents), and we were "American" in our outlook and lives.

In the 1940s and 1950s I recall that there were about eight Japanese-American families in Madison, Wisconsin, where I lived, and we all resided in different neighborhoods. Families would get together monthly so that the grandparents could speak Japanese and play Hana, a card game. That was the only time I saw and played with any Asian children. It was the only time since leaving internment camps that these grandparents had voice and could share culture with their children and grandchildren. As we grew older, we Sansei (third-generation Japanese Americans) talked about our schools and being the only Asian students. We understood ourselves as visual minorities, yet in some ways we were invisible to others. When your non-Asian friends say things like, "You're just like us" or "I don't think of you as a minority" to indicate acceptance or belonging, it isn't congruent with the subtle discrimination and occasional racial epithets directed at you. You learn that, in some contexts you have voice, and in others you are silenced. But it is up to you to figure out when and how to respond because the Japanese interactional style, somewhat adopted by Japanese Americans, tends to be didactic rather than conversational, indirect rather than direct, and hierarchical rather than equal. In short, we were on our own in the white, middle-class American world to communicate as best we could.

Due to the family hierarchy, we as children didn't have "voice," and as I recall were also not allowed to show our emotions (I remember getting in trouble for slamming a door when I was angry and for expressing my own wants and needs). We were taught that others came before us, and that at all times, we needed to consider others when making choices about our behavior (especially in public). My mother had to fight for her voice living with a Japanese matriarch and her number one son. But over the years, I came to discover the strong and intelligent voice of my mother as she encouraged my independence, feminism, and career goals. In private she was quite assertive, but in public reticent and cautionary in her interactions with other non-Asian people. I became the nonconformist, risk-taking child covertly but not openly in public where I was taught to self-monitor my behavior. "You will be noticed because of your Asian face if you misbehave," was the message. In addition, on the outside I was stereotyped by others as the quiet, compliant Asian rather than the woman I became: an intellectual, educator, and professional. In short, I became my father, a university professor, but one with little voice due to gender and minority status in U.S. educational institutions. Like my mother, I feel liberated and assertive inside but cautious and silenced in public.

DEVELOPING VOICE AND IDENTITY

In my Detroit study of Japanese, Chinese, Korean, Filipino, and Hmong families, I attempted to uncover how Asian-American parents socialized their children to understand race and ethnicity and to negotiate their place in school and society (which in most cases was white middle-class suburbia). A salient part of identity formation and self-concept development for children of color rests on their perceptions of self, feelings of efficacy, and opportunity to have "voice" and be heard. The healthy formation of racial and ethnic identity directly affects feeling of efficacy at home, in school, and in the community. During the late 1980s and 1990s, a variety of scholars in multiple fields studied race and ethnicity in relation to Japanese

Americans (Adler, 1998, 1999; Fugita & O'Brien, 1991; Kendis, 1989). In this chapter, *ethnic identity* refers to groups such as the Japanese, Chinese, Korean, Hmong, and so forth, who maintain different languages and cultural traditions. *Racial identity* refers to the socially constructed category called Asian. *Culture* encompasses the norms, values, traditions, and worldview of a particular group and is responsive to group and individual experiences with other groups. *Ethnic awareness* is a precursor to ethnic identity and self-identification and children may participate in their ethnic cultures before acquiring a sense of their own ethnic identities (Lee, 1999). Lee also points out that "although culture is undeniably an important aspect of one's ethnic identity, the equating of ethnicity with culture underestimates the social, political, and utilitarian nature of ethnic groups" (p. 114). Therefore, educators need to consider the impact of racism on the formation of ethnic and racial identity among Asian-American students. In short, according to Lee (1999), "interracial relationships influence the way Asian American students perceive themselves, members of their ethnic group, and others who are not Asian" (p. 118).

Most of the Asian-American parents in my study conducted in the Midwest were adamant about teaching their children about their ethnic culture but were certain that the children would be bicultural or multicultural. Some parents did not speak their ethnic language and either sent their children to visit grandparents to learn it, or resigned themselves to the loss of ethnic language in their family. Language is one indicator of having voice in any social setting. In Asian ethnic communities, some participants felt like outsiders because they were not fluent in the "native" language. They and their children had little voice to communicate.

This language difference was problematic in my Hmong study, conducted in a Minnesota elementary school where there was a substantial Southeast Asian community. The staff felt they absolutely needed translators when communicating with Hmong parents and relied on the ELL (English language and literacy) teachers to bridge academic gaps as well as language differences. Hmong staff, on the other hand, gave Hmong students voice when they allowed them to speak Hmong in class. The school was over half Southeast Asian, primarily Hmong. Although the emphasis was on English and most teachers spoke only English in their instruction, the Hmong students spoke very little in class, except to respond to the teacher's questions. They did, though, actively speak Hmong to their classmates. Only one teacher spoke Hmong in the classroom to help clarify concepts or instructions for the students. This was quite significant because they would have no voice and limited access to knowledge if this wasn't done. Some non-Hmong staff resented this and held to the "English only" policy, thus criticizing their Hmong colleagues. What was seen as culturally relevant teaching by some was considered inappropriate favoritism by other staff members.

Identity for the Japanese Americans settled in the Midwest after leaving intern-ment camps was shaped by the political atmosphere of the time (post–World War II). They sought to find communities that were more tolerant than those on the West Coast. Racism was overt in California at the time, but more covert in the Midwest, where there were fewer Asian families. Many of the Nisei (second gen-eration) expressed sentiments of being "100 percent American" or "All American" in their attempts to assimilate. They told of not congregating together or speaking Japanese, so they would "not draw attention to themselves" (Adler, 1998). These sen-timents and ways of knowing were passed down to the next Sansei generation.

SILENCING AND THE MODEL-MINORITY MYTH

Kincheloe and Steinberg (1997) described the impact of the changing demograph-ics in American society in their book, *Changing Multiculturalism*:

> Without special attention to the racial dynamics of a critical multiculturalism too many teach-ers continue to misunderstand their non-white students. . . . Students who live outside the white mainstream are asked to learn to read and write about culturally unfamiliar topics and abide by behavioral rules that often seem alien to them. A two-fold silencing process occurs in these cultural mismatch situations: the first involves loss of voice of those culturally dif-ferent from the unnamed white school culture; the second involves the silencing of any dis-cussion or naming of racism within the schools. (pp. 204–205)

This silencing process for Asian Americans in public schools has existed from the time Chinese and Japanese children on the West Coast were sent to separate schools, to the assignment of Southeast Asian refugee children to ESL (English as a second, or sheltered, language) classrooms. Proposition 227, the "English only" mandate, continues to silence Asian-American children in California schools. This persistent movement toward assimilation rather than cultural diversity creates two worlds for Asian-American children, rather than providing opportunities for accul-turation and cultural transformation in both the home and school environments. As a result, there appears to be a cultural mismatch between many Asian-American stu-dents and their mainstream teachers and schools, despite the assumption, held by some teachers, that Asians are "model" students (see Lee [1996] and Wu [2002] on the "Model-Minority" myth). Asian-American parents are rarely asked to share their views on racial and ethnic differences, and on their expectations of the schools for helping their children develop healthy racial and ethnic identities.

Lee (1996), in her book *Unraveling the "Model Minority" Stereotype: Listening to Asian American Youth*, points out that this myth is a hegemonic device masking the diversity of Asian-American success in schools. Her research indicated a diversity of achievement and valuing of public education among various Asian ethnic groups. Lee (1996) wrote:

> The model minority stereotype is dangerous because it tells Asian Americans and other minorities how to behave. The stereotype is dangerous because it is used against other minority groups to silence their claims of inequity. It is dangerous because it silences the experiences of Asian Americans who can/do not achieve model minority success. And finally, the stereotype is dangerous because some Asian Americans may use the stereotype to judge their self-worth; and when this happens, we/they may, as one student reminds us, "just lose your identity . . . lose being yourself." (p. 125)

Sue and Okazaki (1990) took a relative functionalism perspective and claimed that the valuing of education is societal more than cultural and that areas such as leadership, entertainment, sports, and politics, where education does not necessarily lead to positions and careers, were not open to many Asian Americans. As a result, they turned to education as a means of upward mobility. My studies indicate that, although some cultural traits may be congruent with success in the mainstream educational setting, linguistic differences, political labeling, and degree of assimilation also play significant roles in school success.

Most recently, Frank Wu (2002) in his book, *Yellow: Race in America Beyond Black and White,* has done a comprehensive appraisal of the model minority myth. He points out that the stereotype has the "twin virtues of being true and being benevolent," yet he contends that "It relies more on acquired behavior than on inborn biology" (p. 48). Wu suggests using behavioral characteristics or nonracial categories that refer to conduct to separate groups of people:

> Ironically, the less race matters for Asian Americans, the less—not more—the model minority myth holds true. As Asian Americans approach whites, the less special we are. An Asian American is successful for the reason any person is successful, such as doing homework, rather than successful because of race. The model minority myth gives the opposite impression. It turns some activities into Asian activities. It gives them racial connotations. At the extreme, to study is no longer to study but to be Asian American. Study makes a person Asian American; Asian Americans as a group are defined by study. Making study the racial activity of Asian Americans does not serve to encourage it among others. If anything, it is likely to be counterproductive. (p. 56)

If two groups, one Asian American and the other European American, were given identical support by families, had highly educated parents with modest incomes; came from communities that support scholarship, with schools that have teachers who recognize these good pupils, are good role models, and give positive feedback and provide support networks, and the Asian Americans scored higher than the European Americans, then, according to Wu (2002), we would have a REAL model minority.

Given these descriptions of the model minority myth and the resulting categorization of Asian-American children by teachers as quiet, respectful, hard working, and compliant, silencing occurs within the framework of this stereotype. As Wu points out, these behavioral attributes become descriptions of and expectations for Asian-American students. An assumed focus on intellectual development (the nerd syndrome) and high academic achievement cast Asian-American students as a stereotypic group rather than individuals with voice, personality, goals, and varied abilities. They have been silenced as a minority of color and a monolithic ethnic group.

AUTHENTIC VOICES
OF ASIAN-AMERICAN CHILDREN

The theme of "naming one's own reality" is a significant part of critical race theory and serves as both interpretive structures by which we organize our experiences and as a "psychic preservation of marginalized groups" (Ladson-Billings & Tate, 1995, p. 57). Asian-American parents need to name their own racial and ethnic realities and teach their children to speak from their own perspectives and experiences. As parents begin to articulate these "realities" and grapple with their own racial and ethnic identities, they influence the identity development and self-concept of their children. If reality for Asian Americans includes covert racism and discrimination, they should begin to articulate this from a proactive, problem-solving position rather than from one of victimization. Schools also need to reciprocate with antibias and multicultural curriculums. But most importantly, researchers and school staff need to be cognizant of situational silencing based on social dynamics and acculturation of families.

Situational silencing occurs when immigrant or minority children respond in ways that are culturally appropriate for them but may be inappropriate or ineffective in cultural contexts different from those familiar to them. For example, students not acculturated to Western competition may become silenced and reserve utilizing observational skills congruent with their family cultural style. Over time and with experience, they may become bicultural and learn multiple ways to respond in new social situations. It is an opportunity for them to accommodate new skills such as competitiveness without sacrificing their own ways of behaving within their families and communities. This leads to healthy multiculturalism rather than assimilation and acknowledges the voice of those who may not readily conform to mainstream ways of knowing and performing. In seeking "authentic" voices of Asian-American children, educators need to consider the diversity *within* Asian ethnic groups, the family immigration and generations in the United States, and the children's sense of racial and ethnic identity. It will take effort on the part of educators to develop new cultural knowledge relevant to their students and to reflect on their own perspectives on race and ethnicity, which influence their classroom expectations. This is the challenge of teaching in a diverse society. Future research can focus on ways in which classroom teachers interrupt this silencing by listening with an open mind for those quiet voices that seek to be heard.

REFERENCES

Adler, S. M. (1998). *Mothering, education, and ethnicity: The transformation of Japanese American culture.* New York: Garland.

Adler, S. M. (1999, April). Understanding racial and ethnic identities of Asian American children. Paper presented at the American Educational Research Association Annual Meeting, Montreal, Canada.

Adler, S. M. (2001). Racial and ethnic identity formation of Midwestern Asian American children. *Contemporary Issues in Early Childhood, 2*(3), Retrieved November 25, 2003, from http://www.triangle.co.uk/ciec

Fugita, S. S., & O'Brien, D. J. (1991). *Japanese American ethnicity: The persistence of community.* Seattle: University of Washington Press.

Kendis, K. O. (1989). *A matter of comfort: Ethnic maintenance and ethnic style among third-generation Japanese Americans.* New York: AMS Press.

Kincheloe, J. L., & Steinberg, S. R. (1997). *Changing multiculturalism.* Philadelphia: Open University Press.

Ladson-Billings, G., & Tate, W. F. (1995). Toward a critical race theory of education. *Teachers College Record, 97,* 47–68.

Lee, S. J. (1996). *Unraveling the "model minority" stereotype: Listening to Asian American youth.* New York: Teachers College Press.

Lee, S. J. (1999). "Are you Chinese or what?" Ethnic identity among Asian Americans. In R. S. Sheets, R. H. & E. R. Hollins (Eds.), *Racial and ethnic identity in school practices: Aspects of human development* (pp. 107–121). Mahwah, NJ: Lawrence Erlbaum.

Sue, S., & Okazaki, S. (1990). Asian-American educational achievements: A phenomenon in search of an explanation. *American Psychologist, 45,* 913–920.

Takaki, R. (1989). *Strangers from a different shore: A history of Asian Americans.* Boston: Little, Brown.

Takaki, R. (1993). *A different mirror: A history of multicultural America.* Boston: Little, Brown.

Tobin, J. (1991). Front and rear (omote and ura). In B. Finkelstein, A. E. Imamura, & J. J. Tobin (Eds.), *Transcending stereotypes: Discovering Japanese culture and education.* Yarmouth, ME: Intercultural Press.

Wu, F. H. (2002). *Yellow: Race in America beyond black and white.* New York: Basic Books.

Zia, H. (2000). *Asian American dreams: The emergence of an American people.* New York: Farrar, Straus, and Giroux.

CHAPTER TEN

ROMA CHILDREN:

Building "Bridges"

AGGELOS HATZINIKOLAOU
AND SOULA MITAKIDOU

The exclusion of Roma ("Gypsy") children from public education in Greece is the result of many social and institutional factors. A discussion of two of them, child labor and the problem of housing, will show their direct consequences to school attendance. At the same time, implementation of another pedagogic and didactical approach with characteristics of social solidarity and critical analysis of the situation aims at (a) fighting school dropout patterns and school failure as well as social exclusion they often have as a result, and (b) building bridges of integration by everyone involved in the educational process—educators and Roma children—using the problems they confront as teaching material, seeking to share them at every opportunity. These approaches are used to address issues of power and voice in working with young Roma children in both pedagogical and research contexts.

The title of this chapter was inspired by the fact that the Roma settlement in the focal community is separated from the small town of Halastra (in northern Greece) by a deep canal. Two small Roma children have drowned in this canal. Since we believe that bridges can be solid even if their foundations are not firmly rooted in the ground, we have tried to create the bridge to school. At this moment, all the children of the settlement go to school while the municipality tries to contribute as much as it can to improving the living conditions of Roma families in its district.

The Roma pupils dictated the subject of this chapter to me. Its purpose is to show (a) how one of the many factors, the lack of housing, leads to dropping out of school or school failure and eventual social exclusion of many Roma children and (b) how the housing problems as a factor of exclusion were used as a teaching subject, as part of a social justice curriculum.

It is helpful to emphasize that during recent years, there has been significant activity regarding the education of Roma children in Greece and other European nations. The fact that many Roma children are enrolled in schools and in some cases they attend preparatory or "reception" classes only partially addresses the complex educational problems that these children face at school, the source of which are the social problems they experience in conditions of poverty, hardship, and social exclusion.

This chapter is based on the assumptions that some of the problems that the children face at school (e.g., school failure, low grades, etc.) could be eliminated and that effective teaching in classes with Roma children depends on how much the dominant school culture embraces the multicultural reality, rejects the culture of ethnocentrism, and is planned in a way that serves the idea of an antiracist pedagogy (Tsiakalos, 2001). Such pedagogy, from this perspective, should have the following characteristics: (a) the creative participation of the Roma children themselves for (b) critical awareness (Freire, 1976) so that all children could point to the factors that lead to their exclusion, and, finally, (c) the formulation of ideas, attitudes, and behaviors of solidarity from everyone involved in the educational process. This approach is intended to eliminate factors that lead to the exclusion of Roma children and enable them to absorb the public and social wealth, part of which is education.

As a consequence of these three characteristics, for one to speak about the education of Roma children, he or she must consider the living conditions of their families and the regulations of arrangements and settlements of the sociopolitical and state institutions that concern regulations that have direct consequences in the education of these children. These regulations involve the whole network of bureaucratic and authoritative structures of education and society. These structures shape attitudes and behaviors in each one of the schools and in every local community where the Roma live. Local administration, schools, and parent associations formulate views, attitudes, and behaviors that affect the permanent settlement of Roma and the possession of a house, which influence directly the children's regular school attendance and, consequently, their education.[1]

Thus, it is important to make general reference to extracurricular variables, factors, and parameters that are directly or indirectly related to the Roma in ways that cause them to experience many negative results. Failing to recognize this may lead to schools being cut off from the social surroundings of Roma families, further contributing to their social exclusion. This distance from the Roma environment results in the adoption or reproduction of dominant false or unsubstantial opinions and data by the school that lead most of the time to wrong conclusions. For example, the school often takes into consideration only whether the children do their homework at home. Pupils and families are blamed, but the fact that many of these children live in sheds with no electricity and no basic furniture and with humidity that destroys books and notebooks is not taken into consideration. In the case of the education of Roma children, this danger is always visible, especially if one isolates the educational problems from the general problems that these children face daily.

From the above it becomes obvious that educators should always have in mind that when they work in the class or anywhere else, they work with people and they have to handle many situations that not only result from their personal interaction with the children but mostly result from influences outside the school environment. These situations influence both the organization and the application of any educational intervention. In other words, the teaching method is not something that exists by itself. The main social factors that influence the daily school reality and shape our instructive intervention with Roma children are the forms of social exclusion and the racism that these children face. Defining the boundaries of social exclusion is a turning point, since it will influence our daily educational intervention. Regarding the context of our intervention, social exclusion is the prevention from the absorption of public and social wealth (Tsiakalos, 1991, 1998). Its correlation with racism is identified in that racism leads to subordinate living conditions. Moreover, racism is a network of views, attitudes, behaviors, and statutory rules that force certain people into subordinate living conditions only because they belong in a discernible category of people (Tsiakalos, 2000).

PLANNING AND ORGANIZING THE TEACHING OF THE RIGHT TO HOUSING UNIT

Based on the above, we can refer to a set of procedures that will take place from planning of the teaching until its completion. Planning curriculum that reflects the situations Roma people experience also implies organization and planning to identify these situations. As a result, my presence as a teacher in the areas where Roma children live is deemed necessary. For many hours each day, I go to the settlements or the neighborhoods of Roma children to better understand the factors of exclusion.

CRITICAL CONSCIOUSNESS AND SOLIDARITY AS EDUCATIONAL INTENTIONS

The success of the educational work depends largely on an appropriate choice of goals that are connected to the social and cultural conditions that Roma children

experience. The educational intentions and the goals for the instructive intervention influence the results of the educational approach. The way in which they will
be stated will set the boundaries for the accomplishment of the expected results
(Noutsos, 1983), and at the same time, they will give all the dimensions of the
course's content, in this case the right for every child to have a house, as well as the
strategies or methods of the teaching practice. For this reason, special emphasis is
given in this chapter to the level of goals. The formulation of the goals and intentions is included in a two-dimensional web including (a) the sociopolitical goals as
they were defined at the beginning of this chapter and (b) the cognitive goals that
Roma children should learn to use Greek, which is not their mother tongue, as their
second language in actual communicative acts.

In both cases, the formulation of goals and intentions is influenced by the
dominant social point of view or commonsense assumptions with respect to the
housing problem of Roma; namely, that Gypsies cannot live in houses. This is a
viewpoint that reinforces the fictionalization of reality, keeping Roma's life in the
dark on the basis of the logic of cultural origin, which in the case of Roma is bio-
logically determined. At the same time, at the political and social level, better-fund-
ed housing programs are being implemented for the Roma. These programs have
limited results, however, since the housing policy is developed without the involvement of the immediately concerned parties.[2] We must avoid the folkloric outlook
that housing for the Rom should maintain characteristics that are considered "normal" for the Rom (Fatouros, 1995; Karathanasi, 2000; Mouheli, 1996; Pavli &
Sideri, 1990).

If education regards the housing difficulties that Roma pupils face as its own
problem and treats these children as children that experience oppression and social
exclusion, then the educational process acquires dimensions of "cultural action" for
the disclosure of the problems ensuing from the exclusion from housing and the
achievement of freedom (Freire, 1977). These procedures are actions of knowledge
acquisition, in which Roma children are the subjects, meaning the true creators, of
knowledge. The disclosure of the conditions in which they live is, according to Freire,
an act of courage. It is a process of courage through which people that were once
alienated and oppressed begin to emerge with critical thinking and awareness
(Freire, 1977).

If a society is characterized by oppression and social exclusion, it means that
there are relations of dominance and subordination that exclude Roma children from
education. In fact, Roma as a subordinate group lives in "silence," because whatever it says is an echo of the dominant voice (Freire, 1977), something that Freire
(1976) called "the culture of silence" because it usually does not respond to the voice

of the subordinates. Our goal then, working with Roma children and communities, is the emergence of the Roma voice, whose subordinate living conditions combined with the lack of education make the Roma a vulnerable cultural minority that does not have the power to make decisions as the dominant groups do (Grant, 2001). So, the children create and their creation is culture and response to any enforcement of silence. Moreover, culture as a procedure does not include only folkloric dimensions of Roma's life that the mass media selectively promote to strengthen the self-evident and to perpetuate false images. For us, culture is the special form in which Roma find their expression using as materials all these social elements that have been created from historic, political, economic, and social interventions. So, culture is not complete, a given situation, but a constantly creative process, a constantly evolving communication for survival and the dimensions of the right to have a house, which will be learned by the children, is part of culture and social dignity. If people understand culture in the sense of a procedure and not of a system of fossilized values that tie down individuals and institutions, then education can contribute to the search procedure for Roma "voice" and to questioning the dominant point of view that insists that "the Roma cannot live in houses."

That means that the educational goals, curriculum, and teaching approaches will be constantly negotiated at school. Educational research offers many such examples of educational interventions, which increase excluded children's opportunities to experience a rewarding school life, often by questioning taken-for-granted assumptions about "at risk" versus "at promise" of children (Swadener, 1999).

The constant negotiation of the teaching organization contributes to strengthening the Roma children's identity. Besides, our method aims at the continuous strengthening of the children at school by showing appreciation and respect for whatever each child brings to school. In that context of emancipatory interaction, Roma children learn to take the initiative and to be creative, with great chances for success. In this case the pedagogic intentions are that the linguistic and cultural background and the experiences of Roma children that are connected with schoolwork increase these children's abilities to analyze and comprehend the social truth of their lives in an effort to develop their texts and their discourse (Axelsson, 2001).

Thus, in our approach, Roma children are the focus of the instructive proccess and there is an attempt to find situations familiar to them. The children consider communication with me as well as with the non-Roma educational contributors necessary. In this framework of communication, everyone has to identify some of the dimensions of the housing problem that the Roma students experience. These dimensions are the main ideas of the lesson and definitely draw the children's interest.

ROMA CHILDREN CONSTRUCTING CRITICAL PEDAGOGY

The meaning of the situations that Roma children experience becomes the object of discussions during which children are invited to express their opinions. The first priority in these interactions is in the content of the students' thinking. Grammatical and syntactical corrections in the students' utterances are also attempted, and every time, we make the necessary corrections and point out a grammatical phenomenon or teach the meaning of the word *house* (Haralampopoulos, 2001; Haralampopoulos & Hatzisavvidis, 1997). The following brief vignettes provide more specific examples of how the children co-construct the critical pedagogy described in the previous paragraphs.

In 1994–95, we organized daily lessons in a shed of the settlement in Evosmos. Children learned the word *home*. We used this word to discuss issues such as how our life would be in a house and what dangers the children face in the settlement without houses (e.g., rats, water shortage, diseases, security, heat or cold depending on the season). At the end we learned a song by Hatzinasios and Tsanaklidou: "The children paint on the wall two hearts and a sun in the middle . . ." The words of young Paraskeva still echo in my mind: "Sir, we don't have a wall. Where shall we paint? This is not fair!"

In 1997, the children of the Halastra settlement made their own first sentence for the right to have a house: "I am a child in the slum and I don't have a house"[3] and some time later, combining the right to have a house with the right to rest, the same children said, "I go to my house and I don't sleep in bed, because I don't have a bed." These children live in sheds and yet they know the meaning of *house*, which they identify with the shed.

While using children's books and Greek textbooks in learning about housing, several very moving discussions transpired. For example, while the children of the Halastra settlement and I were looking at comfortable homes as depicted in magazines and books, Erato observed, "These are expensive [homes], we could never afford them." Emra added, "We are poor, so the mayor does not give us such homes." Gioultza intervened to express her complaint: "Why can't we own a house, aren't we human?"

The comfort and luxury of the homes depicted in one of the children's textbooks initiated a discussion of the necessity of personal space for every family member. "The rooms in these homes are big and they have chairs and beds so the people can rest," Abdoula observed. Susanna added, "Each one of the children have their own rooms!" to which Abdoula responded, "We have no beds so all of us sleep on the floor. We put the baby in the cradle that is hanging from the roof of the shed above."

Sener also expressed his wish: "I would love to live in such a home, sir, but how can my grandpa buy it?"

While examining the chapter for the house from the textbook *We and the World* more recently, the children of the preparatory class made some comparisons between the content of the books and their life and they saw the injustice against poor people, including themselves. Since they were learning how to read and write, some of them thought that they had to write something. "At home I can't study because they yell all the time. If I had my own room I could read and play."

Further examples of children's writing, translated from Greek, regarding housing are discussed next. The first example was typical of the children's writing when we began this unit.

"Our Houses"
The children of our class have small houses. They have only one room and they sleep on the floor and they don't rest.

After one year at school, the children of Halastra settlement started to write more complete texts, as follow.

"My Own House"
I live in a very small house, it is a shed.
My house has . . . meters length and . . . meters width. It is all . . . square meters.

"Children's Room"
The child must have its own room.[4] In this room it has its toys and it plays. When the child is tired, it can lie down and rest in its bed. In the children's room the child has its books and can read. We don't have our rooms.

In this way, we examine our language as a sociocultural mediating product together with the Roma children. They participate actively in the process of language learning and they enjoy the opportunity to learn more substantially. Since they are actively involved, they find the process of acquiring knowledge meaningful, so at a next level they engage in claiming their rights. The children of Halastra decided to paint how they would like their houses to be, and they sent the pictures to the mayor along with a simple letter that described the housing problem they faced.

"A Letter to the Mayor"
Mister Mayor,
We are the children from the slum. We have many problems there. We want houses that will have lights and taps with clean water.

Other writing projects over the years have focused on rights to health care, water, and safety. All are anchored in a socially embedded pedagogy that builds on the everyday experiences of the children and foregrounds their voices.

FINDINGS

All the above examples caused me to reassess my role as a teacher on a daily basis. We educators are usually members of the dominant group, and such a reassessment of our role focuses on ways that education might allow us the possibility of reviewing our opinions, attitudes, and behaviors. According to Cummins (1999), every educator, typically as a member of the dominant group, has the possibility of reproducing or questioning authority; in other words, to assume or state a position about the problems that his pupils experience, to decide whose side he is on. During the teaching hour, we create with the Roma children those conditions of dialogue that reveal an attitude of self-criticism and solidarity. At the same time, through our method, everybody in class, including me as the teacher, has the opportunity to comprehend how political power works and the reasons why the housing problems of Roma have not been solved for so many years, something that has been repeatedly pointed out in meetings or conferences regarding Roma.

In this framework, we hope that we may start working together so that the Roma children will start acting to challenge, complain, and claim their physical, political, social, and economic rights from which they are excluded and to demand equality of access, opportunities, and confrontation. With critical thinking, we daily seek to gain awareness with the specific aim of influencing our lives. By questioning many of the things that Roma children read in the books or any information that promotes a certain aspect of life (Fragoudaki & Dragona, 1997), Roma children who have created their own texts about the right to have a house have changed radically the meaning of literacy, despite the fact that they have not used their mother tongue, which for many and various reasons, such as ethnocentrism and uniformity of the Greek education, has not been recorded by the official state, and the few efforts that have been made to record it have not been encouraged.[5]

Therefore, apart from learning Greek, Roma children need knowledge appropriate to discovering and comprehending themselves and their cultural values and at the same time reinforcing their self-definition (Tressou & Mitakidou, 2001). Freire (1976) believed that literacy is a liberating procedure, and the aim of the educational practices is strengthening through critical awareness. This goal can become a principle of questioning the dominant ideology that aims to control the lives of minorities.

CLOSING REFLECTIONS

For many years now, the homeless Roma are characterized as "nomads" and are not taken into consideration in the planning of housing programs. Even when they have settled in state areas, for example, former military camps, their settlement was not considered permanent by the state.[6]

On the other hand, no matter how positive the demonstrations of solidarity are, we must keep in mind that racism is fought mainly through the improvement of the living conditions of Roma as well as all other groups or minorities that are victims of this phenomenon. It is often the bad living conditions of Roma that lay the foundations for prejudices, contempt, and discrimination against them. The Roma usually consider the issue of descent housing their main problem.

In conclusion, we would like to comment on the title of this chapter, Roma Children: Building "Bridges." The inspiration for this title was Nikos Kazantzakis (2002; paraphrased from quote p. 34), the famous Greek novelist who described the ideal teacher as the person who becomes a bridge so that his students will cross over to the other side and when he will have helped them pass, he happily tumbles, encouraging the students to build their own bridges. Along with the Roma children, we daily take care to build these bridges with new materials because the factors of exclusion and racism are so powerful that they daily try to demolish them, successfully most of the time. The daily building of the bridge between the Roma settlements and the school is a promise on my part, which as a "pedagogic promise" demands determination "to change the world in which the Roma children come to live," a world of cruel injustice and inequality (Tsiakalos, 2001). I have shared with you a simple and small situation in terms of the teaching material, a situation that is basically an unfulfilled promise on my side. I believe that the "educational promise" is realized only when the teachers are able to make known to the world the problems that the children—our students—face daily in conditions of racism, social exclusion, and poverty.

NOTES

1. (a) The negative attitude of the mayor of Evosmos regarding the Roma of his district had many consequences in the children's life and attendance at schools of Evosmos. The mayor's negative statements in the prefectorial council of Thessaloniki, 9–7-1997. Newspaper *Aggelioforos:* 18–7-1997. Confrontation between municipalities regarding the relocation of gypsies. (b) The city council's positive position influenced the school attendance of Roma children in Halastras settlement. (c) Efforts made by the parents' association and the school principal influenced positively the children's school attendance in Halastra settlement.

2. (a) In May 2001, the Minister of the Department of Internal Affairs announced in the Conference of the Panhellenic Inter-municipal Network ROM a housing program for the Roma of a budget of 40 billion drachmas. (b) In many cases, the housing problem of the Roma has been characterized as urgent, but immediate and effective programs for the housing of the Roma have not materialized. Department of Environment, Country Planning & Public Works, General supervision of urban planning, Supervision of Residential Policy and Resident/ no. pr. 10.021/4/27.12.1995.

3. From the children's book "My Rights, Our book (A' and B')" that was written by Roma children of the Halastra settlement with the supervision of their teacher A. Hatzinikolaou, in 1997–98.

4. *Child* is a gender-neutral term in Greek, thus in translation is referred to as "it."
5. We are referring to the efforts of the Linguistics Department of the School of Philosophy of Aristotle University of Thessaloniki, with Mr. Tzitzili in charge. We are also referring to Mr. Marselo's efforts to record the language of Roma, which were not completed, however, due to his death.
6. Report by the assistant to the Prefect of Thessaloniki and application for allotment of makeshift housing, 9–12–1999.

REFERENCES

Axelsson, M. (2001). Basic factors in the education of children of linguistic minorities in an environment of majority. In E. Tressou & S. Mitakidou (Eds.), *The teaching of language and mathematics: Education of language minority children* (pp. 77–82). Thessaloniki, Greece: Paratiritis.

Cummins, J. (1999). Negotiating identities. In E. Skourtou (Ed.), *Education for empowerment in a diverse society* (S. Argiri, Trans.). Athens: Gutenberg.

Grant. C. (2001). Language, literacy and teaching of minorities. In E. Tressou & S. Mitakidou (Eds.), *The teaching of language and mathematics: Education of language minority children* (pp. 139–151). Thessaloniki, Greece: Paratiritis.

Fatouros, D. (1995). Gypsies in local communities: A seminar on matters of social exclusion and integration of Gypsies. A collaboration of the program Ecos Ouverture and the Primary Education Department, Aristotle University of Thessaloniki, Greece, January 20–22.

Fragoudaki, A., & Dragona, T. (1997). *What is our country? Ethnocentrism in Education.* Athens: Alexandria.

Freire, P. (1976). *Pedagogy of the oppressed* (G. Kritikos, Trans.). Athens: Rappa.

Freire, P. (1977). *Cultural action for freedom* (S. Tsami, Trans.). Athens: Kastanioti.

Haralampopoulos, A. (2001). Teaching Greeks in the minority schools of Thrace. In E. Tressou & S. Mitakidou (Eds.), *The teaching of language and mathematics: Education of language minority children* (pp. 456–463). Thessaloniki, Greece: Paratiritis.

Haralampopoulos, A., & Hatzisavvidis, S. (1997). *Teaching the functional use of language. Theory and practical application.* Thessaloniki, Greece: Kode.

Karathanasi, Å. (2000). *Gypsies' houses. Biospace and social space of the Gypsies.* Athens: Gutenberg.

Kazantzakis, N. (2002). *Askitiki* [Asceticism]. (16th ed.) Athens: Kazantzakis Publishing.

Mouheli, A. (1996). Gypsies and social integration. In *Dimensions of the social integration* (pp. 502–504). Athens: EKKE.

Noutsos, M. (1983). *Educational goals and curricula.* Athens: Dodoni.

Pavli, M., & Sideri, A. (1990). *Gypsies in Agia Barbara and Kato Ahagia.* Athens: G. G. L. E.

Swadener, B.B. (1999). "At risk" or "at promise?": From deficit constructions to building stronger alliances with children and families. In proceedings from the *Human dignity and social exclusion* conference (pp. 131–187), N. Poulantzas Society. Athens: Ellinika Grammata.

Tressou, E., & Mitakidou, S. (2001). Mathematics in linguistic contexts. In E. Tressou & S. Mitakidou (Eds.), *The teaching of language and mathematics: Education of language minority children.* Thessaloniki, Greece: Paratiritis.

Tsiakalos, G. (1991). Educational work from planning to materialization. In *Educational work. Questioning, planning, materialization, evaluation* (pp. 68–86) Athens: OLME.

Tsiakalos, G. (1998). Social integration; Definitions, context and importance. In K. Kasimati (Ed.), *Social exclusion. The Greek experience* (pp. 39–65). Athens: KEKMOKOP, Gutenberg.

Tsiakalos, G. (2000). *Guide of antiracist education*. Athens: Ellinika Grammata.

Tsiakalos, G. (2001). Intercultural education and social integration. In *Intercultural education* (pp. 47–47). Ministry of Culture—Friends of Melina Merkouri's Institute.

CHAPTER ELEVEN

KENYAN STREET CHILDREN SPEAK THROUGH THEIR ART

BETH BLUE SWADENER

It is that Third Space, though unrepresentable in itself, which constitutes the discursive conditions of enunciation that ensure that the meaning and symbols of culture have no primordial unity or fixity; that even the same signs can be appropriated, translated, rehistoricized and read anew.

—Homi Bhabha (1994, p. 37)

While spending a year in Kenya, as a visiting researcher with the National Centre for Early Childhood Education in Nairobi, I had the opportunity to volunteer with street children and their mothers in a street-based feeding and tutoring program, which has since grown into an informal school and rehabilitation program (Swadener, 2000). Since that time, I have returned each summer to work with this children's program and with a mothers' self-help group in a neighboring slum, while completing further research on impacts of neoliberal global policies on children and families in Kenya (Swadener & Wachira, 2003). I had come to Kenya in the mid-1990s to study impacts of rapid social and economic change on childrearing and was carrying out a national study that involved working with twenty-one local early childhood collaborators and interviewing over 460 parents, grandparents, children, teachers, and community leaders in eight districts (Swadener, Kabiru, & Njenga, 2000). I interviewed eighty-two children (ages eight to twelve) in contrasting settings in Kenya. They were older siblings of children under three, whose care was a major focus of our study. Similar to research I had done in the United States with children, we began the interviews by asking children to draw pictures of their family, their home (*shamba* in rural areas), and things they liked.

Although this chapter does not focus on the interviews, which were part of our childrearing study (Swadener, Kabiru, & Njenga, 2000), I will draw some comparisons between their artwork and that of children with whom I was volunteering throughout the same year. In writing this chapter, I have attempted to re-view these research and volunteer experiences through the lenses of first-, second-, and third-space perspectives.

Using expressive arts, including visual arts, drama, songs, and storytelling, children mapped the terrain of their daily lives and appeared to enter spaces of possibility and vision for different futures—and here-and-nows. Although much of their art expressed a language of possibility, it also reflected the harsh realities they faced (e.g., being beaten, shot at by police, or placed in neglectful "remand homes"[1]). The "classroom," like the children, had to be constantly on the move—just ahead of the vigilant gaze and regulation of the local authorities. Many youth returned the gaze assertively and experienced culturally typical rites of passage, reframed in an urban landscape with age mates on the street, versus in rural seclusion. Drawing from both cultural geography and decolonizing methodologies, I use examples from this experience to explore the use of expressive arts as a vehicle for negotiating issues of power and voice in work with young people.

The chapter begins with a "firstspace" or material perspective on how I came to work with street children and then shifts into a "secondspace," or more analytic/comparative perspective, focusing on the artwork and children's descriptions of its themes. In the concluding section of the chapter, I draw from Soja's (1996) notion of "thirdspace" and Sibley's (1995) discussion of "geographies of exclusion," particularly his work on mapping the "pure and the defiled," and on the roles of boundary enforcement on social exclusion, to deconstruct children's multiple modes of communication regarding spaces of possibility and resistance. This section uses the stories of two young men who have successfully used the arts to get "off the street" for significant periods of time, and transform their visions of self and future in what were likely unimaginable ways. I further argue that marginality itself, as problematized and reappropriated by such writers as bell hooks and feminist ethnographers including Tsing (1993), offers a vision of such possibilities. This reassessment of the often subtle power and critical resistance of marginality is tempered, however, with cautions from Gandhi (1998) and Spivak (1993, 1999) that even as the "margins have thickened with political significance" (Gandhi, 1998, p. 84), the margin is still in the service of the center—which has persistently tried to define it. Finally, I consider the role of personal representations and self-expression in creating such spaces of possibility as a dance between youth and "allied other" (Rogers & Swadener, 1999), in this case, the volunteer/researcher.

TEACHING ON THE STREET

I came to work with street children as a result of several experiences during previous visits to Kenya. The first was something that happened to a colleague at the City Market in downtown Nairobi. When a young girl with a baby on her back approached her for money, my colleague gave her a few shillings, which the girl threw to the ground. The young girl then picked up a stone and hurled it, just missing my colleague's head. I was also attending an International Social Studies conference during that week, and there were many similar stories shared by conference participants who had earrings pulled out of their ears or necklaces taken while walking near the conference hotel. Several of the colleagues who had experienced these incidences were African-American academics, and we discussed ways to make meaning of what had happened. During the same summer, I was going home briefly and then returning to Kenya with my family for a year. Thus, I resolved not to hold "street children" as objects of fear, but rather to find a way to get involved in some sort of volunteer work with them.

Such an opportunity came the first week after we moved to Nairobi. I asked the *escari* (guard) in our apartment compound whether he knew of any programs working with street children and he told me about an American woman who lived literally across the street from us. She had begun by providing hot meals outside her compound a couple of days a week, and then had moved the "program" to a grassy area near areas in which street children lived and worked. One of the things I would learn over the course of the year was that programs such as this one kept changing location as we did not have an official permit.[2] When I first came to volunteer, the program had grown to include a feeding program three days a week, which began with tutoring using some Kenyan primary texts and small notebooks and focusing on math, Kiswahili, and English. This was followed by a group time in which there were discussions of the dangers of sniffing glue, AIDS, what to do about police, and Bible lessons. Finally, came a hot meal of local food and, on some days, soccer in a nearby university playing field. The numbers of children participating in this open-air, all-volunteer program grew to between seventy and ninety children and youth, mostly boys.[3] Several Kenyan volunteers were facilitating different aspects of the program, including serving as youth counselors and in a live-in position in a group home.

I began by bringing thirty loaves of buttered bread every Monday. I also brought storybooks, helped correct math problems, and worked with children on English (which, along with Kiswahili, is the language of instruction in Kenyan public schools). I also quickly began to bring art supplies and cardboard "desks" or drawing boards to the program. This was a turning point for me in the work. Children, youth, and homeless adults who came to the feeding program were enthusiastic about drawing with pencils, crayons, and markers. The first time I brought watercolor paints, I had not anticipated their thirst for drinking water. After that day, I brought clean drinking water and separate jars of water for painting. Children had unique styles and themes in their work. A number of common themes could be found in their work, which I discuss in the following sections.

USING ART IN RESEARCH WITH CHILDREN

Before turning to descriptions and initial interpretations of the children's artwork, I want to raise some issues and recommendations for using art in attempting to better understand the life experiences and perspectives of children and youth. The advantages include providing a pleasant and engaging activity for children. This includes giving them sufficient time to plan what they want to express and to complete at least one drawing. Children should not be rushed, and with interview or other data to be collected, there are often pressures to hurry this process. Other advantages include children's "semiotic sense" or ability to show things that they cannot always name or discuss. Children's drawings become a source of dialogue through which others may begin to enter their world. I like to draw alongside of children, making it less of a one-way process. I also encourage them to "interview" me about my artwork, family, and life. The street children did this more than the primary school children who were completing the interviews with us on "school time."

Disadvantages or cautions include overinterpreting children's artwork, reading too much into the artwork of children, who may just be drawing what they think will please adults—including the researcher. Children who have attended traditional schools in Kenya or other neocolonial settings also tend to have been instructed in copying illustrations out of the textbook, tracing with pencil before using any color, and being rather "structured" in their artwork. Thus, the artwork alone does not typically reveal as much as the combination of art and dialogue. I worked with translators fluent in the mother tongues of the children, which also helped put them at ease and did not force them to express ideas and experiences in their second or third language. Having taught expressive arts and social studies for over a decade, I truly value the arts as a vehicle for learning, self-expression, and growth. I take delight in children's artwork and do not hide this enthusiasm! They, in turn, appeared to thoroughly enjoy the various media that I made available. They concentrated, worked hard, and took pride in their work, often writing "Artwork by . . ." and signing their name, as I had told them artists did. I always referred to them as artists and also tried to bring a number of Kenyan artists to the feeding and tutoring program, so that the children would have them as role models. I found that the arts were an accessible way for children who were on the margins of an increasingly print-literate society to express themselves with the depth and maturity that many of them had reached at an early age. Finding the promise in all children is not difficult when they are involved in the visual and performing arts.

THEMES IN THE CHILDREN'S ARTWORK

A number of themes were apparent in the drawings and paintings made by children on the street in Nairobi. The first was depictions of housing, both traditional *shambas* and newer, more middle-class homes. Many have parts of the compound labeled, including *a choo* or toilet, granary, or well, much as a social studies textbook might label a map or illustration. As they talked to me about their artwork, several boys discussed their rural homes or a desire to escape the difficulties of being homeless and out of school in the city. The children were of several different ethnic backgrounds, mainly Kikuyu, Luyha, Kamba, and Maasai or Samburu. Children coming from the latter, more "traditional" or pastoralist cultures tended to draw more animals in their pictures of housing, which is understandable given that animals are the wealth of such ethnic groups. Others talked about how their homes in Nairobi slums were very crowded, how they might be abused or neglected, and about a large number of younger siblings who needed the care of their mother or grandmother. Some of these children gathered paper or other recyclable materials, sold small items in shopping area parking lots, or begged during the day, then returned home every few days (or more frequently) with whatever they could share with their family. It was interesting to juxtapose their stories with those of some of their mothers in the self-help group.

Many of the young artists had "trademark" or signature aspects of their art (see Figure 1). These included Munyao's distinctive (Matisse-like to my Western eyes) use of color in houses and flowers, James's intricate style of drawing flowers and birds (often combined with buses or airplanes), and Gidraf's stylized pigs and suns. Zachariah liked to make his art *"kubwa sana"* (very big), and Chicago used cartoons and a graffiti-like approach, which incorporated popular culture images ranging from Woody Woodpecker to Coca-Cola. The few girls who came to the program typically drew flowers and buildings where they had been served (e.g., a church that provided a home for unwed mothers or *"Tunsa Dada"* (Rescue Sister, a housing and vocational program for street girls in Nairobi). Other artwork was both playful and metaphysical, including Steve Kimani's rural roads (*bara bara*), which became the long necks of birds, giraffes, and other wild animals. Another example was Moses Watene's use of allegory. One day he came to visit me and brought a picture made with some art supplies I gave him when he went to live in a large vocational training program for street children. Things were not working out well for him there, and he illustrated this in a drawing in which a young person is being chased up a tree (which he had started to cut down) by a lion. A crocodile is heading toward the shore and a snake is in the tree. I arranged the following week for him to move into our newly opened arts apprenticeship group home.

Another very frequent theme in the artwork of the children was transportation—particularly *matatus* or minivans, buses, and lorries (large trucks). They also liked to draw planes, both large airliners and military aircraft. Types of work that a number of the boys were interested in was becoming in the future included being a driver, a "turn-boy" (copilot), or a "tout" on a *matatu*. Since these provide the majority of Kenyans with transportation, work is plentiful and the minivans, as in many places in Africa, play loud music and have creative names (e.g., Street Justice, Chicago Bulls, Foxy Lady, and Sensi). Many older youth who were not likely to get sponsors in order to attend school expressed interest in learning to be mechanics, as well as drivers. Living, working, and hanging out on the street also put the children in close proximity to lots of vehicles, which appeared in their artwork in detailed, intricate ways. They always drew from internalized visual images and only rarely (and twice at my tentative suggestion) drew people or things that they could see while drawing (e.g., landscapes or portraits).

People represented another theme in the children's artwork, although not as often as in that of the primary students we interviewed. Children and youth participating in the street tutoring program tended to draw athletes, boxers, religious figures, and girls. Often they drew traditional Maasai or Samburu warriors (*morans*) or other symbols of age sets and their rites of passage. Several of the boys who lived most of the time on the street returned to rural areas between the ages of twelve and fourteen for their initiation into adulthood, including circumcision.

Animals, including wild animals, which have come to symbolize Kenya to many tourists, were featured in some of the children's art—especially when they were preparing greeting cards or paintings for sale to *wazungu* (white people/foreigners, including tourists and expatriates). These tended to be stylized or even idealized representations that were popular pieces in our Kenyan exhibits, which are beyond the scope of this chapter but entailed many border crossings, as the children entered usually forbidden settings to display and discuss their work.

VIOLENCE IN DAILY LIFE

> Ragpickers dealt with residues and were themselves residual, socially and spatially.
> —David Sibley (1995, pp. 100–102)

Another theme of some of the children's artwork was violence. Children were violated on virtually a daily basis in various ways, including fights with older youth on the street, sexual abuse, and being chased and often whipped or beaten by guards or police. Many of the children I worked with had spent time in remand homes in which few of their basic needs were met. In fact, one aspect of the program I worked with was visiting children in such "youth prisons" and taking them blankets, clothing, and food—often the only food they got for long periods of time. Shortly after I began to volunteer with street children, a child was shot multiple times in the back by a police reservist. The reservist bragged that this was the sixth street child he had killed, and was on trial for murder. Two of the young men in our program were witnesses to this murder and testified against the reservist. He was found innocent, with the testimony of several eyewitnesses being deemed by all three judges as "questionable" due to their lifestyle. The young men who had testified were in immediate danger and we hastily opened another, temporary group home that served as a safe house. We did not reveal their location, and they lived there for several months.

Other children died or were injured when hit by buses or taxi cabs and one of the things our program did, through its Kenyan volunteers, was track down the families of any boys who were seriously ill or who were killed. In the case of one boy who was hit by a matatu, we learned that his family was in Tanzania. Three volunteers took the body home for burial, and I met the boy's father several months later. He came to the street feeding site to thank everyone for returning his son. When I returned to Kenya in 1999, a drop-in recreation and literacy center for older street youth had been opened and named after him, and was still open when I visited in 2003. At the time of the earlier deaths, children's artwork included images of the bus hitting the street boy, a demonstration held by his friends, and also showed "avenging" themes similar to superhero images. These were strong male figures who were going to fight for the cause of street children so that their friends would not have died in vain.

I also worked with the children to write an anonymous group letter to the editor, expressing their feelings about the loss of their friend and the "not guilty" verdict, in the case of the murdered street boy, Simon. Art was one vehicle for expressing loss and ideas for revenge, and oral discussion another. When their letter and my guest editorial appeared in two newspapers, we translated both into Kiswahili and read them to the children, who cheered that their "voices" were in the paper. Since that time, as is in evidence in the following newspaper excerpt, many of the youth have become far more "media savvy" and have planned demonstrations in front of the major newspaper office, demanded that photographers document abuses they have suffered, and have worked with volunteers to have their own work (including prose and poems) published.

All of these tensions and stresses of daily living became subtexts, if not explicit texts, of much of the artwork the children made. Children on the street became overdetermined signs of their frequent vocation—ragpicking and recycling. They became, in Sibley's words, residue—to be contained, violated, and hidden from sight and consciousness.

ART AS AN OPENING TO THIRDSPACE POSSIBILITIES FOR YOUNG PEOPLE

Beyond their role in daily life and in research with children in difficult circumstances, the arts provide openings and access to previously unavailable narratives for children living on the street. As I began to bring art supplies to the street-based feeding and tutoring program, I noticed that children (and homeless adults) literally appeared hungry for expression. They sprawled out on the grass, using the cardboard "desks" I had cut, and concentrated on their drawings. Another view of this event was that drawing was more than just a pleasant diversion from difficult life circumstances and was an opening of space for another, unimagined future of here-and-now experience. As children drew traditional homes, detailed lorries and *matatus*, or rural scenes, they appeared to be transported to another time and place. Occasionally, someone would ask to borrow a pencil and some paper, but usually the art was reserved for our times together, three days a week. In fact, when I offered art supplies to some of the older youth in the program, they refused, saying that nothing was safe and they preferred that I kept their artwork and supplies safe and sound until next time.

If thirdspace can be constructed as drawing from the work of Black intellectuals such as Cornell West and bell hooks (Soja, 1996, p. 84) in "the formation of multiple communities of resistance, polyvocal political movements capable of linking together many radical subjectivities and creating new 'meeting places' and real-and-imagined 'spaces' for diverse oppositional practice," I reflect now on the oppositional practices and yearning for unimagined spaces that the children and youth on the street appeared to bring to their art. Philip Kilbride and others have written about ways in which traditional rites of passage are reenacted on the street, with active resistance to the colonizing adult world of police, shop owners, taxi drivers, and tourists ... and with seemingly contradictory desires to continue with their education, yet enjoy the freedom of living on their own and with their friends. Given that Soja's dissertation focused on "The Geography of Modernization in Kenya," I think it is interesting to apply his more recent work to the urban geography of street life in Nairobi. While Kilbride and colleagues gave Nairobi street children cameras to document where they traveled and slept in the course of a day, I gave children art supplies and encouraged them not only to express daily reality, but also to imagine other possibilities.

Having discussed the more general themes of children's artwork in a previous section of the chapter, I would like to turn now to some specific youth who embraced the arts project and are continuing to make art as they attempt to leave the street and make their way as young adults. I will focus on two of the young men described earlier, who showed great promise and passion for the arts: Moses and Ibrahim (ages twenty and twenty-one, respectively, at the time of this writing). Moses was often called a "Maasai" by the other youth, as his father is Samburu and his mother, deceased, Kikuyu. Ibrahim is Kikuyu (the largest ethnic group in Kenya, located primarily in the Rift Valley). A third young man, Chicago, was part of the arts apprenticeship group home, but died at the age of eighteen. All three were close friends on the street, living together with other youth in various places with names including "Sabima" (which they playfully first told me meant "beautiful place" and later admitted meant "place of shit") and "Viet Nam" (the name for the squat that I heard about in 1999). All three boys were living and working on the street when I met them in August 1994. Shortly after that they were actively involved in the arts program and were beginning to mentor the younger children in their use of arts media, as well. Thus, when I was leaving Kenya in June 1995, they were the three young men I took "off the street" to live and study with a well-known Kenyan sculptor, Foit. There were two other young men who were part of the program at various times, as well.

Applying the notion of thirdspace to the lives of Moses and Ibrahim, one of the unimagined spaces was clearly the world of art exhibits, sales, and personal identity of "professional artist." It was this strong identity that Ibrahim greeted me with on my return to Kenya in 1999. After some brief greetings and several hugs, he stated simply, "I am an artist now . . . I will make art all my life. I am learning to be a professional artist." He echoed these feelings many times during my stay, and clearly demonstrated a vision for the future, which was one with risks, yet powerful possibilities. After leaving the arts group home in early 1997, Ibrahim had returned to the streets, staying in the squat called Viet Nam. He had never stopped making art, however, and at the peak of his work in the arts to date, he had work on display in the contemporary art gallery of the National Museums of Kenya and sold a piece of sculpture for 10,000 Kenya shillings (about $160). Unfortunately, a local newspaper story featuring his "success story" led to his eventual return to a lifestyle of the street, and he was later convicted of robbery and served three years in prison. He is presently living in a rural area near extended family, and I remain hopeful that he is continuing to make art.

Moses offers a parallel, yet contrasting story. Moses has communicated with me for sometime through art (and more recently through letters and one videotape made by a visiting colleague from my university). A vivid example, described earlier, occurred in 1995, after Moses had left the street to be part of a large "rehabilitation" and training program for street children. He was bored with the program and was also concerned about returning to the street after a number of violent incidents, including the death of a friend. He showed up at my gate one Sunday afternoon with a drawing he had made depicting the theme of "no place to turn" and multiple dangers surrounding the boy in the picture. Shortly after that visit, we arranged for Moses to join Chicago and Ibrahim in the smaller, rural arts apprenticeship program.

Though Moses enjoyed the arts, it was to be an avocation and not his chosen vocation. Thus, another volunteer and I sponsored him for driving school and a two-year course in auto mechanics in a vocational boarding school. We also assisted him in finding employment in one of Nairobi's best auto repair shops, a job he held for just under a year. He told me that he would always make art, but did not see that he could ever make a living doing art, the way that Ibrahim likely could. He has kept in touch with his art mentor and the social worker in our children's program. When I was last in Kenya, summer 2003, he presented me with a beautiful wood-carving he had made. Unfortunately, he was also arrested for being in an area in which he had hung out with other street boys over the years and was in jail awaiting trial at the time of this writing. Although the latest chapter in his story is a sad one, his letters to me over the years and conversations during my annual visits have always indicated that he has a "thirdspace" vision of improbable yet desired possibilities for his future.

Much of what I describe in this section has happened in spaces created and nurtured by "Morris Foit" (Joseph Njau), artist, magical mentor, "trickster," and third-space creator. Having come of age during the "Emergency" preceding Kenya's Mau Mau war for independence, Joseph had found himself on the street early in life. A Czech sculptor who lived in Kenya at the time took him in, teaching him a skill he could use for life—woodcarving. After many years working for the prison system, having five children, and so forth, Joseph returned to his first love—making sculpture—and took the name of his mentor, Morris Foit. Since that time, Foit's magical creatures, including surrealistic lizards, birds, and figurative work, have gained prominence in not only the Kenyan art world, but have been sold to art collectors in Europe, China, Japan, and the United States. We got to know Foit shortly before his wife died suddenly, leaving him with five young children (in late 1994). His children were raised for several years by their grandmother on the family's rural *shamba* (farm), and the opportunity to take in former street boys in an arts apprenticeship program presented itself the following year. He mentored Ibrahim, Moses, and two other young men, one of whom died in the second year of the arts group home "experiment."

As Soja (1996) quotes from bell hooks, there is a "definite distinction between the marginality which is imposed by oppressive structure and that marginality one chooses as site of resistance, as location of radical openness and possibility," (hooks, 1990, p. 149, quoted in Soja, p. 98). Yet, I (like Leela Gandhi, Gayatri Spivak, and Michelle Fine) would not want to romanticize resistance from the borderlands, which have not been directly part of my experience. To quote Gandhi (1998, p. 84), "the metropolitan *demand* for marginality is also troublingly a *command* which consolidates and names the non-West as interminably marginal." Indeed, as Gayatri Spivak suggests (cited in Gandhi, 1998), the margin is at the service of the center. In the present case, the tendency to emphasize the pathos, difficult circumstances, and brutality of the lives of street children—potentially rendering them poster children illustrating their own posters—needed to be mediated by respect for their bravado, vision, and ability to cross many complex borders in order to survive.

The potential binary oppositional categories of passive victim–generalized other and romanticized resistor of postcolonial systems of oppression were also difficult to transcend. In other words, in telling others of my experiences in Kenya, I often felt that my work could easily be interpreted as possessing a missionary zeal that ranged from a pitying discourse to an extreme view of the notion "children at promise," which has been written about for many years (e.g., Swadener & Lubeck, 1995). My intent was to be that "allied other" (Rogers & Swadener, 1999) to which I referred earlier in the chapter. I could never transcend my privileged, postcolonial power position, or "otherness," however. I could not even have conversations in Kikuyu or KiKamba with the children with whom I worked so closely. The language we shared, to at least some degree, was the language of art.

As I reflect on my difficulties in completing this chapter, and on the conference paper on which it was based, I am struck again that I did not enter the community of street children as a researcher, postcolonial theorist, or even advocate. I came as a volunteer in my own ethnically mixed (predominantly Asian) suburban neighborhood. I came with white privilege, expatriate protections, buttered bread, and art supplies. The only "data" I collected were stories, artwork, photographs, and letters once I returned home. I was, in many ways, a development tourist who wandered in for a few months and has wandered back in ever since.

Did the expressive arts offer openings for a thirdspace of unimagined possibility for some of the many children who participated? Was much of the artwork done to please me or those who might purchase it when we had exhibits? To what degree did children's art reflect their lives, their sense of the cultural geography, and their identities? I cannot answer these questions. I can, however, recall the excitement about working with art media that all but the most exhausted or sick children and youth conveyed when it was time for "art class" on the street. The tough, street-wise demeanor or glue sniffing–induced daze often appeared to fade away as individuals picked up pencils, paper, crayons, markers, or paintbrushes. Even in a school without walls or a roof, a safe space was usually created in the program—a space where it became possible, even if for only a few minutes a day, to imagine the unimaginable possibilities of thirdspace.

NOTES

1. Remand homes are overcrowded juvenile detention settings with little or no food provided and frequent abuse. Street boys would frequently "re-cycle" through remand homes, running away when they could. The founder of the program I volunteered with brought food to children in remand homes and tried to get boys from the program released.

2. Legal issues facing street children and adults who work with them are beyond the scope of this chapter.

3. For a more detailed description of the population of children we worked with, see the work of Aptekar, Cathey, Ciano, and Giardino (1995) and Kilbride, Suda, and Njeru (2000).

REFERENCES

Aptekar, L. (1994). Street children in the developing world: A review of their condition. *Cross Cultural Research, 28*(3), 195–224.

Bhabha, H. K. (1994). *The location of culture.* London: Routledge.

Gandhi, L. (1998). *Postcolonial theory: A critical introduction.* New York: Columbia University Press.

Kilbride, P., & Kilbride, J. (1990). *Changing family life in East Africa: Women and children at risk.* University Park: Pennsylvania State University Press.

Kilbridge, P., Suda, C., & Njeru, E. (2000). *Street children in Kenya: Voices of children in search of a childhood.* Westport, CT: Bergan and Garvey.

Rogers, L. J. & Swadener, B. B. (Eds.). (1999). Reflections on the future work of anthropology and education: Reframing the field. *Anthropology and Education Quarterly 30*(4), 436–440.

Sibley, D. (1995). *Geographies of exclusion: Society and difference in the West.* London: Routledge.

Soja, E. W. (1996). *Thirdspace: Journeys to Los Angeles and other read-and-imagined places.* Malden, MA: Blackwell.

Spivak, G. C. (1993). *Outside in the teaching machine.* New York: Routledge.

Spivak, G. C. (1999). *A critique of postcolonial reason: Toward a history of the vanishing present.* Cambridge, MA: Harvard University Press.

Swadener, B. B. (2000). "At risk" or "at promise"?: From deficit constructions of the "other childhood" to possibilities for authentic alliances with children and families. In L. D. Soto (Ed.), *The politics of early childhood education,* pp. 117–134. New York: Peter Lang.

Swadener, B. B., & Lubeck, S. (1995). *Children and families "at promise": Deconstructing the discourse of risk.* Albany: State University of New York Press.

Swadener, B. B., Kabiru, M., & Njenga, A. (2000). *Does the village still raise the child? A collaborative study in changing childrearing and early education in Kenya.* Albany: State University of New York Press.

Swadener, B. B., & Wachira, P. (2003). Governing children and families in Kenya: Losing ground in neoliberal times. In M. N. Bloch, K. Holmlund, I. Moqvist, & T. S. Popkewitz (Eds.), *Governing children, families and education: Restructuring the welfare state*, pp. 231–257. New York: Palgrave Macmillan.

Tsing, A. (1993). *In the realm of the Diamond Queen: Marginality in an out-of-the-way place*. Princeton, NJ: Princeton University Press.

Weisner, T. S., Bradley, C., & Kilbride, P. L. (1997). *African families and the crisis of social change*. Westport, CT: Greenwood.

PART THREE

LINGUISTIC AND CULTURAL IDENTITIES

CHAPTER TWELVE

BILINGUAL BORDER-CROSSING CHILDREN'S IDEOLOGICAL BECOMING

LOURDES DIAZ SOTO AND JULIANA LASTA

to survive in the borderlands,
"you must live *sin* fronteras be a crossroads"
Gloria Anzaldua (1999, p. 217).

The children whose drawings you will view are bilingual border crossers within multiple contexts and multiple layers for their families, themselves and their community. Their border-crossing ability can be seen in the ways they create bridges/crossroads for their families with words. Bahktin (1990 a,b) discussed the process of selectively assimilating the words of others by using different categories of discourses that leads to the "ideological becoming of a human being." The drawings and interviews with young children give us insights into how we might analyze the "ideological becoming" of children who demonstrate love for their families, peers, and the "other."

This slice of the project shares drawings and spontaneous conversations with young children living in the metropolis. Juliana gathered the drawings and conversations. The cohort consists of four to five-year-olds attending a public school kindergarten. Their depictions continue to demonstrate the possibilities of *help*ing behaviors (altruism) similar to a previous cohort (reported elsewhere, Soto, 2002a). This research with children is reminiscent of Kohlberg's (1981, 1984) highest levels of moral reasoning, Alfie Kohn's (1990) "brighter side of human nature," and

Robert Coles' (1992) interviews with children. Children's drawings can give us insights into daily-lived realities.

Young children's depictions of their own bilingualism move beyond dualisms and underscore how we can rid the world of oppression. Children's gifts of bilingualism are leading to an interpretation of agape love as opposed to a "burden of bilingualism/biliteracy." The children *help* to illuminate the needed new directions for a post-border-crossing society sin fronteras (without borders).

The emerging themes from the interviews include:

1. The desire to help the other(s)
2. The role of parents as models of prosocial behaviors
3. The meaning of empathy, love, sharing, and commitment to Other(s)

For the purposes of this chapter we will first share selected drawings and narratives from this slice of the research, then we will contextualize the themes, and finally we will explore the notion of ideological becoming. We realize the limitations of this work and that these areas will ultimately benefit from continued research and analyses about "children's ways of knowing" and more specifically conducting research with border-crossing children.

BORDER-CROSSING YOUNG ARTISTS

Aldo and Charlie's illustrations depict conversations/translations in Spanish and English and vice versa. In the first illustration we see a conversation where Aldo is translating for his younger brother.

Figure 1 "what he is telling in English I tell him (brother) in Spanish"
For the illustration Juliana asks Aldo:

Juliana:	What does this heart mean here?
Aldo:	That everyone is in love, in this whole city . . . There is love, they like each other . . . Hay amor (There is love).
Juliana:	. . . Why is there a heart in this drawing?
Aldo:	Que esos dos son . . . que se quieren. . . . .se gustan mucho, muchisimo

"that everybody is in love in this whole city"
Aldo included hearts in his drawings. He illustrated smiling faces and used a variety of colors in each of his depictions. His drawings are as expressive *and inspirational* as denote examples of a loving community.

Alondra (five years-old) recounts how she "*helps*" her younger brother with the alphabet. Figure 2 shows Alondra with her brother and the letters he is writing she tells us that even though he may make mistakes she will still "*help*" him because she wants to. "Como hace mal la tarea, yo lo ayudo para que el lo haga/entonces el la

Figure 12.1. "what he is telling in English I tell him (brother) in Spanish"

Figure 12.2. Shows Alondra with her brother.

Figure 12.3. Alondra introduces us to the other children she teaches.

Figure 12.4. Tracy is helping a cousin.

hizo conmigo. Lo ayudo porque quiero . . . y cuando el lo hace mal yo todavia lo ayudo."

In Figure 3 Alondra introduces us to the other children she teaches, "Andy, su hermanito, le ensono ABCD Y sabe como llegar hasta 100." ("Andy, and his brother I teach them ABCD and he knows how to count to 100.")

Tracy in Figure 4 (five years-old) is "*Help*ing cousin. . . . He is from Santo Domingo nacido (born) en PR. I *help* him by getting the bread when he cannot reach it, I get into a chair and I stand up and I get the bread. I *help* my little cousin to take a bath." Tracy also shares how "When somebody speaks Eng to him . . . I *help* him."

"I *help* my MOM," she continues to tell us how much she *help*s her family and her peers, "I turn it into Spanish. I '*help*' my MOM and she *help*s me . . . She makes me feel good, she makes me feel nice, she makes me feel happy. I *help* her by telling her what others say when it's in English. She buys some things and then when she wants to pay she doesn't understand the number and I tell her." " I turned it into Spanish for my mom. I like to *help* people that *help* me. I *help* my friends when they don't know how to spell a word I *help* them, and I *help* them when they need my *help*, and they fall down I *help* them to get up. I *help* them feel better by drawing pictures for them. When you share with them that makes them happy."

Tracy continues, "My grandma taught me how to speak Spanish but she died. I *help* my mom sometimes and she *help*s me sometimes, she *help*s me clean my room . . . when I can't find the soap, she finds it for me so I can wash my hands . . . when I go to the park and fall she *help*s me walk and she puts band-aids . . . she makes me feel comfortable, she makes me feel good and she makes me feel happy. My father *help*s me by making coffee. And then when we found a dog we return it back and I said to my mom, Can we buy a dog? And then she bought it for me."

Juliana: How does it feel when you help someone?

Sometimes it feels a little cold in the inside, hot on the outside . . . you get embarrassed and then you (be)come friends and then you *help* each other. This is what being a friend is all about about *help*ing each other. I share my fruits with my friends Celine, Amy, Lily, Ashley.

Jesus (five years-old,) also "*help*s" his mother who does not speak English.

Figure 5 "I'm *help*ing my mother with the phone, I tell her—when you need *help*—tell me!

I *help* her with the dates, carry this, or pick up my brother on the bus. I tell her . . . how to speak English. She was calling me . . . she gave me the phone and I tell people that my sister is not here. I am *help*ing my mother to speak in English."

Jasmine illustrates in Figure 6, "This my house—me, my baby brother, and my sister. I'm teaching them Spanish and English. I *help* them to understand the

Figure 12.5. Jesus (five years-old,) also "helps" his mother who does not speak English.

Figure 12.6. Jasmine with her baby brother and sister.

language. I talk Spanish to the people who speak Span and with the people who speak Eng I speak Eng."

In Figure 7, Amy tells us that "One day I turned 6. . . . one day: to teach English. I teach my grandmother how to speak English a lot and she could say all the things that I was saying, she was repeating it right!" "When somebody speaks Spanish only, we CAN teach them how to speak English. I think, you have to '*help*' them to speak English . I teach all the people—I ask one of them to speak and they speak . I went Spanish-English, Spanish-English, Spanish-English, that's what I am trying to do."

Amy: "I speak to my grandpa . . . and to my grandma—And I ask him, "Do you want to speak to person that speaks English?"—and he said, "Si." I want to draw flowers . . . for my grandpa because I really like him. . . . and I love my grandma too." "I have been teaching him how to play tag a little bit, we run around the house, though, I was just running slowly, that way he could catch me and tag me . . . so he just won the game because I don't want him to lose. I want him to win. . . . I just wanted him to win because I love him a lot."

Figure 12.7. Amy tells us that "One day I turned 6. . . . one day: to teach English.

Figure 12.8 Francisco (four years-old) is helping his parents to speak English.

In Figure 8 Francisco (four years-old) is helping his parents to speak English. In this illustration he is with his mother at the supermarket. "Mi y mi mama en el Mercado. Estamos comprando-yo le digo en Ingles lo que dice mi mama, se lo repito en Ingles. (My mother and I at the supermarket. We are buying and I tell (them) in English what my mother says and I repeat it in English.)" Francisco adds, "Ayudo a mi papi-Cuando pedimos algo de comer y el no sabe como se dice yo lo le pido que me de el telefono y yo lo digo." (I *help* my father. When we order something to eat and he doesn't know how to say it, I ask him to give me the telephone and I say it.)"

THE DESIRE TO *HELP* THE OTHER(S)

Young children's *help*ing/altruistic personalities emerged in their conversations and drawings. Altruism can be understood as an intentional behavior carried out and intended to benefit or helping another without contemplation for internal personal gain (Batson, 1991; Hoffman, 1981, Eisenberg, 1979) and for no other purpose than the desire to improve recipient's welfare (Staub, 1986).

The children were very clear when they explained to us that the main benefit of being bilingual (border-crossing) subjects was being able to *help* others (class-mates, family members, friends). This deliberate, voluntary behavior intended to benefit others was found in almost all of the children. These are some of the examples from the conversations with the children. The children presented themselves as concerned about the well-being of others and with the will to *help* the other(s).

> " I like to *help* people . . . I want them to feel good."
> "I tell her when you need *help*, tell me."

Their depictions express forms of socially desirable actions and behaviors such as: teaching, translating, and helping in general, all instances of true altruism. These altruistic behaviors are somewhat paradoxical as "in spite of their colonized existence, [they] express love-altruism for the other[s] (Soto, 2002a, p. 599). Children face daily challenges in their homes and communities, particularly with issues of language, power, and culture that are intertwined in their existence and mark their lives. Their "gift of bilingualism" (Soto, 2002a) leads them to prosocial behaviors as becomes evident from such words as, "I *help* them when they need my *help*." As Bakhtin (1984) points out "there are no 'neutral' words . . . each word relates to the context in which it has lived its socially charged life" (p. 293). In explaining the world to their parents, the children themselves acquire power and courage. "I *help* them understand the language," thus helping them to live in the world conceived by their own words. Language is not a neutral and objective conduit of description of the "real world" . . . but serves to construct it.

The adult, often a mother who lives within their home (Latino) culture, relies on her view of the surrounding, English-speaking society, filtered through the view of a five-year-old. The child, in effect, acts as a translator of different values, traditions and culture(s); in other words, *different languages* in the Bakhtinian sense of *world views*.

IDEOLOGICAL BECOMING

Children are shaped (ideological becoming) at the beginning of their lives by the values of certain adults; with parents playing a determinant role in their children's prosocial behaviors. Prosocial behaviors are affected by two environmental determinants: modeling and reinforcement. Parents are conceived as role models in their altruistic behaviors of helping others, by exposing and encouraging their youngsters in a variety of ways. In order to teach altruism it is fundamental that adults show and express love and sensibility to others.

These border-crossing bilingual children seem surrounded by prosocial behavior that extend from their parents to siblings and grandparents. Valdes (1996) explains that *education* for English speakers means school or book learning whereas *educacion* in Spanish has a much broader meaning and includes both manners and moral values. She further argues that culturally diverse Spanish-speaking mothers consider "la educacion de los hijos (the moral education of their children) to be their primary responsibility" (p. 125). Thus, moral education is embedded in the culture and worldviews of the children and their community members.

The meaning of empathy, love, and commitment to other(s)

"It feels nice [to help someone] . . .
sometimes it feels a little cold in the inside and hot in the outside . . .
It's like when somebody helps you and
you get embarrassed that you don't know them,
so then you meet them and
then you come friends and then you help each other . . .
that is what being friends is all about, helping each other . . .
that way you make them feel better. . . .
I found it all by myself" (Tracy)

Tracy's words become an example of empathy and love. Helping and sharing are both types of altruistic behaviors that society applauds and tries to encourage in children. Educators and psychologists are interested in understanding how children perceive the behavior of others. The depictions of these children shed light on those areas of a child's moral development that are linked to comprehension of moral issues and principles.

In their attempt to make sense of the world, these children, with their words and drawings, express the struggle they face in a monolingual society that blindly negates the pluralistic nature of the U.S. context (Freire & Macedo, 1987). Their depictions also demonstrate their willingness to *help* others thereby contributing to their own ideological becoming and the ideological becoming of those around them.

Dialogic interaction constitutes the sphere where languages live because "as a living, socio-ideological concrete thing . . . language . . . lies on the boundaries between oneself and the other. The word in language is half someone else's" (Bakhtin, 1984, p. 293). We are inseparable from language with the dialogic interactions characterizing our lives. Other people's words have far-reaching consequences in our lives (Moraes, 1996).

Children provide us with a model to be followed by societies that are faced with multiple challenges. The positive and encouraging effects of allowing children to contribute in the communities where they live plays a vital role in the child's educational future (Soto, 1997). The children in this study continue to reach out to the "other" with love and compassion (Soto, 2002b, p. XXIV).

As Freire (1985) described, "love is an act of courage . . . love is commitment to others" (p. 71). At a time when our society is characterized by violence and intolerance between people and groups' children's knowledge and deep commitment and concern about the well-being of others emerge as much needed wisdom.

CONCLUSION

How might we analyze the possibilities that are contributing to the "ideological becoming" of human beings?

It is clear that additional research exploring research methodologies with children is needed as is the ways of interpreting the children's perspective in ways that will afford power to children's voices, perceptions, and wisdom. Affording children the opportunity to be an integral part of the work as co-researchers opens possibilities for theoretical and methodological explorations. Our sense is that children's ideological becoming is affected by multiple contexts and multiple players nested within a dialogic reciprocal process.

The search for an emancipatory existence leading to the egalitarian treatment of border-crossing children includes the notion of, not only the post-modern, but also a post-border-crossing/crossroads society. It is fundamental to understand and contextualize the lives of children, as their language/illustrations/depictions give us valuable insights into how they make sense of their own social existence in the world.

The daily lived realities children experience create complexities emphasizing the need to move beyond essentializing elements that begin to build upon border crossing communities of difference (rather than obliterating them). A democratic society is one, which values cooperation, participation, contribution, equity, and choice. Justice needs to be continually created, constantly struggled for as a way to overcome the complex ways in which power operates to dominate and shape consciousness.

As scholars/teachers we can continue to engage in critical knowledge production that comes from reflection, action, and popular participation. As Freire (1985) pointed out . . . it is not enough to analyze the problem . . . it is a continual process of reflection, action, reflection. It is a process that will allow people to understand and to act toward creating a better world for all of our border-crossing children.

As Tracy so eloquently pointed out

It feels nice [to *help* someone] . . .
sometimes it feels a little cold in the inside

and hot in the outside. . . . . .
that is what being friends is all about,
*help*ing each other . . .

REFERENCES

Anzaldua, G. (1999*). Borderlands/La Frontera: The New Mestiza.* San Francisco: Aunt Lute Books.

Bakhtin, M. M. (1984). *Problems of Dostoevsky's Poetics.* (C. Emreson, ed. and trans.). Minneapolis: University of Minnesota Press.

Bakhtin M. M. (1990a). *Speech genres and other late essays.* Austin: University of Texas Press.

Bakhtin, M. M. (1990b). *Art and answerability: Early philosophical essays.* Austin: University of Texas Press.

Batson, C. D. (1991). *The altruism question: Toward a social-psychological answer.* Hillsdale, NJ: Lawrence Erlbaum Publishers.

Coles, R. (1992). *Their eyes meeting the world.* New York: Houghton Mifflin.

Eisenberg, N. (1990). Prosocial development in early and mid-adolescence. In R. Montemayor, G. Adams, & T. Gullota (Eds.), *From childhood to adolescence: A transitional period?* Newbury Park, CA: Sage.

Eisenberg-Berg, N. (1979). Development of children's prosocial moral judgment. *Developmental Psychology*, 15, 128–137.

Freire, P. (1985). *The politics of education.* South Hadley, MA: Bergin & Garvey.

Freire, P. & Macedo, D. (1987). *Literacy: Reading the word and the world.* South Hadley, MA: Bergin & Garvey.

Hoffman, M. L. (1981). The development of empathy. In J.Rushton & R. Sorrentino (Eds.), *Altruism and helping behavior.* Hillsdale, NJ: Erlbaum.

Kohn, A. (1990). *The brighter side of human nature: Altruism and empathy.* New York: Basic Books.

Kohlberg L. (1981). *Philosophy of moral development: Essays in moral development,* Vol. I. San Francisco: Harper.

Kohlberg, L. (1984). *Psychology of moral development.* San Francisco: Harper.

Kohn, A. (1990). *The brighter side of human nature.* New York: Basic Books.

Moraes, M. (1996*). Bilingual Education: A dialogue with the Bakhtin circle.* New York: State University of New York Press.

Soto, L. D. (1997). *Language, culture, and power: Bilingual families struggle for quality education.* New York: State University of New York Press.

Soto, L. D. (2002a). Young bilingual children's perceptions of bilingualism and biliteracy: Altruistic possibilities. *Bilingual Research Journal, 26,* 599- 609.

Soto, L. D. (Ed.). (2002b). *Making a difference in the lives of bilingual/bicultural children.* New York: Peter Lang Publishers.

Staub, E. (1986). *A conception of the determinants and developments of altruism and aggression: Social and biological origins.* Cambridge: Cambridge University Press.

Valdes, G. (1996). *Con respeto, bridging the distances between culturally diverse families and schools: An ethnographic portrait.* New York: Teachers College Press.

CHAPTER   THIRTEEN

VOICES OF ENGLISH LANGUAGE LEARNERS

MIN HONG AND CELIA GENISHI

AMERICANS ARE WHITE: INTRODUCTION (MIN)

Alex:	That's a nice book [referring to a book about America]. I'm American.
Kate:	If you're American, then you're white.
Alex:	I'm not white.
Kate:	You're kinda white.
Alex:	But I'm not. That means I'm not a American?
Kate:	[shrugs her shoulders] I know that Americans are white.
Alex:	I'm Chinese but I'm American [whispers to himself as he walks away], I think?

(Audiotape [AT] 4/02)

The first graders in my classroom are used to talking freely about what they believe. Kate and Alex know I can hear this conversation, and their comfort with my listening to them has grown since the first day of school. Something else that happens on the first day of school is that many of my children assume that their teacher is "Chinese"—this is based on my appearance and my last name, *Hong*. (In fact, I am of Korean heritage.) I am always surprised, after being a part of my school community for the last thirteen years, that I must continue to teach my children and their families about avoiding stereotyped responses. My children and their families learn eventually that an Asian person is not always and only "Chinese." And they also come to the realization that authentic Chinese food is not chicken wings and fries (a popular take-out special). Perhaps because their teacher is a person of color, they learn to accept issues of diversity, and many easily talk about race and culture.

Kate and Alex's conversation illustrates this point clearly. Although Kate's perception of an "American" is someone who is "white," Alex is uncertain of her theory because for him, his Chinese culture and tradition are what make him an American. But on this day, Kate challenged Alex's understanding of his own identity. From Kate's point of view, if you are not "white" or "light skinned," you are not American. It was an interesting concept she concocted on her own, and she always stuck to this rule. When I told her that I was Korean and American, she told me that I couldn't be both—that I was Korean.

According to their teachers, both Kate and Alex entered prekindergarten as English language learners (ELLs), speaking their home languages (Kate spoke Spanish, and Alex spoke Chinese). Kate spent most of her prekindergarten year using nonverbal cues and often had difficulty communicating with her teacher and peers. Alex, on the other hand, learned how to speak English by midyear of prekindergarten. By the time both children entered my class (first grade), they were able to speak the English language fluently.

This chapter focuses on how I have challenged my own identity of "teacher" and have grown increasingly comfortable with a particular aspect of my identity, that of teacher–researcher or sometimes that of collaborator with my children. In dialogue with Celia Genishi, I describe parts of my journey of coming to listen carefully to children's voices, as a classroom teacher and as a teacher–researcher. As readers, you will learn about my background as an English language learner, as well as Celia's. The processes of writing and revising were shared by both of us, as our names in parentheses show. Our shared goal, however, is to place children's voices in the foreground, within the framework of one teacher–researcher's story.

WHAT IS THE QUESTION? (CELIA)

As we developed this chapter, we thought about how we could best contribute to this volume on children's voices. We have both published work that incorporates what children do and say (Genishi, Stires, & Yung-Chan, 2001; Hong, 2001); indeed, we have a hard time imagining our work without the presence of children's voices. Still, along with other contributors to this volume, we are rethinking the power of these voices and how we might offer a new perspective on them. So, we asked ourselves a number of questions that we answer in the remainder of the chapter:

- ▶ Which children's voices are we most concerned with?
- ▶ In what contexts did we listen to these voices?
- ▶ For Min, the teacher–researcher, how did the context influence what she heard, how she listened, and what she learned through her research?
- ▶ What about our identities? Did we see children's identities shifting as they worked and played in the classroom, and what did we as coauthors learn about our own identities?

WHICH CHILDREN'S VOICES ARE WE MOST CONCERNED WITH?(MIN)

When we enter an early childhood classroom where children are encouraged to express, share, and talk about their life stories and experiences, we might wonder who is in charge and where the teacher's voice is. This is the kind of classroom I try to provide for my young and active learners. They enter a room where their individual and collective voices shift and shape what they are to learn. My classroom is a place where children's voices have a clear impact on the development and outcome of lessons and curriculum. However, among these voices, the voices that concern me the most are always those of ELLs. My concern in wanting to make these voices more audible stems from my own experiences as an ELL.

I immigrated to the United States with my family at the age of seven from Seoul, Korea. We moved around the Washington, D.C., area for two years until my father found a job in New York City. Unlike my brother, I learned to speak the English language within three months of our arrival. People marveled at the speed with which I learned to speak the new language. Despite my gifts for acquiring the language, as a student attending inner-city public schools in New York City, I was consistently labeled "English as a Second Language" (ESL). This meant that although I was fluent in the English language, I would forever be labeled as an "ESL" student in the school system.

CELIA'S STORY

With Min and the ELLs in her room, I share an identification with those whose home language is not English. I was born in 1944, as World War II was ending, in an internment camp for Japanese Americans in California where many of the internees spoke Japanese. Thus, although there is little of the language now in my memory, Japanese was my first language, and I have a long-standing interest in ELLs, the processes of becoming bilingual and bicultural, and issues of social justice. Like many ELLs, I stopped speaking my home language and thus forgot it once I started school. Then, as now, English was the generally accepted language of "Americans." As a high school student, I began to learn Spanish with an excellent teacher named Jean Torre Garretson and later became a secondary Spanish teacher, before changing careers and becoming an early childhood educator. Like Min, my interests in ELLs and social and educational issues related to them stem from my family story and early childhood experiences.

IN WHAT EDUCATIONAL AND RESEARCH CONTEXTS DID I LISTEN TO THE VOICES OF ELLS? (MIN)

Both Celia and I believe that part of the teacher's role, regardless of the age of her or his students, is to continually improve in our work as educators. To do that, teachers must see themselves as *active* researchers. It is not possible to evolve or transform as a teacher without looking at our practices over time. For me, this can most effectively happen when I am immersed with children in the joyful world of teacher research. However, conducting research in one's own classroom doesn't happen naturally, and for me it did not come easily.

In my beginning years as a teacher, my own misconceptions about teaching ELLs may have kept me from fully servicing my students. The home language of the majority of my students is Spanish, a language I neither speak nor understand. Therefore, although I never view any of my students as "at risk" or less than capable, I initially thought that the ELLs in my class were at a disadvantage because I didn't speak Spanish. Despite my inabilities to communicate in the children's home language, I proceeded to plan and implement a language and literacy program that consisted of informal and formal instruction. I also encouraged learning through socialization and play with peers and insisted on children using their home languages.

Over time, I became one of those teachers who thought that I knew all that I could know about my children, until one day when I was faced with a group of eighteen first graders (out of twenty-eight) who began the school year not knowing any concepts about print, the alphabet, or how to write their names. I realized that I needed to learn about children who were different from the "typical" first graders that I had taught in the past; this year I was blessed with a group of children who needed me in new ways.

I did not know these children well enough to teach them successfully because routine assessments from the past were not adequate to guide my practices. This challenging situation provided the context for my first research study as a classroom teacher. Until this time, I sometimes placed more importance on the product or end results (i.e., getting the children to read on grade level at the end of first grade) than on the process (i.e., recognizing what each child brings to the experience of learning how to read and how he or she progresses over time). I had a hunch that it was important to follow individual children's processes, but until I systematically studied what children did and said, I did not have data that showed me how much each child brings to all that he or she learns. As a result of this year-long inquiry, Brenda Steele (my principal at the time) and I decided that I would also teach this group of children in the second grade, to give continuity to their learning processes in a new year.

At the same time, I was learning about qualitative research with young children and working with my mentor, Celia Genishi. I learned to listen more carefully as I became more systematic about studying how children were taking different paths to learning. Looking back on the process, it seems that I was gradually reconstructing the meaning of "at risk." I struggled with this term *at risk* and felt strongly about unpacking a label for children who are not meeting grade-level standards. Often, children with this label were ELLs. (Interestingly, the term *ELL* came about because the terms *English as a Second Language* [ESL] and *Limited English Proficiency* [LEP] had become negative stereotypes.) The term *at risk* has a similar connotation—the child is judged to be deficient based on socioeconomic background or on not meeting grade-level standards. However, what I learned through my research is that when we allow children "at risk," including ELLs, to draw on their own resources or "funds of knowledge" (Moll, 1992; Volk, 1999), they more easily connect to the learning experiences at school and encounter success.

The examples we share in this chapter are illustrations of how children have taught me about their learning and how we have come to co-construct contexts for learning and for appreciating differences in each other. Because purpose-driven learning happens throughout the day, I listened to children's talk in the contexts of typical school days, including contexts of play.

WRITING WORKSHOP: POWER PUFF GIRLS VERSUS PUCCA (MIN)

The children love to write about popular characters on television. Writing about "what's in" is a cool thing to do during writing workshop. And if you are good at drawing certain cartoon characters, you are popular among your peers. While the boys labor over drawing and writing about *Pokemon* and *Dragon Ball Z* (two popular Japanese cartoon series), the adventures of the Power Puff Girls fill the writing folders of most of the girls in class. *Power Puff Girls* (PPG) is a popular cartoon on a cable channel. The characters include three girls (not human) who were created by their scientist father in a laboratory. They each have their particular talents and they are called upon by the mayor to save the world from criminals and monsters. Pucca is a cartoon character created in Korea. Although her series can only be seen online, she, too, is a popular character who is a strong woman figure. In the following example, Cierra, bilingual in Spanish and English, and Ali, bilingual in Mandarin and English, talk with me about Pucca and the PPG:

Cierra:	Why do you like the PPG so much?
Min:	They remind me of another character that I really like.
Cierra:	What?
Min:	She's called Pucca.
Cierra:	Huh?
Min:	She reminds me of the PPG.
Cierra:	Why?
Min:	Pucca is a girl who knows what she wants.
Cierra:	Is she strong like the PPG?
Min:	Absolutely. She also likes this boy.
Cierra:	Yuck! The PPG don't like boys, they're too busy saving the WORLD. I don't think they're the same, Ms. Hong.
[Ali who has been sitting at the same table joins the conversation.]	
Ali:	She's the doll on your phone, right, Ms. Hong?
Min:	Yes. How did you know that?
Ali:	I saw it a lot. She looks like the PPG but I don't think she is like them.
Cierra:	Can I see?
[I walk to my closet to get my cell phone. I show it to the girls.]	
Ali:	See, Cierra. She looks like the PPG, right?
Cierra:	No. She has weird eyes. [Pucca's eyes are slanted.] She doesn't look like the PPG at all. Maybe she's strong like the PPG.
Ali:	She [Pucca] doesn't have weird eyes. The PPG has weird eyes. You always have to draw the eyes as big as their heads. Now that's WEIRD.
Min:	Cierra, describe why do you think Pucca's eyes are weird?
Cierra:	It's like this. [She uses her fingers to pull up both of her eyelids. The children at the table start laughing.]
Ali:	I don't think that's funny. You should say sorry.
Cierra:	Sorry.
Min:	Why are you sorry, Cierra?
Cierra:	Don't know, but Ali's mad.
Min:	Do you know why she's mad?
Cierra:	Because I did this to my eyes?
Ali:	Anyway, I don't care what you say. I think that Pucca is stronger than the PPG!
Cierra:	NO WAY!
Ali:	There's three PPG that fights crime but there's only one Pucca. She can fight by herself so she's stronger. Ms. Hong, can I borrow your doll? I want to go draw her.

(AT 6/02)

Ali is typically vocal about culture and issues of equity. She takes great pride in being Chinese and asks if she can sit in during parent–teacher conferences to translate for her father. Ali is sophisticated enough to distinguish the differences between speakers of different languages, such as Alex (Cantonese), me (Korean), and herself (Mandarin). She is also sophisticated enough to sense when an action, like making your eyes "slant," might be racist. In choosing to draw Pucca instead of the PPG, Ali seems to be standing up for what she believes, just as she makes it clear to her friends that certain actions offend her.

Remember the conversation at the beginning of this chapter when Alex and Kate are discussing whether Americans are "white," and remember that Alex walked away from Kate feeling confused? As his teacher, I knew that Alex would not question a peer. Since I feel strongly about addressing inequities and matters of race, I encouraged Alex to talk to his close friend Ali, who was very comfortable about confronting her peers about things that are unfair. Alex and Ali did have a talk.

Ali also takes pride in her family. She proudly tells her friends that her younger sister is still in China and will be coming to school the following year. When asked why she is separated from her sister, she replies, "Well, no one can take care of her here while we're all busy at work. She's too little for school and when she comes next year, she'll learn to speak just like me." Indeed, Ali was right about her sister—she did come at the beginning of last year, entered prekindergarten speaking only Mandarin, and in three months learned how to speak English.

MATH WORKSHOP: DO YOU WANT TO HAVE A PLAYDATE? (MIN)

Sasha and Kia (ELL) are in the block area working on a block town that is part of the Geometry Unit. The two of them are engaged in a conversation about how they love playing together. Kia speaks Albanian fluently and is just learning how to speak English. Sasha has become a valuable "buddy" for Kia as she is learning a new language. In this conversation, Sasha is quite concerned that her mother will not be able to communicate with Kia's mother in order to set up a playdate:

Sasha:	Isn't this fun?
Kia:	Yes.
Sasha:	We should play after school. Do you want to come over my house?
Kia:	I want to come.
Sasha:	How will I tell your mom?
Kia:	Okay. I tell my mom.
Sasha:	But my mom will want to talk to your mom. That's what she always does when I have a playdate with my friends. She likes to talk to the moms.

Kia:	Okay. I tell mom.
Sasha:	I know. We can draw a picture of the two of us playing in my room. We'll ask Ms. Hong. Ms. Hong, can you make copies of this drawing for us? We want to give it to our moms.
Min:	[Nods.]
Sasha:	Okay. Let's go draw a picture and we can give it to your mom and my mom, and then we can have a playdate.
Kia:	Today?
Sasha:	Maybe.

(Fieldnote 2/02)

Clearly the interaction above pushes us to reconstruct the term "at risk" for Kia, an ELL. She assures Sasha that she can tell her mom about the possible playdate, as if she is used to being the interpreter or linguistic mediator between school and home. However, Sasha knows that her own mother will not grant permission for a playdate without speaking first to Kia's mother. Sasha extends their conversation by suggesting a different form of communication, a drawing. Here both children are resourceful communicators, solving a problem so that they can enrich their social lives.

WHOSE IDENTITIES ARE SHIFTING? SIDE-BY-SIDE RESEARCHERS (MIN)

The children and I often talk honestly about my role as a teacher–researcher. To share with them the benefits of doing research, I say that studying what they do helps me to plan and be thoughtful about what they should learn in school. For example, I tell the children that I would never know about things like PPG or PlayStation 2 if I didn't study things that interested them. When the children realize that research informs me in ways that make learning more enjoyable for them and that they are the ones teaching me, they are thrilled.

Of course, there are aspects of my identity of teacher–researcher that are not obvious to the children. For example, I pay a lot of attention to "volume control" in my classroom. As a teacher and participant observer, I try to make sure my own voice is not too soft or too loud. I lower my own voice when I hear myself interfering too much in children's talk and play. This then increases the volume of the children's interactions so that their voices are at the center of the research. At other times I increase my own volume when it seems necessary to push an overall agenda (as I did above with Alex and Ali). These examples show how my identities as teacher and researcher are always shifting, sometimes from moment to moment.

I sometimes discover how seriously the children take my researcher identity and our conversations about research. One day, Mary, a teacher who was visiting my classroom, told me:

> I shared with Christian that I was going to write notes and that he shouldn't look up at me or let me get in the way of his learning. I went on to describe why I was doing this, informing him that I'm in your class to learn—to become a better teacher. And Christian looked up at me and said, "I know, my teacher does it all the time; she calls it research."

Mary was surprised that a child could so easily identify my role as a teacher–researcher. She also observed that the children must feel comfortable with the dual role of teacher and researcher. Because my first graders have been so accepting of the researcher role, I feel that they have allowed me over time to capture their true voices. In other words, they have been instrumental in helping me grow into the shifting identities of teacher and researcher.

When children see their teachers being researchers, they, too, might want to be researchers. One year, Marlena, a first grader, was curious about whether her peers liked school. Because she had come to see herself as a researcher, instead of asking me to investigate, she became the principal investigator of the study. Armed with her clipboard, she created a survey, asking the children, "Do you like school?" She spent most of her writing-workshop time asking her classmates questions and writing up her findings. Marlena's research led to honest remarks by the children. Not all children liked school; two children shared with Marlena that school was "boring." If I had been the one to ask the question about school, the two children might have responded less truthfully to spare my feelings.

Other children also have become very comfortable seeing themselves as researchers. One year we inherited a brand-new shelf that we used to store our writing workshop materials. The shelf came with wheels and although at first glance I thought the wheels were a bonus, over time it proved to be a problem (as the shelf moved throughout the day). I encouraged the children to observe this problem, investigate why it was happening, and suggest what we could do to fix this problem.

The children were fascinated, and some of them created a graph and tallied each time the shelf moved. After several observations, two children stated that the wheels on the shelf were the cause of the problem and encouraged the rest of the class to find solutions. Some of the children thought that if the shelf were moved away from a busy area, it wouldn't move as much. Some said to take off the wheels, whereas others said if it moves, move it back to where it was. And Rivkah said, "Just get rid of it."

When we show children the purposes of research, they may feel empowered to follow our lead and voice what they have learned. Children do many things well—

they naturally build beautiful and complicated block structures; they're honest when conversing with their friends; and they're quite capable of being the principal investigators of their own research. The power of classroom research is that the teacher can enable children's voices, especially those of ELLs, to be in the foreground. Teacher research is a valuable tool to help educate the growing number of ELLs in our schools.

DID OUR OWN IDENTITIES SHIFT?(CELIA)

The processes of doing research add to our identities as speakers, learners, teachers, and participants in classroom life. We have felt our own identities shifting in an everyday sense: Over the years, we have shifted from being a speaker of a home language to English. I lost my home language and became bilingual in Spanish and English; Min maintained her home language and quickly became bilingual in Korean and English. We have also added the identity of researcher to the others. I have been primarily a university teacher and researcher who is not a participant in the classrooms I have studied, although I'm currently studying a college class that I am co-teaching (Genishi, Huang, & Glupczynski, in press). Min has been primarily a teacher–researcher, although she recently took on the role of nonparticipant researcher when she completed her dissertation (Hong, 2003). We have also felt the shift from my identity as Min's adviser to that of peer and collaborator; Min's identity as student has similarly shifted to that of peer and collaborator.

These shifts are not automatic and, of course, happen over time. They push us to think about how much having a public voice matters in asserting our identities and sharing the power that comes with gaining knowledge through research and then sharing that knowledge through writing for publication. Although it is tempting to think in terms of fixed identities such as "teacher," "student," and "researcher," our work on this chapter has demonstrated anew that our identities are anything but fixed. They shift back and forth within the same classroom space, and the shifting both enriches our work and makes it more challenging.

As teachers and researchers, we appreciate opportunities to foreground children's voices for their own sake and also for the sake of coming to new understandings. An important understanding is the rethinking, what we could call the retheorizing, of the term *at risk* in light of Min's students, especially her ELLs. Through careful observation and analysis, we see through her eyes and hear in the children's voices that ELLs are resourceful. They have impressive communicative skills, along with deep concerns about who they are, who their friends are, and how people respond to their racial and ethnic identities. Thus the practices unfolding in Min's first grade illuminate and challenge taken-for-granted, deficit-oriented theories underlying the term *at risk*. Children's voices, foregrounded by a teacher–researcher, push us all to retheorize problematic terms in a practice-grounded way.

Min and I also think about understandings that come to us from outside the classroom, in a complex backdrop grounded in theory. Postmodern theories of identity and power are a good match for the processes of identity creation and shifting that we have experienced (Grieshaber & Cannella, 2001). We have a deeper understanding of how fluid our identities as teacher and researcher are—we don't have a teacher hat or a researcher hat that makes us *either* a teacher *or* a researcher, or makes children in Min's room *either* child *or* researcher; rather, we all wear multiple hats—minimally as teacher, researcher, learner, writer, listener, critic, friend. This fluidity carries over as well to our deepening understanding of power, not as belonging to one person or group, but as circulating in large part through talk (Dyson, 2003; Tobin, 1995). Hearing the children in Ms. Hong's first grade vividly reminds us that young children share with us the power to take on difficult topics such as race and ethnicity, as well as multiple identities.

REFERENCES

Dyson, A. H. (2003). *The brothers and the sisters learn to write: Popular literacies in childhood and school cultures.* New York: Teachers College Press.

Genishi, C., Huang, S.-Y., & Glupczynski, T. (in press). Learning to teach for social justice in an early childhood teacher education program. In S. Ryan & S. Grieshaber (Eds.), *Postmodern theory and early childhood education.* Greenwich, CT: JAI.

Genishi, C., Stires, S., & Yung-Chan, D. (2001). Writing in an integrated curriculum: Prekindergarten English language learners as symbol makers. *Elementary School Journal* (special issue), *101*(4), 399–416.

Grieshaber, S., & Cannella, G. S. (Eds.). (2001). *Embracing identities in early childhood education: Diversity and possibilities.* New York: Teachers College Press.

Hong, M. (2001). *Teaching first grade.* New York: Scholastic.

Hong, M. (2003). *Kindergartners' literacy-related talk: Case studies of three English language learners.* Unpublished doctoral dissertation, Teachers College, Columbia University, New York.

Moll, L. C. (1992). Bilingual classroom studies and community analysis: Some recent trends. *Educational Researcher, 21*(2), 20–24.

Tobin, J. (1995). Post-structural research in early childhood education. In J. A. Hatch (Ed.), *Qualitative research in early childhood settings* (pp. 223–243). Westport, CT: Praeger.

Volk, D. (1999). The teaching and the enjoyment and being together: Sibling teaching in the family of a Puerto Rican kindergartner. *Early Childhood Research Quarterly, 14*(1), 5–34.

CHAPTER FOURTEEN

BILINGUAL CHILDREN IN LITERATURE DISCUSSIONS

CARMEN MARTÍNEZ-ROLDÁN

It is easy to imagine talk in which ideas are explored rather than answers to teachers' test questions provided and evaluated; . . . in which students themselves decide when to speak rather than waiting to be called on by the teacher; and in which students address each other directly. Easy to imagine, but not easy to do. Observers have a hard time finding such discussions, and teachers sometimes have a hard time creating them even when they want to.

(Cazden, 1988, p. 54)

This chapter offers a glimpse into a qualitative study in which the researcher, working collaboratively with an elementary bilingual teacher, organized the kind of successful literacy event described by Cazden, above. Within the context of bilingual literature discussions, minority students were able to express themselves through their own language and perspectives.

While early childhood researchers have examined the literacy development of English Language Learners (ELLs), the tendency has been to focus on basic oral English skills, which they believe support students' literacy development. Scholars studying ELLs' development of biliteracy have expanded that body of work by highlighting the important role of students' first language as an intellectual resource that supports their literacy development. Less attention has been paid, however, to the equally important aspect of ELLs' critical readings and discussions of texts during their primary grades. The sparse representation of young bilingual children's voices and perspectives in early childhood literacy research, especially as it relates to children's interactions with texts, led me to conduct a one-year qualitative study (Denzin & Lincoln, 1994; Merriam, 1998) in which I examined the nature of bilingual children's discussions of literature in a second-grade bilingual classroom (Martínez-Roldán, 2000, 2003). The students were from low-income working-class families, described by some as "children at risk" and by others as "children and families at promise" (Swadener & Lubeck, 1995). I wondered if, by making their first language an essential part of the research methodology, we could more accurately represent bilingual students' perspectives, and better understand how they learn and talk about texts. I also wanted to explore how the integration of the children's language and interests might affect the quality of their discussions about the texts. Since the purpose of my study was to listen to the children's voices and try to understand them, this study placed their voices at the center.

Throughout the chapter, I share the challenges and promises of a research paradigm that places children's voices at the center. I describe the ways in which their voices were foregrounded, and how the children's roles shaped the study. Below, I provide a brief description of the classroom context in which the study took place, and the literacy event that was the focus of the study. A more comprehensive description of the study, its theoretical framework, methodology, and data analysis can be found in Martínez-Roldán (2000, 2003).

A BILINGUAL CLASSROOM

The setting for this study was a bilingual second-grade classroom in a neighborhood school in the U.S. Southwest. There were twenty-one seven- and eight-year-olds, all of Mexican descent. Ten were English-dominant, and eleven were Spanish-dominant, as determined by the school's classification of language proficiency. Julia López-Robertson, a bilingual teacher for five years, decided to integrate bilingual literature discussion groups as part of her language arts curriculum, a process in which we worked collaboratively (Martínez-Roldán & López-Robertson, 1999). In this study, literature discussion groups or circles are defined as small groups of students who read or listen to the same book (or several books related to a single theme or broad issue), and then meet to discuss their ideas and opinions about the text with one another (Short, 1997; Short & Pierce, 1998). Literature circles not only provide students with a place to listen, value, and consider each others' voices and perspectives, but they are also a place for teachers and researchers to listen to what students have to say. Small group literature discussions in this study served the following purposes:

1. They were intended to provide students with an aesthetic experience with literature (Rosenblatt, 1995), to help students make connections, pose questions, and develop their own taste in books. Students had the opportunity to pay more attention to their responses to the books while learning to evaluate literature.
2. They encouraged thoughtful discussions about books with all the children, regardless of their reading proficiency or language dominance. In other words, they provided the students with the opportunity to develop an opinion about social issues, enabling them to stand up for their own ideas while listening to others and considering different perspectives.
3. They offered a particular space where Spanish language (oral and written) was valued, supported, fostered, and where everyone—English- as well as Spanish-dominant students—was encouraged to be bilingual.

When Julia and I organized the literature circles, we encouraged students as individual readers and as small groups to have a variety of responses to literature. Inspired by Rosenblatt (1978, 1995), we believe that rather than approaching a piece of literature for the first time by analyzing its literary elements, students should be allowed to experience the literary text aesthetically, making meaning and responding in different ways. Therefore, we did not assign roles for the students to perform in the literature circles. The discussions were twenty to forty-five minutes long and took place each week or every other week. I participated in the classroom from one to three times weekly, whenever we had literature discussions, organizing and facilitating the discussions together with Julia, who became a teacher–researcher.

Below, I describe how the children's voices and perspectives were placed at the center of the study. I first discuss the decisions we made before beginning the study, as I negotiated the focus of the study and the organization of the small group literature discussions with the teacher and the children. Second, I present excerpts from a bilingual literature discussion, illustrating how the students engaged in meaningful discussions and how their active role shaped the process.

FOREGROUNDING STUDENTS' VOICES AND PERSPECTIVES

One of the ways in which this study incorporated children's voices into its design was by integrating children's interests into the focus of the literature discussions. Julia and I did that by exploring their perspectives and interests in relation to a larger, organizing topic the teacher and I had already chosen. We decided to learn about issues that mattered to the students, then seek out texts that might help them engage in inquiry. We needed, therefore, to create a context where they had time to think and to find issues that could be the focus of the discussions. We created that context before the actual organization of the literature circles, as we negotiated the curriculum and the focus of the discussions, and as we chose the texts. We believe that for the students to have meaningful discussions of texts, the texts themselves should reflect and raise substantive questions.

BEFORE THE STUDY BEGAN: NEGOTIATING THE CURRICULUM

Before beginning the phase of intense data collection, I had several concerns. I wanted the study to be embedded in the curriculum, not an isolated literacy activity. As part of the mandated curriculum that required the study of the desert in second grade, Julia and the students were planning a visit to the school district's outdoor learning center in the desert. Julia was also interested in using picture books by author/illustrator Eric Carle to expose the children to his style as an illustrator. Julia and I agreed that the literature circles should be related to social issues, which we thought would provide an appropriate context for students to think together about critical issues. I wanted to examine how the children would talk in such a context. The challenge ahead of us was how to integrate those different perspectives and interests into the research design.

After speaking with other colleagues, we decided to organize the curriculum around the broad concept of "sense of place and sense of belonging," which we translated in Spanish as *sentido de pertenencia o sentirse parte de un lugar.* We felt that this broad concept would allow for the integration of the various aspects of the curriculum, the teacher's and the students' interests, and also my interests as a university researcher. For example, people might experience a sense of place or belonging at home, in a physical location (e.g., in the desert), or within a culture. They can find a sense of place within a family (a topic the children often brought into classroom activities), within a community, through their memories, and in their relationship with other people and with animals (another topic the children were drawn to, since they had a lizard in the classroom).

We wanted to create a context where the students could gain familiarity and make connections to that broad concept, a context where they could express their opinions and "wonderings" (Lindfords, 1999). By listening to the children, we also hoped to find specific issues that mattered to them and to integrate those into the readings of the literature circles. As a researcher, I characterize this phase of the study as a time of uncertainty. Several questions came to my mind: Would these young students connect with the broad concept of sense of place and belonging? Could we find quality bilingual children's literature relevant to the children's understanding of the broad concept? Would the students engage in meaningful discussions of those texts? By letting the students actively influence the focus of the literature discussions, I relinquished "control" of the process and entered into a process of discovery and learning along with the teacher and the students.

Over the course of two weeks, four major activities helped facilitate the integration of the students' perspectives into the study. The four activities supported the students and our exploration, negotiation, and understanding of the broad concept that guided the organization of the literature circles. First, we read aloud many picture books that presented different ways in which people find their sense of place or belonging, such as *Amelia's Road* (Altman, 1993), *Evan's Corner* (Hill, 1967), *Lost* (Johnson & Lewis, 1996), *The Cactus Wren and the Cholla/El reyezuelo y la cholla* (García, 1997), and *The Mixed-Up Chameleon* (Carle, 1984). By using Venn diagrams in both languages, Julia pointed to the different ways in which the characters felt their sense of place and belonging, and helped students to visualize the connections they were making among the texts.

Second, emulating one of the characters in *Amelia's Road*, the students each created a box with special things in it. Five students shared their "treasure boxes" with the class each day. Julia and I shared our boxes first, explaining how the objects represented who we were or where we belonged. The students brought photos of their relatives, baby pictures of themselves, blankets, toys given by special relatives, letters from relatives, and so forth. It was obvious that they derived their sense of belonging from their families, their own history and growth, and the people they loved.

For our third activity, we gave the children time over the course of a week to browse more than fifty picture books presenting different perspectives on the broad concept. As the students browsed the texts displayed on the tables, they were asked to write questions they had about the books on index cards, and to put the cards in a box. These seven-year-old students generated 105 questions, which I then categorized by theme and used to organize discussion topics for the literature circles. The children addressed three major social issues through their questions: moving/immigration, discrimination, and children who work. Appendix A includes some of the books the children browsed. Each title is followed by some of the questions posed by the children. This activity provided us with an opportunity to see what issues the children were exploring.

Last, in one of the most important activities before beginning the literature discussions, we prepared a visual representation of the broad concept. We invited the students in a whole class discussion to share their initial understandings of what

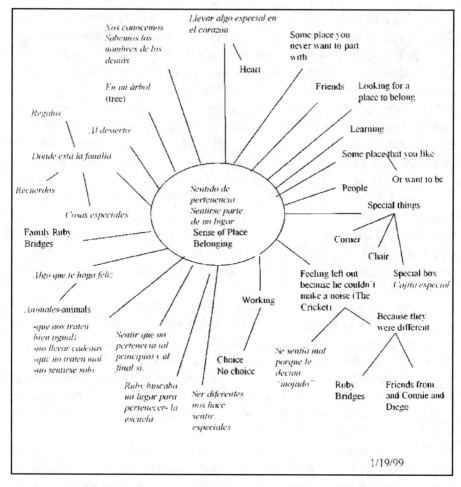

Figure 14.1. Web of children's understanding of the concepts "sense of place" *(sentirse parte de un lugar)* and "sense of belonging" *(sentido de pertenencia)*

"sense of place" and "sense of belonging" meant to them through a graphic web. Figure 1 represents the resulting web. Italics are used for the Spanish text.

These two last main activities—generating questions after browsing different texts and preparing a web around the concept of "sense of place"—enabled the children to express clearly their thinking and interests. The children's connection to the issue they called "feeling left out," "feeling out of place," or "why do some people laugh at others" provided the basis for the organization of the literature circles around issues of discrimination.

The teacher and I decided to begin the discussions with a focus on "feeling left out" or "discrimination" based on racial differences and on language, and we continued to listen to the students' responses and interests as we organized new literature discussions. For instance, after the first literature discussions, Julia and I decided to pull together a set of books for a literature discussion dealing with gender issues after Amaury, one of the students, asked, "What does gender equity mean?" We decided to offer the children the opportunity to talk about gender issues, and the small group discussions seemed to be the perfect place for having such a conversation. In this way we incorporated students' interests and concerns not only at the beginning of the study but throughout the process, as we planned each round of literature discussions. The students' evolving interests shaped the course of the study.

During the Study: Negotiating Texts, Language, and Meanings

The children had an active role in shaping the development of the study through their choices of texts and their negotiation of language(s) and meanings within each literature discussion. About one week before each discussion, the children made choices from a selection of four books available in both languages. Each text was

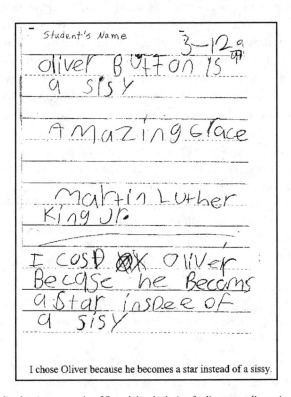

Figure 14.2. Unedited written sample of Steve's book choice for literature discussion on gender issues

read aloud to the students before the discussions, alternating languages by days. Figure 2 is an example of one student's choices and reasons he gave for his selection.

The small groups were, therefore, organized based on the students' choices of texts—four groups in each literature discussion—and were grouped heterogeneously, with English-dominant students and Spanish-dominant students in each group, and different "levels" of reading proficiency. The decision to organize the groups heterogeneously and based on students' choices of texts represented a challenge for the study. For the purposes of comparison over time, there would be a clear advantage to keeping the same groups of students throughout the year, especially given the sociohistorical–cultural theoretical framework of the study (Vygotsky, 1978, 1987). However, controlling the groups for the study would have reduced students' choices and voices, thereby negating one of the central concerns of this literacy development project.

SHARING ROLES: TEACHERS AND STUDENTS AS FACILITATORS AND MEDIATORS

While the teacher and I shared the role of facilitator, the children often took on that role as well. The analysis of 30 percent of students' conversational turns coded as "nonliterary responses" illustrates that the children acted as facilitators of the discussions by asking questions of each other, inviting others to participate, and directing the group's attention to other topics for discussion. They negotiated turn taking and language and monitored their discussions. In the following section, I use an excerpt from one of the discussions I facilitated, to illustrate the active role these seven-year-olds played in leading and shaping the discussions.

While I was fixing the video camera to record the literature discussion of *Oliver Button Is a Sissy*, the children initiated their discussion without any prompting on my part. Amaury, Helena, and Steve were English-dominant speakers, and Ada and Johaira were Spanish-dominant. (The Spanish text will be displayed in italics and translation in brackets will immediately follow the Spanish words.)

1 Helena: I'm going to say it in English. Leave this [the microphone] right here.
2 Ada: I'm going to say it in Spanish.
3 Steve: I know.
4 Helena: Wait. Let's do it like that [indicating with her finger the order she was proposing for turn taking]. We're going to read the book for the literature discussion *Over Button Is a Sissy*.
5 Amaury: Not "Over Button": Oliver! Oliver!
6 Ada: OK. Now it's my turn. *Estamos leyendo* literature discussion book *y éste se llama* Oliver Button es un nena. [We are reading a literature discussion book and this is entitled *Oliver Button es un nena*]

7 Helena: OK. *¿Quién está aquí?* [Who is here?] My, Helena.
[The children said their names for the recording.]
14 Ada: *Y Carmen.*
15 Helena: And Carmen.
16 Amaury: Your name is Steven in English, Steven [inaudible].
17 Helena: Carmen, but she's not here yet. [Giggles]
18 Steve: Alright, whoever finds theirs first, shares theirs.
19 Amaury: Wait! I found it first. I'm right here.
20 Ada: I already found mine!
21 Steve: I already found mine! I already found mine!
22 Amaury: Whoever found theirs is [inaudible].
23 Helena: I felt happy when . . .
[I joined the discussion and the students commented on what they had done so far, and Helena continued sharing the parts of the story she liked.]
29 Helena: *Cuando el niño, el niño andaba agarrando flores y los otros niños andaban jugando con la pelota. Y también me hizo sentir mal cuando su papá dijo que vaya a jugar con la pelota y que no era (que era) una* sissy. Who's going next? Amaury. [When the boy, the boy was picking flowers and the other boys were playing with the ball. And it also made me feel bad when his dad told him to go to play with the ball and that he wasn't (was) a sissy. Who's going next? Amaury.]
(Excerpt from literature discussion on *Oliver Button Is a Sissy*, 3/18/99)

This excerpt illustrates how the seven-year-olds had appropriated ways of participating and talking in small group literature discussions. The students decided the order in which they wanted to talk and the language(s) they wanted to use: English, Spanish, and code switching.

As the discussions unfolded, the students sometimes needed to negotiate turn taking so that they could participate without needing to raise their hands. Negotiating who was going to take the floor of the discussion was not always a successful process. Sometimes students' talk overlapped and no negotiation was involved. Other times they were more focused on talking than on listening. The students developed listening skills over time, after many opportunities for practice during their group discussions, but it was not a linear process. Sometimes their disposition to listen varied depending more on the activities for the school day, their interest on the text, and the specific combination of students within a small group. As a researcher facilitating the discussions, it was not always clear to me when to step back and when to control the turns strategically so that all of the students could participate.

The following excerpt from the same discussion illustrates the kind of talk young children are able to engage in when they have meaningful questions to pursue. Amaury wanted to know why playing dress-up was considered something that only girls do, and he used the written text to present an alternative explanation to Steve's response:

58 Amaury: What was the girly about playing dress-up?
59 Steve: I didn't hear you very good.
60 Amaury: What was so girly about playing dress-up?
61 Steve: I don't know.
[The discussion continues]
65 Steve: Probably he likes to play girls' games.
66 Amaury: But he said, it says in the book that he was pretending to be a star.
67 Steve: I know. Wait. What page are you on? This one?
68 Ada: He got it too [pink sticky notes to mark the pages].
69 Steve: [Reading from the text] Then he would sing and dance and make believe he
             was a movie star. "'Oliver,' said his papa, 'Don't be such a sissy! Go out and play
             baseball or football or basketball. Any kind of ball!'"
70 Amaury: So, do you know the answer?
(Excerpt from literature discussion on *Oliver Button Is a Sissy*, 3/18/99)

When Amaury asked, "What was the girly about playing dress up?" (#58) Steve responded that, "Probably he [Oliver] likes to play girls' games" (#65). Steve accepted the argument of those who called Oliver a sissy and introduced the issue of gender stereotypes and gender polarization into the discussion. Amaury rejected that interpretation and used the same book to support his point about questioning the view of dressing up as a girls' game (#66). I then introduced a question to challenge and support the children's discussion: whether they thought that there are boy games and girl games:

88 Ada: No. I don't think that. I think he dresses up because the boys dress [up] too.
89 Amaury: Steve played dress up before.
90 Steve: I know. I'm not a girl.
91 Amaury: I know.
(Excerpt from literature discussion on *Oliver Button Is a Sissy*, 3/18/99)

Ada positioned herself as favoring Oliver's gender border crossing: "boys dress [up] too" (#88). Amaury extended Ada's comments, confronting Steve with his own reality when he said that, "Steve played dress up before" (#89). Steve realized that it is true, he liked to dress up and was drawn into disequilibrium in the Piagetian sense. From this point on, Steve tried hard to understand "that boy and girl thingy."

CHALLENGING THE ADULT'S STANCE

In the process of making sense of gender issues and roles, the children expressed strong opinions and even challenged my interpretations. As the discussion on gender unfolded, it became evident that Ada, one of the girls, had an emergent awareness of the inequality in the possibilities open for women and for men. She mentioned many perceived differences between what men and women can do in terms of clothes, jobs, giving birth, and so forth, to highlight the inequality:

399 *No hay [mujeres en el Army] porque mi hermano fue y no había nada de mujeres.* [There are no women in the Army because my brother went there and there wasn't a single woman.]
451 *Los hombres no tienen* babies. [Men do not have babies.]
518 *Yo no puedo ser presidente; no'más hombres pueden.* [I cannot be president; only men can be].

The members in the small group—including myself—challenged each one of Ada's examples based on our experiences (and values), but Ada sustained her opinions, even if those were contrary to everyone else's opinions, including those of the adult in the group. She stated, "OK, *pero lo que yo estoy diciendo también* is true." [OK, but what I'm saying is also true.] The context created in the literature discussions, in which every member in the small group could share his or her opinions, was well established, so my opinions as the adult and the researcher did not silence Ada's voice. She used both Spanish and English to get her ideas across and to make sense of the issues raised by the text. Indeed, Ada demonstrated that she was not only reading the words of the text but that she was very perceptively reading the world surrounding her (Freire, 1970/1993).

FINAL THOUGHTS: RESEARCH THAT SUPPORTS A DEMOCRATIC LEARNING CONTEXT

The students' discourse documented in this chapter represents a significant shift from traditional classroom discourse. The typical classroom corresponds to a banking model, where the students are seen and learn to see themselves as recipients of the knowledge residing in teachers and in books. Cazden (1988, 2001) points out the cognitive benefits of creating a classroom social organization where children's voices are heard and peer interactions are fostered. She also highlights how deliberately including opportunities for such interactions in the curriculum contributes to the development of democratic relationships. Scholars working with language minority students have advocated the creation of such contexts to support ELLs who traditionally have been excluded from receiving a meaningful and quality education (Darder, 1995, Moll; Diaz, Estrada, & Lopes, 1992; Nieto, 2000).

In this classroom, the children had an opportunity to express their opinions and to make many decisions related to the books they wanted to read, the language they wanted to use, and the questions they wanted to pursue; literature discussions nurtured the ongoing development of student identity, voice, and participation. This study offers an example of the potential of educational research in early childhood classrooms for ELLs, not only for foregrounding students' voices, but also for supporting an emancipatory education for young children.

REFERENCES

Cazden, C. (1988). *Classroom discourse: The language of teaching and learning.* Portsmouth, NH: Heinemann.

Cazden, C. (2001). *Classroom discourse: The language of teaching and learning* (2nd ed.). Portsmouth, NH: Heinemann.

Darder, A. (1995). *Buscando América:* The contributions of critical Latino educators to the academic development and empowerment of Latino students in the U.S. In C. Sleeter & P. McLaren (Eds.), *Multicultural education critical pedagogy, and the politics of difference* (pp. 319–347). New York: State University of New York.

Denzin, N., & Lincoln, Y. (1994). Introduction: Entering the field of qualitative research. In N. K. Denzin & Y. Lincoln (Eds.), *Handbook of educational research* (pp. 1–17). Thousand Oaks, CA: Sage.

Freire, P. (1970/1993). *Pedagogy of the oppressed* (rev. ed.). New York: Seabury.

Lindfords, J. W. (1999). *Children's inquiry: Using language to make sense of the world.* New York: Teachers College Press.

Martínez-Roldán, C. (2000). *The power of children's dialogue: The discourse of Latino students in small group literature discussions.* Unpublished doctoral dissertation, The University of Arizona, Tucson.

Martínez-Roldán, C. (2003). Building worlds and identities: A case study of the role of narratives in bilingual literature discussions. *Research on the Teaching of English, 37,* 491–526.

Martínez-Roldán, C., & López-Robertson, J. (1999). Initiating literature circles in a first-grade bilingual classroom. *The Reading Teacher, 53,* 270–281.

Merriam, S. B. (1998). *Qualitative research and case study applications in education.* San Francisco: Jossey-Bass.

Moll, L. C., Díaz, S., Estrada, E., & Lopes, L. (1992). Making contexts: The social construction of lessons in two languages. In M. Saravia-Shore & S. F. Arvizu (Eds.), *Cross-cultural literacy: Ethnographies of communication in multiethnic classrooms* (pp. 339–366). New York: Garland.

Nieto, S. (2000). *Affirming diversity: The sociopolitical context of multicultural education* (3rd ed.). New York: Longman.

Rosenblatt, L. M. (1978). *The reader, the text and the poem: The transactional theory of the literary work.* Carbondale: Southern Illinois University Press.

Rosenblatt, L. M. (1995). *Literature as exploration* (5th ed.). New York: The Modern Language Association of America.

Short, K. G. (1997). *Literature as a way of knowing.* York, ME: Stenhouse.

Short, K. G., & Pierce, K. M. (1998). *Talking about books: Creating literate communities* (2nd ed.). Portsmouth, NH: Heinemann.

Swadener, B. B., & Lubeck, S. (Eds.). (1995). *Children and families "at promise."* New York: State University of New York Press.

Vygotsky, L. S. (1978). *Mind in society: The development of higher psychological processes* (M. Cole, V. John-Steiner, S. Scribner, & E. Souberman, Eds.). Cambridge, MA: Harvard University Press.

Vygotsky, L. S. (1987). Thinking and speech. In L. S. Vygotsky, *Collected works* (R. W. Rieber & A. S. Carton, Eds.; N. Minik, Trans.; Vol. 1, pp. 39–285). New York: Plenum.

CHILDREN'S REFERENCES

Adler, D. (1989). *A picture book of Martin Luther King, Jr.* Illus. Robert Casilla. New York: Holiday House.

Altman, L. J. (1993). *Amelia's road [El camino de Amelia]*. New York: Lee & Books.

Carle, E. (1984). *The mixed-up chameleon*. New York: Crowell.

dePaola, T. (1979). *Oliver Button is a sissy*. San Diego, CA: Harcourt Brace Jovanovich.

dePaola, T. (1991). *Oliver Button es un nena*. Madrid: Susaeta.

García, M. (1987). *The adventures of Connie and Diego/Las aventuras de Connie y Diego*. Illus. Malaquías Montoya. San Francisco: Children's Book Press.

García, V. C. (1997). *The cactus wren and the cholla/El reyezuelo y la cholla*. Illus. Fred Barraza. Tucson, AZ: Hispanic Books Distributors.

Henkes, K. (1991). *Chrysanthemum [Crisántemo]*. New York: Greenwillow.

Hill, E. S. (1967). *Evan's corner*. New York: Holt, Rinehart & Winston.

Johnson, P. B., & Lewis, C. (1996). *Lost*. New York: Orchard Books.

Picó, F. (1991). *La peineta colorada [The red comb]*. Río Piedras, PR: Ediciones Huracán.

Tabor, N. (1995). *We are a rainbow/Somos un arcoiris*. Watertown, MA: Charlesbridge.

APPENDIX A

EXAMPLES OF STUDENTS' QUESTIONS AFTER BROWSING BOOKS PRESENTING DIFFERENT PERSPECTIVES ON SENSE OF PLACE AND BELONGING. JANUARY 14 &15, 1999

AMELIA'S ROAD [EL CAMINO DE AMELIA] (ALTMAN, 1993):

¿Por qué se movían mucho? ¿Por qué se cambian de casa a casa? [Why do they move from house to house?] Why do they have to move a lot?

¿Por qué trabajan? [Why do they (the children) work?] Why does Amelia have to work before school?

CHRYSANTHEMUM [CRISÁNTEMO] (HENKES, 1991):

¿Por qué la niña está llorando? [Why is the girl crying?] Why did she cry? Why are they laughing at her?

THE ADVENTURES OF CONNIE AND DIEGO/ LAS AVENTURAS DE CONNIE Y DIEGO (GARCÍA, 1987):

¿Por qué nacieron de colores? [Why were they born with different skin colors?]
¿Por qué gritaron sus hermanos? [Why did their brothers scream?]
How come the twins ran away from home? *¿Por qué se escaparon?* [Why they ran away?]

LA PEINETA COLORADA [THE RED COMB] (PICÓ, 1991):

¿Por qué parecen pobres? [Why do they look poor?]
¿Por qué la niña trabajaba? [Why does the girl work?]

WE ARE A RAINBOW/SOMOS UN ARCOIRIS (TABOR, 1995):

Why do the kids are different colors? *¿Por qué las gentes son de diferentes colores?* [Why do people have different colors?]

A PICTURE BOOK OF MARTIN LUTHER KING, JR. [UN LIBRO ILUSTRADO SOBRE MARTIN LUTHER KING, HIJO] (ADLER, 1989):

¿Por qué trataban mal a los niños negritos? [Why were the little black boys mistreated?]

CHAPTER FIFTEEN

CHILDREN'S RETELLING

CATHY GUITIERREZ-GOMEZ

In listening to young children's responses to storybooks, teachers or early childhood researchers can often miss the connections young children make to the storybook because they may be too preoccupied in their search for a given answer or some other aspect of the process itself. We can become so focused on gathering certain pieces of information that we become oblivious to children's voices and the truly rich connections that children are constantly making between their prior knowledge and new experiences. Often, during classroom observations for this study, I noticed that the teachers were so focused on getting through all the activities on the daily schedule that everything seemed to be rushed. At the end of the day it was difficult for these teachers to focus on how individual children had performed or made connections. What happens to children's voices then? In essence, we are rendering them powerless.

An analysis of data gathered over 2 months on the literacy of sixty-three preschool children (ages three to five) proved to be much more enlightening when utilizing an interpretive research process and reviewing the data a second time (Gutierrez-Gomez, 1996). Interpretivism acknowledges that the researcher is exercising the freedom "to recognize what is happening, using herself as an instrument to determine what counts or is important" (Jipson, 2000, 167). I observed more prudently and listened more intently to *everything* the children said. This included dialogues or comments, in English or Spanish, that occurred before, during, and after data collection periods. A closer examination of responses from the children's perspectives allowed me to recognize, and be able to convey, a more comprehensive interpretation of children's voices and how they express what they know, or what they have recently learned, and how they make important connections.

In addition to videotaping children's retelling and reenactment responses to a storybook, I had also videotaped them during routine classroom activities, including morning circle and learning center time. Having these videotapes made it possible for me to watch and listen to them multiple times and transcribe the children's exact words for content analysis. This time, however, I decided to also incorporate detailed descriptions of the children's body language, including their facial expressions. I made this decision after I had started transcribing the videotapes, though at the time I was uncertain about my own motives. I believe that I inadvertently sensed that this could prove to be quite informative. Today I'm wondering why I didn't think of this before.

SOCIOCULTURAL CONTEXT AND PERSPECTIVES HELD BY THE CHILDREN

My presence in this preschool eventually became ordinary and the children grew accustomed to seeing me in different classrooms and involved in the daily classroom routines. However, with each of my initial visits to each classroom came the same questions: "Whose mama are you?" or they would ask if I was a specific child's mother, "Eres la mamá de Jessica?" (Are you Jessica's mom?). I began to document what I was hearing and interpreting as potential examples of children going through basic processes and making connections based on their own sociocultural contexts (Nieto, 2002; Siegler, Deloache, & Eisenberg, 2003, p. 159). It is possible that some of the children may have wondered if I was another teacher. However, previous experience had taught them that when an adult female, besides their teachers, walked into the classroom and that woman looked a lot like most of the children (dark skin and dark hair) and she spoke the same language, she was probably someone's mama.

For two months I was often in one of the four classrooms early in the morning and helped to set up for the day or interacted with the children. While I had been introduced as "another teacher" who was going to be "visiting" for a few weeks, I do not believe the children perceived me as a visitor for long. Right away they expected me to conduct myself like the other teachers by looking to me for comfort, assistance, or direction. A couple of weeks after my arrival at this preschool, I read the storybook *Coyote: A Trickster Tale from the American Southwest* (McDermott, 1994), and their perception of me changed some more. I was now referred to as "the teacher who reads *Coyote*" or "la que lee del Coyote" (the one who reads about Coyote). Though the children were always friendly, after I involved them in some reenactment and retelling activities related to the Coyote book, they seemed to smile at me more and I was definitely getting embraced more. Was this their way of showing gratitude for what I was doing? Indeed, they were letting me know they enjoyed it when I read to them and they were having a good time with the activities I brought in. Additional interactions with the children continued to provide insight to research-related data.

DOCUMENTATION OF CHILDREN'S RESPONSES

The documented responses are those that were captured on videotape when I began interacting with some of the preschoolers two days after I had conducted formal assessments to complete my study on reenactment and retelling. Part of the agreement with the program where I was conducting my research was that I would do workshops for a certain number of days in exchange for permission to do research. On those days that I served as a consultant, I continued to carry my video camera and record my interactions with the children whenever it was convenient. In addition to our conversations, I was able to capture some of their body language and facial expressions as we talked about the *Coyote* storybook or some of the related activities.

The following is an excerpt of an impressive conversation with three-year-old Brandon when I went back to visit his classroom:

B (Brandon): [Sees me, runs to hug me, and yells] "Coyote!"
C (Me): You remember the story I read to you?
B: Coyote [with a big smile].
C: Yes, the story about Coyote.
B: Can I weed it?
C: You'll get to read it later. Do you remember who else was in the story?
B: Snake, . . . umh buds [birds], . . . umm, Coyote.
C: Wow! That's great, do you remember anybody else?
B: [Shrugs] Umm, umm . . . [looks up, puts right forefinger on lips, like "thinking"]
C: Can you tell me the story of Coyote?
B: [Nods yes; two other boys come stand next to me and listen.)
C: OK, tell me what happens in the story about Coyote?
B: Uh, Coyote flies [extends arms to sides], Coyote falls [brings right arm up and down in quick swoop], and Coyote waits for de udder buds to fly.
C: And then what happens?
B: Den he staht on fiya [start on fire], and he was twapped [trapped?] up . . . he,
. . . he dat ting was pulling his nose off [pinches his nose; remembering when Badger bites Coyote's nose]
C: And then what happens?

B: He fell on de flo, . . . and he go like dis, POW! [brings hand up and starts to bring it down, down, and slaps the floor]

C: Oh my, tell me what happened next.

B: Coyote, he, he wanna to fly again.

C: Coyote wanted to fly again? Did he?

B: [Nods yes.]

C: And what happened?

B: He stahted on fier [started on fire], he's up in de sky [motions with right hand up; when he looks up he notices a broken light) Look, who break dat?

C: I don't know. He was on fire and up in the sky and then what?

B: He fell! [shrugs shoulders, both hands with palm up]

C: He fell?

B: Yeah—like dis, BAM! (Brandon falls facedown onto the floor.)

C: Oh—my goodness, just like that?

B: [Grinning and nodding yes as he picks himself up and sits on a little stool.]

C: Oh-oh, be careful Brandon. So, Coyote fell hard, right?

B: Yup, he fall . . . like dis . . . [Brandon falls again] . . . uhh.

C: And then what?

B: Das all, he goed away.

C: That was the end of the story?

B: [Nods yes.]

This particular event was impressive for several reasons. First of all, I was delighted at how much of the story three-year-old Brandon was able to recall several days after the storybook reading. Brandon had been in a group that had only had one reading in English and had only done one drawing session, based on the storybook, as a follow-up activity. According to my records he had not remembered much (about 20 percent) during the research assessment interviews that I had conducted immediately following the storybook readings and follow-up activity. For an instant I wondered if I was mistaken about what group Brandon had been in. Had he been in the "reenactment classroom"? Is that why he was able to recall and retell as much of the story as he had? He remembered most (approximately 80 percent) of the major events in the story along with recalling three out of five of the major characters. What happened? I was puzzled and decided to investigate this matter some more.

My conversation with Brandon continued and I asked him if he had read the book again or if a teacher had read it to him. He said no even when I asked him a second and third time:

C: None of the teachers have read the book to you?

B: No.

C: OK.

B: Jessie take it.

C: Who is Jessie?

B: Jessie! Jessie! [Looks at me like I'm suppose to know who Jessie is.]
C: OK.
B: He mama weed it.
C: Jessie's mama read the book? To you and Jessie?
B: [Nods yes]

Miss Jenny, Brandon's teacher, verified that Jessie had borrowed the book from his teacher and taken it home for two nights. She also explained that Jessie was Brandon's five-year-old cousin and he was in the classroom down the hall. Jessie was in Miss Donna's class and they had participated in the study as a reenactment classroom. The two reenactment groups that participated in the original study had been involved in an activity where I directed the reenactment of the *Coyote* storybook. Miss Donna shared how Jessie had loved the story about Coyote and, since they had the extra books I had provided for them, she was letting the children borrow them. Miss Donna also informed me that Jessie's mom picked up Brandon at the same time that she got Jessie. She told the teacher that she had probably read the book to the boys about five times. She had also shared that Jessie and Brandon played "coyote," which consisted mostly of Jessie, or "Coyote," chasing Brandon around in the backyard.

Even though Brandon's storybook-related experiences were not planned experiences, they nevertheless substantiate research findings that focus on practices that can impact children's developing literacy skills and abilities. Some of those practices include reading aloud, revisiting favorite storybooks, and interactions between the reader and the child (Jalongo, 2003). Brandon could demonstrate a higher level of literacy skill and ability than before because he had additional experiences with the same storybook. At least two adults had read the *Coyote* storybook aloud and his requests for repeated readings had been honored by Jessie's mom. In addition, the storybook-related interactions between Brandon and possibly as many as three adults afforded him supplementary practice in learning how to have conversations about the storybook (Jalongo, 2003).

There were at least half a dozen other instances where children were involved in extended storybook-related activities. Even though those instances may not have been as in-depth as what Brandon experienced, they still helped to reinforce what was previously learned. None of these activities were planned or teacher directed, and they all took place during learning center or free play time. Five of the children showed me samples of drawings or paintings they had done. They had all drawn different versions of a blue or gray coyote and they all included an episode where Coyote was in trouble. Listening to the children's descriptions of what they had drawn or painted revealed what they remembered most about Coyote's antics. The three- and four-year-olds, including Brandon, typically did not re-create the exact story sequence even if they had experienced repeated readings, which some researchers suggest is due more to development than to practice (Aldridge & Geist, 2002; Engel, 1995). The following dialogue with four-year-old Elizabeth provides an example of a child explaining her drawing and her understanding about what happened to Coyote in the story:

> C: What was happening here?
> E (Elizabeth): The coyote, he fell down.
> C: He fell down? Oh, that's why he looks like that. Is that water?
> E: He got to a, . . . a pool.
> C: And then what happened?
> E: The birds were laughing.
> C: Oh, I see, this is the bird laughing. Coyote looks gray.
> E: He got mad. [frowns]
> C: He got mad? And what did he do?
> E: He turned into gray.
> C: He turned into gray? How come he turned into gray?
> E: Because he wasn't listening.
> C: Because he wasn't listening?
> E: [Nods yes; pauses.] The birds said, "No Coyote!"

Several other children had made similar comments about Coyote and the idea that he was not listening, but it was only until this conversation with Elizabeth that I began to question their rationale. Elizabeth, like some of the other children, interpreted Coyote's constant capacity for trouble as a consequence of his failure to listen. In the storybook there is no episode where the birds said, "No Coyote!" like Elizabeth recalled; however, her response was similar to how one group of children had responded during one of the storybook readings:

> C: He went up to take a look. [reading p. 5 of Coyote book]
> Boy 1: He's gonna get in trouble again.
> Boy 2: He's a troublemaker. [Both boys shake their heads]
> C: Let's see what's going to happen next. [I continue reading.]
> Boy 1: See! There he go, to see the Indians.
> Boy 2: Stop, Coyote, they're gonna bite you! [Part where Coyote is looking at the birds.]
> Girl: He's not gonna stop.
> Boy 2: Nope, he's not gonna stop.
> C: You don't think he'll stop? Why?
> Boy 1: Cause he don't listen too good.
> Boy 2: Nope, he don't listen too good.
> Girl: That's why they call him Wild Coyote!

My immediate assumption to the children's comments about "listening" was that they were reflecting the school behavior that was being taught in the classroom. This assumption changed after a majority of the children responded to another question, "Does your teacher tell you to listen?" As expected, the children acknowledged that their teacher was often reminding them to listen. Before long, however, it became evident that instructions to "listen to the teacher" or "hágale caso a la maestra" (mind the teacher) were coming from home, as Maria's (age five) comments demonstrate:

> C: Tu maestra te dice que escuches or que pongas atención?
> (Does your teacher tell you to listen or to pay attention?)
> M: Si, pero yo, yo si, umm, yo le hago caso.
> (Yes, but, I, I yes, umm, I listen to her.)
> C: Le haces caso a la maestra? Que bien, eres buena estudianta.
> (You listen to your teacher? Good, you're a good student.)
> M: Si, porque si no, si no, mi mamá, mi mamá, se enoja.
> (Yes, because if not, if not, my mama, my mama, gets mad.)
> C: O tu mamá se enoja? Que te dice?
> (Oh your mama gets mad? What does she say?)
> M: Ella dice, "Maria, haces caso Maria?"
> (She says, "Maria, do you listen Maria?")

Similar responses from other students supported the premise that the children were reflecting their funds of knowledge (Moll, 1992; Riojas-Cortez, 2001) or what they were being taught at home about school or appropriate school behavior. One message these children seemed to be getting from their parents was that education was important and that they needed to listen and pay attention at school. In addition, they expressed a sincere appreciation and respect for their teachers when they talked about them. According to Miss Donna, she felt the children appreciated her and she attributed the lack of behavior problems to the support she received from parents.

BODY LANGUAGE AND SOUND EFFECTS

Young children respond to literacy experiences in much the same way they respond to other information or stimuli, with their entire bodies. In addition to responding to questions about a storybook with an assortment of body movements, they also react with facial expressions and vocal sound effects that may help them express a point. The boys that I videotaped appeared to use more exaggerated physical movements in conjunction with vocal sound effects when they were retelling or talking about the *Coyote* story. In a number of instances, like this one with Sam (age five), they were quite animated as they retold parts of the story that they remembered:

> C: So, he was really mad and he went running after the crows and tripped?
> S: "I tripped too! Ugh!" (He falls back and lands on his bottom.)
> C: Oops! Careful, Sam. So, Coyote tripped and he went tumbling in the dust?
> S: "I tumble too! Vooom!" (He rolls on the floor a couple of times.)

Some body language or movements were consistent among all the children. They all spread their arms out in a similar manner to demonstrate "birds flying" and most of them flapped their "wings," too. They all touched or tapped the part of the body that the book referred to. For example, when the children retold about Coyote getting his nose bitten, they would touch or tap their nose, or when retelling about the birds putting feathers on Coyote, they children would touch or tap their arms.

Along with using very colorful language, the children laughed and made the most humorous gestures when Coyote's tail catches fire. When referring to Coyote's tail, they used terms like "bootie," "butt," and "butt tail," and in Spanish, "cola," or "colita," all of which were followed by laughter or giggling. Though most of the girls refrained from making rough and noisy movements with their entire bodies, they did use more of an assortment of facial expressions and hand gestures to retell or talk about the story. While most of the children pointed at or patted their bottoms, there were a few who went a bit further. Alejandra (age five) seemed to especially enjoy this part of the retelling:

C: Y luego que paso?
(And then what happened?)
A: Y luego pues . . . se quemo la cola! [eyes wide, points to her bottom]
(And then well . . . he burned his tail!)
C: Se quemo la cola?
(He burned his tail?)
A: [Laughing, hand over her mouth] Si, se quemo la colita,
[stands up and wiggles her bottom]
Se quemo la colita, ha-ha-ha, ha-ha-ha [sort of sings]
(Yes, he burned his little tail, he burned his little tail, ha-ha-ha, ha-ha-ha.)

REENACTMENT AND RETELLING WITH LANGUAGE-DIVERSE CHILDREN

Storybook reenactment and retelling, along with other types of story reconstruction, are believed to have positive effects on language-diverse children (Morrow, 1993). Most of the participants from the original retelling and reenactment study had come from homes that the teachers had identified as bilingual, Spanish/English (twenty-five children) or predominantly Spanish-speaking families (twenty-three children). In addition, there were four children whose families had indicated that, though the children spoke English, the home language was different. One child came from a home where some family members spoke Navajo, while three came from Pueblo Indian families where some family members spoke Keres. These children were able to communicate well in English and participate in the retelling and reenactment activities. Their language skills or degree of proficiency in the native languages spoken in their homes were not assessed. One child was Vietnamese and, according to her teacher, she was beginning to learn English as a second language. The opportunity to listen to her speak never occurred and her participation in the storybook readings was limited mostly to listening to the storybook readings and observing the other children.

Interacting with and listening to some of these language-diverse children validated the belief that involving them in storybook reenactment and retelling activities encompasses significant benefits (Vukelich, Christie, & Enz, 2002, p. 85). Alberto and Marcos, both 5-year-old Spanish speakers, provide two vivid examples of how second-language learners responded to the storybook:

Example #1

C: Le pusieron plumas? Por que le pusieron plumas? [taps both shoulders]
   (They put the feathers on him? Why did they put the feathers on him?)
A: Umm, porque el perro queria volar. To fly. [flaps arms like a bird]
   (Umm, because the dog wanted to fly.)
C: El perro queria volar? To fly?
   (The dog wanted to fly?)
A: Si, queria volar! [laughs and shrugs shoulders]
   (Yes, he wanted to fly!)
C: Y volo el perro?
   (And did the dog fly?)
A: No, no pudo, se callo . . . para bajo [points to floor], no pudo volar,
   no, no, no. [Exaggerates the sound of "no" in English; shakes right forefinger and head no]
   (No, he wasn't able to, he fell . . . down, he wasn't able to fly, no, no, no.)
C: No pudo volar? Y luego que paso?
   (He was not able to fly? And then what happened?)
A: Y luego cuando se puso café, se cayo haci y se dio gueltas y gueltas y gueltas!
   Fall, fall, fall! [makes quick, large circular motions with right arm]
   Haci, verdad? Si?
   (Then after he turned brown, he fell like this and he went in circles, circles, circles! Fall, fall, fall! Like that, right? Yes?)

Example #2

C: Dime otra vez. (Tell me again.)
M: Que le dice "gimme dat, gimme dat." [pretends to pluck feathers from arm]
   (What he says "gimme dat, gimme dat.")
C: Oh, cuando le quitaron las plumas?
   (Oh, when they took the feathers from him?)
M: Si, y el coyote grita, "I can fly me too." [spreads his arms out]
   (Yes, and the coyote yells, "I can fly me too.")

Both of these boys started the beginning of the school year as monolingual Spanish speakers, and with two months left in the school year, they were demonstrating some acquisition of English. Though no formal assessment was conducted to determine to what degree they had acquired English, their teacher predicted that they would be able to say some full sentences by the end of the year. For the rest of the school year, the teachers were going to be immersing the children in English to prepare the non-English speakers for kindergarten. According to Ms. Donna, they were directed to speak to the children in Spanish only if it was absolutely necessary. This revelation raised concerns about whether the children's present stage of second-language acquisition or skills in first language were being acknowledged.

Dialogues with Alberto and Marcos, and some of the other Spanish speakers, support the belief that most of these children were in what Ramsey (1987) described as the "transition to production" stage of second-language learning. Some of the children were comfortable enough with the new language to begin practicing words, such as when Alberto repeats, "Fall, fall, fall!" or try short phrases, such as when Marcos says, "I can fly me too." The children were also able to answer occasional short-answer questions, especially if they had the storybook to look at. One example would be when they were asked, "Who is this?" while pointing to the picture of Coyote in the book. All the children were able to respond with "Coyote" or "Blue Coyote."

It is important that teachers or programs recognize the language skills that children possess in their home language. These children were quite able to communicate their ideas proficiently, and in a comprehensive manner, using their first language. They understood the basic structure of story and were able to convey this understanding as they retold how the story started, relayed episodes that took place in the middle, and recalled how the story ended (Jalongo, 2003). The children also displayed other behaviors associated with emergent readers, including asking for repeated readings, connecting the storybook to personal experience, and asking questions about the storybook (Jalongo, 2003). To ensure that language-diverse children become successful readers and writers of English, it is highly recommended that children's first languages be respected and used as a foundation on which to build further learning (Rinehart, 2000; Vukelich, Christie, & Enz, 2002).

Teachers need to critique potential children's books carefully and be aware of stereotypical images or messages. The book I read to this group of children, *Coyote: A Trickster Tale from the American Southwest*, is an excellent example of why we need to be careful in our selection and use of children's books. In this storybook, there is an Old Man Crow and a group of crows throughout most of the story. Though the book never states that the birds are American Indians, they all wear a headband and their feathers have American Indian types of designs on them. Old Man Crow is also wearing a turquoise necklace with a medallion. The birds chant or sing and dance by hopping from one foot to the other. These are three examples from at least ten instances where the children made statements indicative of how they perceived the birds as "Indians":

Example 1
C: Who else was in the story with Blue Coyote?
Boy 1: Umm, a snake, umm . . . a Indian . . .

Example 2
C: Who were they?
Boy 2: Hey, ye-ye-ye.
[holds right hand next to his head, forefinger pointing up, like feather?]
C: Who said that? Who was it?
Boy 2: The birds, the Indian birds.

Example 3
C: Porque dijo eso Coyote? Porque dijo "Ouch, ouch, ouch!"?
(Why did Coyote say that? Why did he say "Ouch, ouch, ouch!"?)
Girl: Porque los Indios, los pajaros, umm, le pongen las plumas haci, *poing-piong*! [pretends to stick feather in arm]
(Because the Indians, the birds, umm, they put the feathers like this, *poing-poing*!)

During the reenactment and retelling activities, there is one part that most vividly reveals that some of the children perceive that the crows are Indians. For example, in the first of four groups that reenacted the storybook, I asked the children how they thought the crows were dancing. Jacob (age five) quickly responded, "Like Indians!" When I asked him how Indians dance, he replied, "Like dis, wah-wah-wah!" as he proceeded to jump and whoop while using his hand over his mouth. A couple of other boys followed Jacob's example. My response was quick and simple:

C: Do Indians really dance that way? [the boys stopped]
J: Yeah.
C: Well, I know that's probably what you've seen on TV or the movies?
But, do you think they really dance that way?
[Group responses varied: "Yeah," "No," "I dunno."]
C: Have any of you seen the dances at some of the pueblos?
[A few children nod or say yes.]
Girl 1: My grama dance like . . . like dis [she sways slightly]
C: Can you show me how?

After a short while the children and I were doing a round dance, an American Indian social dance, and then we went on to finish our discussion. In a second group event, a similar experience took place, only this time it was initiated by Tara, a four-year-old Pueblo Indian girl. When I asked the group of children how they thought the crows were singing, Tara started to sing very softly; it sounded something like, "He-he ya hey, he-he ya hey." When we all looked at her, she became very embarrassed and did not want to sing anymore. Then one of the boys starts prancing and whooping in much the same fashion as Jacob had done. I noticed that Tara looked puzzled as she watched the boy jump around. Again my reaction and response were similar to the previous ones; I used the opportunity as a teachable moment. Then I said, "I think Tara gave us a good idea about how the crows might have been singing because I have uncles and aunties that sing like that too." With Tara's help we imitated her song and finished the reenactment activity. I have no way of knowing what kind of impact my lessons had on the children's previous perceptions of Indians and how they dance and sing. Though it was very difficult to assess any impact and there were no more opportunities to follow up on this event, the implications for the need for research in this area subsist. Stereotyping of American Indians continues to prevail in the media and in school materials (Jones & Moomaw, 2002). Teachers need to be more aware of stereotypes or misrepresentations of American Indians in children's storybooks and other curriculum materials. The field would benefit immensely from studies that focus on investigating how children respond to stereotypical images of a diversity of people in children's books.

CONCLUSION

Every minute we spend reading storybooks to young children can have an impact on them, particularly when children are afforded multiple opportunities to understand and respond to them in culturally and linguistically relevant ways. Inherently, this type of responsive curriculum incorporates children's voices, thereby acknowledging that their perspective is critical to providing quality educational experiences. When storybook readings are followed by reenactments, retellings, and other forms of extended literacy activities in the home language, the benefits can be very worthwhile.

My conversations with the children were informative as well as immensely entertaining and enjoyable. Their words, their voices, their faces, along with their gestures and body language expressed to me that they were eager and trusting participants. Communication is much broader than language; therefore, children's body movements, including eye contact, hand gestures, and facial expressions, need to be considered when interpreting what children are attempting to communicate verbally. Communication, or, more precisely, successful communication, is dependent on having a good listener, interpreter, or both.

More conversations with the children to tap their existing funds of knowledge need to be included in daily literacy activities. These thoughts kept surfacing as I dedicated more time and listened to the voices of children that I had studied. It was during those conversations that I became most aware of how some Spanish-speaking children, who may have remained silent or struggled through a response in English, were quite proficient when responding in their own language. Another impression these children left with me is that they already possess a great deal of knowledge, including perceptions that may be incorrect.

Children are constantly acquiring new knowledge that supports or challenges previously formed ideas. One challenge for us as educators is to find ways to dedicate more thought and effort toward promoting an awareness of children's voices within quality curriculum. Research relative to perceptions and practices regarding children's voices and their place within curriculum would be timely given some current trends toward more structured curriculum. Teachers give power to children's voices when they listen and respond to them, ideally by incorporating what they have learned into the daily curriculum. By incorporating what is learned, teachers acknowledge that what the children bring with them, including funds of knowledge, have value.

REFERENCES

Aldridge, J., & Geist, E. (2002). The developmental progression of children's oral story inventions. *Journal of Instructional Psychology, 29*, 33–39.

Engel, S. (1995). *The stories children tell: Making sense of the narratives of childhood.* New York: W. H. Freeman.

Gutierrez-Gomez, C. (1996). *Effects of English and bilingual storybook reading and reenactment on the retelling abilities of preschool children.* Unpublished doctoral dissertation, College of Education, University of North Texas, Denton.

Jalongo, M. R. (2003). *Early childhood language arts* (3rd ed.). Boston: Allyn & Bacon.

Jipson, J. A. (2000). The stealing of wonderful ideas: The politics of imposition and representation in research in early childhood. In L. D. Soto (Ed.), *The politics of early childhood education* (pp. 167–177). New York: Peter Lang.

Jones, G. W., & Moomaw, S. (2002). *Lessons from Turtle Island.* St. Paul, MN: Redleaf Press.

McDermott, G. (1994). *Coyote: A trickster tale from the American Southwest.* San Diego, CA: Harcourt Brace.

Moll, L. C. (1992). Bilingual classroom studies and community analysis: Some recent trends. *Educational Researcher, 21*(2), 20–24.

Morrow, L. M. (1993). *Literacy development in the early years: Helping children read and write* (2nd ed.). Boston: Allyn & Bacon.

Nieto, S. (2002). *Language, culture, and teaching: Critical perspectives for a new century.* Mahwah, NJ: Lawrence Erlbaum.

Ramsey, P.G. (1987). *Teaching children in a diverse world: Multicultural education for young children.* New York: Teachers College Press.

Rinehart, N. (2000). Native American perspectives: Connected to one another and to the greater universe. In L. D. Soto (Ed.), *The politics of early childhood education* (pp. 135–142). New York: Peter Lang.

Riojas-Cortez, M. (2001). Preschoolers' funds of knowledge displayed through sociodramatic play episodes in a bilingual classroom. *Early Childhood Education Journal, 29*(1), 35–40.

Siegler, R., Deloache, J., & Eisenberg, N. (2003). *How children develop.* New York: Worth.

Vukelich, C., Christie, J., & Enz, B. J. (2002). *Helping young children learn language and literacy.* New York: Addison-Wesley-Longman.

CHAPTER SIXTEEN

LOS POETAS

CARMEN MEDINA, KELLY BRADBURRY, AND SUSAN PEARSON

Estos poemas son mis memorias, mis sueños—mis películas en mi almohada.
These poems are my memories, my dreams—the movies in my pillow.

(Argueta, 2001, p. 1)

Research on language and literacy development for English language learners has provided extensive data and theoretical frameworks to suggest different practices—nonprescriptive or homogenous—to effectively engage these students in successful literacy learning experiences. Among the most relevant to this chapter are sociocultural theories that look at the connections among language, literacy, and culture (Huerta-Macías, 1998; Pérez et al., 1998; Soto, 1997; Trueba, 1990) and the critical role of honoring and welcoming the students' home language and culture into the learning process to develop inclusive and culturally democratic biliteracy spaces (Darder, 1997). Related to this notion of home, language, and cultural democracy is also the idea that students from diverse linguistic backgrounds come to the schooling process with valuable information and experiences from their home and their communities or "funds of knowledge" (Moll, Amanti, Neff, & González, 1992) that should be considered in the development of a relevant curriculum that allows for the students' voices and experiences to be heard and be present (Martínez-Roldán, 2003).

In this chapter we present Mario's voice on a literature-based unit reading and writing bilingual narrative poetry. Mario is a fifth-grade student from Mexico who recently immigrated to the United States and now lives in a city in the Midwest. This instrumental case study (Stake, 2000) was part of a collaborative research project between two teachers and a university professor in an elementary school. On this unit the students read and responded to the book *A movie in my pillow/Una película en mi almohada* (2001), a collection of bilingual poems by Salvadorian author Jorge Argueta. In the book, Argueta uses his life experiences as an immigrant in the United States to write narrative poems connected to his identity. Through a series of curricular explorations, we interpret the poet's voice, images, and intentions to understand how poetry as a literary genre is used as a space to express and create images related to the writer's identity. After an analysis of the author's writing, the students engaged in an "authoring cycle" (Short, Harste, & Burke, 1996) to create their own bilingual poems using their life experiences as a framework. The questions framing the students' writing inquiry were: "If you were going to write a book like *A movie in my pillow/Una película en mi almohada*, what experiences would you like to share? What kind of images and/or words would you use in your poetry?" The students had the choice of writing in English, Spanish, or both.

This chapter presents how through the reading and interpretation of Argueta's poetry Mario began to voice aspects of his experiences of coming to the United States. Modeling after Argueta's poetry on border crossing, Mario worked on writing narrative poetry that voiced his own story of coming to the United States. We used notions such as Anzaldúa's (1987) literary image of border crossing and Igoa's (1995) stages on the "phenomenon of uprooting" to interpret Mario's inner voice in his process of creating the poetry. Our intention here is to share the possibilities of using bilingual Latino/a literature and authors as "cultural modeling" (Lee, Spencer, & Harpalani, 2003) for engaging Latino/a students in multiple and complex explorations of identity and literary genres such as poetry. According to Lee, Spencer, and Harpalani (2003), "cultural modeling" is a "framework for designing instruction that makes explicit connections between students' everyday knowledge and the demands of the subject matter-learning" (p. 7). When we refer to the used of Latino/a literature and authors as cultural models, we are talking about the ways in which authors and students "live culturally" in diverse and complex ways. We agreed with Moll (as cited by Lee, Spencer, & Harpalani, 2003) in that "cultural life consists of multiple voices, of unity as well as discord, including an imperfect sharing of knowledge; of intergenerational understanding; of developing both adaptive and maladaptive practices while discarding others . . ." In our research all students in the classroom shared multiple aspects of their identity through poetry. We found, however, that Mario's voice was among the most engaging.

LATINO/A VOICES AND AUTHORING CYCLES

According to Giroux (1988), "[v]oice refers to the principles of dialogue as they are enunciated and enacted within particular social settings" (p. 199). Voice then is not just a matter of generic talk but the creation of situated dialogues or forms of self-expression that are socially and culturally constructed. The multiple literacy engagements we create in classrooms for students to talk, read, write, and listen are not generic forms of communication but are always socially and culturally situated sites from where to voice and perform in particular ways. Literary explorations and writing, for example, are aspects of the curriculum that we could use to either silence students' voices through meaningless worksheets and generic skills lessons or facilitate a space to speak using the students' social and cultural reality as a framework. This is the case we present on this piece working with bilingual Latino/a students in authoring cycles (Short, Harste, & Burke, 1996) using bilingual Latino/a literature as models for literary understanding and writing.

In an authoring cycle (Short, Harste, & Burke, 1996), students engage in learning inquiries—writing, literary explorations, and other—using their knowledge and interests as the main sources. Students are encouraged to use their immediate world to transform the learning process into something relevant to them. Furthermore, when the structure of the authoring cycles is framed as inquiry into themselves, the students have the opportunity to voice and share critical aspects of their life experiences and identity with the rest of the classroom community naming and sharing their wor(l)d (Freire, 1970/1995). For this reason, we also considered that as we encouraged students to look and write their lives, it was valuable to study authors who served as models both culturally and literarily.

Using Argueta's work was relevant because the process of authoring for many Latino/a literary writers is embedded in multiple intentions connected to their voice, identity, culture, and social locations (Medina & Enciso, 2002). This is significantly important in texts that are considered "critical fictions" (Mariani, 1991) where authors from traditionally marginalized communities explore their identities and cultural experiences as forms of "inner liberation" (Anzaldúa, 1987) to name and make visible their experiences. Among the powerful images explored by Latino/a writers is the complex nature of being immigrant in a new country. For example, Anzaldúa (1987) used the literary image of *la frontera*, the borderland, to describe not only the physical space where many immigrants live close to the border between Mexico and the United States, but also a state of mind where multiple cultural negotiations take place, such as race, ethnicity, and gender. In her literary descriptions of living in *la frontera*, the borderlands, she defines identity as complex and ambiguous. *La frontera* is a contested space where people deal with multiple contradictions as a result of leaving behind a culture and dealing with aspects of a new one.

Using bilingual Latino/a literature as "mentors" for writing (Buckner-DiMuzio, 1999), to look at how their identity is embedded in their writing is one way to support bilingual Latino/a students' writing development. By looking closely at Latino/a writers as models, the students began to explore their writing as ways to acquire a strong sense of voice both in English and Spanish. This process contributed to the formation of bicultural identities and the validation of those identities in schools.

CLASSROOM CONTEXT

The students in this fifth-grade classroom came from a variety of ethnic, cultural, and linguistic backgrounds: six of the nineteen students were Latino/a, one from Angola, who spoke Portuguese; seven were African American; and five were Caucasian. Kelly is the fifth-grade teacher and Susan the English as a Second Language (ESL) teacher. They have been working throughout the year in a shelter classroom model to support the literacy development for English language learners. In a shelter classroom, as opposed to a pull-out model, the mainstream teacher does the class instruction all in English and the ESL teacher is also present to help adapt lessons, assist students, and work in a small group setting within the class with English language learners. It is important to point out that the school district this school belongs to only has English as a Second Language program as opposed to bilingual or dual language programs. Under the law, teachers cannot teach in Spanish; instead, the ESL teacher is charged with teaching students how to read, write, speak, and listen in English. Therefore the research and practice we present on this chapter is in many ways in tension with larger administrative ideologies that do not perceived bilingual education as an effective model to teach linguistically diverse students.

Carmen, a Puerto Rican and bilingual university professor in the area of language and literacy, approached Kelly and Susan to collaborate in a research project. Carmen proposed a study that looks at the students' responses to bilingual Latino/a literature, paying particular attention to the ways in which this literature could facilitate Latino/a students' literary understanding, biliteracy development, and connections and separations to their own cultural identity. She also wanted to see what happened when the creation of bilingual space was open in the classroom where both languages were welcomed into the learning process. Susan and Kelly agreed to participate and suggested a unit on poetry given that it was the one literary genre they had not worked on with the students.

A MOVIE IN MY PILLOW/UNA PELÍCULA EN MI ALMOHADA: A UNIT ON BILINGUAL POETRY

The unit was devised among the three of us. We met and agreed that Argueta's *A movie in my pillow/ Una película en mi almohada* is a powerful collection of bilingual poetry to inspire the students' writing, and used it as the framework for a unit on narrative poetry. The unit lasted one month, meeting three times a week. We began by having a broad dialogue about definitions of culture and aspects of our cultural identity. We created a "culture mural" that collected all the words that defined aspects of our individual culture, and the mural allowed us to see the multiple cultural locations shared in the classroom. After the creation of the mural, we worked on three literature discussion groups with multiple copies of the text for the students on each group. We read the book aloud both in English and Spanish, beginning with the author's introduction where he provides a description of his life experiences and intentions for writing the book that helped us to better contextualize the poems in the book. The curricular engagement "say something" (Short, Harste, & Burke, 1996) was used to share our—students and facilitators—thinking after reading the introduction and each poem by saying what came to our mind. The initial reading was just meant to enjoy and openly respond to the poetry.

The students then met in pairs and chose two poems to respond to using a "graffiti board" (Short, Harste, & Burke, 1996). In a graffiti board, the students record their immediate responses to a text, and in the context of this classroom, the students could choose any language to respond, creating multilingual representations in English, Spanish, and Portuguese. The graffiti boards worked as a way to frame readers' conversations around the text in pairs. Carmen, Kelly, and Susan did not intervene in their creations or dialogues. The students then read the two poems to the class and presented some of their thinking around the graffiti boards.

The unit continued by looking closely at the author's craft and intentions. We asked the students to think of why the author would write/share a specific experience in a poem. In an overhead, we recorded three examples of poems the students chose and webbed their responses. Among the students' choices was the poem "Yo-yo," which was one of the students' favorites mainly because of the rhythm and playfulness that Argueta brings to the poem. The students thought that he would write this poem perhaps because "maybe he wanted one," "he had a yo-yo when he was young," and "he loved to yo-yo." They also chose the poem "Soup of Stars/Sopa de Estrellas." In this poem, Argueta shares his experiences as a child living in El Salvador during the war and the challenges his family lived, such as not having enough food. He uses the literary image of a soup of stars, *una sopa de estrellas*, to share how the family would go up to the house ceiling and watch the stars: "We would look up at the stars—the stars were our soup" (p. 12). The students thought the author "saw the shape of soup in stars," which refers to an illustration, "Instead of eating he would look at the stars," "He is hungry," and "Not a lot of money to buy food." Through this engagement, the students had an opportunity to examine the author's intentions and interpretations of the poetry. From there, we transitioned to brainstorming ideas for their own writing. We asked the students to think of some experiences they would like to share and what specific aspects of those experiences were important to consider.

Once we posed the inquiry questions, the students created graphic organizers similar to the ones we did on the author, to generate and organize their ideas for writing. The students informally shared with us and among themselves all the possibilities, and we moved from there to write the firsts drafts of the narrative poems. The students engaged in a writing cycle where they drafted ideas; we looked at those drafts and generated a series of mini-workshops on elements that could make their writing more powerful; and they revised, translated, published, and presented their final literary products. Bilingual students wrote their poems in English and Spanish, but also English-speaking students asked for help from Spanish-speaking students to have their poems translated. There was a clear shift in the language dynamics in the classroom when Spanish speakers suddenly became the language experts to support English speakers.

Mario's Voice: Cultural and Literary Inquiry

Mario was born in Mexico. Five years ago, his mother and the children left Mexico to live in the Southwest and now live in a city in the Midwest. Mario began the school year extremely quiet, but by the end of the year, he was much louder, for instance, when reading or speaking in front of a group.

Similar to many of the poems in *A movie in my pillow/Una película en mi almohada*, Mario developed his ideas—at the brainstorm stages and in his final poem—to explore multiple aspects of his feelings about moving to the United States. During the poetry unit, Mario found close connections with various of Argueta's poems, such as *When we left El Salvador/Cuando salimos de El Salvador*. On this poem the author narrates his experiences on the day he moved from El Salvador to the United States:

> **When I left El Salvador**
> **by Jorge Argueta**
> When we left El Salvador
> To come to the United States
> Papa and I left in a hurry
> One early morning in December

We left without saying goodbye
To relatives, friends or neighbors
I didn't say goodbye to Neto
My best friend

I didn't sat goodbye to Koki
My happy talking parakeet
I didn't say goodbye to
Miss Sha-sha-she-sha

My very dear doggie
When we left El Salvador
In a bus I couldn't stop crying
because I had left my mama
my little brothers
and my grandma behind (p. 11)

Going to Texas
by Mario
Going by airplane
I see outside
Little cars, little buildings
But leaving Mexico is sad
Because I didn't tell my dad
when I was going to go to Texas.
I cried because I never see him.
Ir para Texas
Ir por avión es divertido
Yo vi afuera
Carros pequeños, edificios pequeños.
Pero irme de Mexico es triste
Porque yo no le avise a mi papá
Cuando me iba a venir a Texas
Yo llore porque yo nunca lo vi más.

Mario identified "When I left El Salvador/Cuando salimos de El Salvador" as his favorite poem because "This poem reminds me when I didn't say goodbye to my dad. I thought Texas was going to be boring but met my aunt, uncle and cousins." The influence of Argueta's poem on his writing was apparent throughout the brainstorm ideas on his graphic organizers, which later on in the process he used to construct his final poem. He developed graphic organizers that included words, images, and ideas for writing his poetry. On these organizers he represented his ideas for writing about "Going to Texas" and those mostly focused first on his narrative and feelings about leaving Mexico and the circumstances that took place, such as leaving his father behind without the possibility of ever seeing him again. He used words and phrases such as "Going to Texas," "sad," "My mom said I had to come here," "Ask my dad when are you going to come here," "He was working," "He said never," "cried," "divorce," "Wanted to stay with my dad," "no choice." Second, he explored his excitement about the airplane with phrases such as "Airplane," "fun," "I see outside," "cars," "buildings," "scared," "fall down," "hold on tight." Third, he shared his feelings about Texas, including friendship, language, and schooling with words such as "fun," "friends," "Cesar," "play soccer," "school," "Speak a lot of Spanish," and "Wanted to learn English."

Once we examined Mario's overall process on this series of curricular engagements, we looked at how Argueta's literary images and voice framed Mario's voice and literary images for his own poetry. Like we mentioned at the beginning of the chapter, he used Argueta's ways of naming his experiences to name his own. Furthermore, when we carefully examined his writing, we realized the complexity of Mario's narrative, particularly as it relates to aspects of border crossing that are explored by many Latino/a writers (Anzaldúa, 1987) and the multiple emotions involved in this experience. We looked for a framework that helped us understand and listen to what he was saying in a deeper manner. We met and realized that many of the *testimonios* Mario shared in his poetry were related to Igoa's (1995) descriptions of the "phenomenon of uprooting," thereby making his writing a powerful example of a literary text where identity and literary work come together.

Igoa (1995) described the "Inner world of the immigrant child": Based on observations of her immigrant students, she identified different aspects—emotional, psychological, and cultural—children live through as they are uprooted from their native cultures and countries to new countries. Those experiences are part of the child's inner world or "the deeper area within the child that can be defined as the truth within (whether or not that "truth" has any basis in reality) or, simply, what the child feels and believes" (p. 46). She organized the process of uprooting in stages, however we looked at her ideas more as descriptors to make sense of Mario's and Argueta's literary writing and that facilitated our ability to listen and understand their poetic voices. The descriptors were used as guide for interpretation and not as static or to suggest generalizations among all immigrant children's experiences. We agreed with Gutiérrez and Rogoff (2003) that in doing research on culture we should avoid generalizations and reductive approaches. The framework was useful to us only after we began analyzing Mario's experience and not before as preimposition. It helped us understand the complex emotional and psychological process Mario went through as he moved to the United States and how creative and culturally situated models of teaching and learning facilitated Mario's self-expression.

For example, according to Igoa's notions of uprooting, immigrant children could experience mixed emotions about the journey. Sometimes those feelings involve dealing with leaving a parents or siblings behind. In Argueta's poetry, he describes his feelings of leaving friends and family behind. Similarly, on Mario's first brainstorm, he described the circumstances that frame the move to Texas. He used the word "sad" at the center to elaborate on his feelings. He then continued by stating, "My mom said I had to come," and asked his dad when he could come to the United States: "Ask my dad when are you going to come here; he was working." His father said never, and Mario finalizes that section with the word "cried." He also used the word "divorce," describing his parents' relationship and also his desire to stay with his father but not having a choice. "Wanted to stay with my dad" "no choice."

Mario demonstrated his mixed emotions as he described his trip on the airplane with a level of excitement about coming to a new place and beginning a new life. Mario thought the "airplane" was "fun," and he could "see outside" "cars" and "buildings." He was also "scared" about the possibility of falling down but he "hold on tight." This combination of sadness, excitement, and fear about the trip are Mario's explorations of his own border-crossing experience.

Once in Texas, Mario describes his experiences as "fun" and includes the name of his friend and playing soccer. On that same figure he includes aspects of his schooling such as speaking lots of Spanish and his desire to learn English. This is also similar to some of Argueta's poetry, such as when he writes about the *Barrio lleno de sol/Neighborhood of sun* to describe his life at the San Francisco's Mission District. Both Argueta and Mario consider the mixed feelings of sadness, excitement, and happiness in their poetic representations. Mario's composition of ideas resulted in a powerful final bilingual narrative poem entitled "Going to Texas."

RESEARCH AND PEDAGOGICAL IMPLICATIONS

Mario's poetic representations voiced multiple aspects of his "inner voice" related to immigration experiences. Furthermore, using Argueta's poetry as a model for writing, Mario used content (border-crossing experiences) and context (bilingual poetry as a literary genre) to develop his own writing of bilingual narrative poetry. Culture, knowledge, and curriculum came together to create learning experiences that supported Mario's development.

It is significant to point out that most of the other students' poetry was powerful also and included multiple aspects of their lives and identity as well. Students wrote about vacations, family, death, pets, and favorite things to do. Using narrative poetry where authors write their lives, like in *A movie in my pillow/Una película en mi almohada*, are powerful literary texts to use as models for writing in the classroom. Furthermore, Latino/a children's literature as a body of literary texts has multiple examples of texts where the authors' identities are embedded in their writing (for specific examples see Medina & Enciso, 2002). These texts have the potential to frame learning experiences that constitute cultural and literary inquiry where students learn how literature is a mirror into our lives and the lives of others.

REFERENCES

Anzaldúa, G. (1987). *Borderlands/La frontera: The new Mestiza.* San Francisco: Aunt Lute Books.

Argueta, J. (2001). *A movie in my pillow/Una película en mi almohada.* Illus. Elizabeth Gómez. San Francisco: Children's Books Press.

Buckner-DiMuzio, A. (1999). Using authors as mentors. *Primary Voices, 7*(4), 7–9.

Darder, A. (1997). Creating the conditions for cultural democracy in the classroom. In A. Darder, R. Torres, & H. Gutiérrez, *Latinos and education: A critical reader* (pp. 331–350). New York: Routledge.

Freire, P. (1995). *Pedagogy of the oppressed* (rev. ed.; M. Ramos, Trans.). New York: Continuum. (Original work published 1970)

Giroux, H. (1988). *Teachers as intellectuals.* New York: Bergin & Garvey.

Gutiérrez, K., & Rogoff, B. (2003). Cultural ways of learning: Individual traits or repertoires of practices. *Educational researcher, 32*(5), 19–25.

Huerta-Macías, A. (1998). Learning for Latinos: The sociocultural perspective. In M. L. González, A. Huertas-Macías, & J. Villamil-Tinajero (Eds.), *Educating Latino students: A guide to successful practices* (pp. 29–45). Lancaster, PA: TECHNOMIC.

Igoa, C. (1995). *The inner world of the immigrant child.* Mahwah, NJ: Lawrence Erlbaum.

Lee, C., Spencer, M., & Harpalani, V. (2003). "Every shut eye ain't asleep": Studying how people live culturally. *Educational Researcher, 32*(5), 6–13.

Mariani, P. (1991). *Critical fictions: The politics of imaginative writing.* Seattle, WA: Bay Press.

Martínez-Roldán, C. (2003). Building worlds and identities: A case study of the role of narratives in bilingual literature discussion groups. *Research in Teaching of English, 37*(4), 491–526.

Medina, C., & Enciso, P. (2002). "Some words are messengers/Hay palabras mensajeras": Interpreting sociopolitical themes in Latino/a children's literature. *The New Advocate, 15*(1), 35–47.

Moll, L., Amanti, C., Neff, D., & González, N. (1992). Funds of knowledge for teaching: Using a qualitative approach to connect homes and classrooms. *Theory into Practice, 31*(2), 132–141.

Pérez, B., McCarty, T. L., Watahomigie, L. J., Torres-Guzman, M. E., Thi Dien, T., Chang, J., Smith, H., Davila De Silva, A., Nordlander, A. (Eds.). (1998). *Sociocultural context of language and literacy.* Mahwah, NJ: Lawrence Erlbaum.

Short, K., Harste, J., & Burke, C. (1996). *Creating classrooms for authors and Inquirers.* Portsmouth, NH: Heinemann.

Soto, L. (1997). *Language, culture and power: Bilingual families and the struggle for education.* Albany: State University of New York Press.

Stake, R. (2000). Case study. In N.K. Denzin & I. Lincoln (Eds.), *Handbook of qualitative research* (2nd ed.) (pp.435–454). Thousand Oaks, CA: Sage.

Trueba, H. (1990). The role of culture in literacy acquisition: An interdisciplinary approach to qualitative research. *International Journal of Qualitative Research, 3*(1), 1–13.

EPILOGUE: WHEN CHILDREN AND YOUTH TALK BACK

Precocious Research Practices and the Cleverest Voices

ERIC MALEWSKI

> We have created the ultimate "Other," a group of human beings not considered able or mature enough to create themselves. We have not analyzed the assumptions and beliefs that underlie our creations. . . . We have not discussed the possibilities that younger members of society may not benefit from living within our constructions of "childhood."
>
> (Cannella, 1997, 19)

Although it seems commonsensical to many, the notion that culture situates knowledge and identity was brought to my attention during the past year as I conducted research in a bilingual, multiracial first-grade classroom. As a faculty member deeply concerned with changing material and symbolic relations both inside and outside schools, I found myself coming to grips with a pressing contradiction: As I came to understand the strength of culture as constituent of the lives of our young, I also witnessed the increased bracketing of culture in relation to knowledge production—research and assessment of learning. This effect I attribute to insurgent conservativism, a phrase I use to describe the interconnected relation of subjugating educational practices occurring within a larger societal crisis in meaning over what constitutes high intellect. Under these conditions, it has been suggested that diversity in representation (physical difference) can be embraced within the context of standardized research methodologies (intellectual sameness): In multilingual, multiracial communities, a single form of investigation is best for all children and culturally relevant research practices are less valued by the general public because they resist generalization, are overly focused on context, and promote inequity by validating less relevant knowledge. In short, it has been at least an implicit suggestion that there is no need for integrative research practices, that culture can be separated from knowledge in ways that will benefit all social groups by making them essentially equal. Is it possible that cultural representations in physical form can exist apart from style and intellect in ways that imply, for example, a classroom of predominantly Latino students from a low socioeconomic background construct and are constructed by knowledge in relatively similar ways to a classroom of predominantly white upper-class students living in the same town, city, or state?

The assumptions that undergird the bracketing of culture in research and assessment as well as curriculum involving children and youth are complicated. On some registers they are problematic as they subjugate the characteristics of those living on the downside of race, gender, class, and age binaries, whereas on other registers they resonate with a democratic ethos. For example, on a cultural level, one typically associated less with public education, the assumptions of standardized research and assessment, including the bracketing of culture, are a concern for those whose values and ways of being are marked less relevant by the criterion for inclusion, for how might research practices bring equality across race, class, gender, sexuality, and age when the differences of those on the downside of the asymmetries are marked as a disadvantage? On the level of moral belief, however, standards and instrumental approaches to research are not nearly as disconcerting as they resonate well with a discourse of human rights and the very underpinnings of public education: a belief in the inherent moral worth of all people; standards as a pathway toward equity; empirical research as value-free; and the disciplines as embodying stable knowledge that exists outside of the intractability of cultural influence. The *public* in public education for many U.S. Americans implies access for all, the partitioning out of difference, and the exclusion of power. But in this context, what are we to make of cultural difference?

What is the relevance of bracketing cultural style and intellect to this brief commentary on Soto and Swadener's edition of perspectives on research with children and youth? This disposition toward public education, that the public space of education can reach its goals if we separate out our differences, is also common in research on its aims. It would seem in most approaches to educational research, particularly at a time where there is an increasing emphasis on large-scale empirical measurement and the discourse of rationality and causality has been successfully grafted onto notions of equity, as well as the separation of cultural differences from research practices, bracketing has become the very terms for distinction. This realization should not be taken as an indication that cultural differences denote unequal moral worth; humanistic discourses on equality are effective at establishing a right to fundamental symbolic and material resources. Rather, that in research with children and youth, methodologies need to be more nuanced, tentative, and illustrative of youthful complexity than decontextual, binary approaches to assessment will allow; it seems impossible that a declaration that research on young human beings be conducted through assessments of zero culture will make the need for culturally relevant research practices go away. Similar to adults but different in form, race, class, gender, and age shape the way knowledge constructs our young as well as the way our young construct knowledge.

In offering the epilogue on this edited book, I turn attention to the title, which draws the notion of voice into relation with children and youth. In fact, precocious research practices—focused on the study of the social construction of children and youth, prone to the intractability that comes with contextualized inquiry, and grounded in the everyday life of young human beings—have elevated the youthful voices in the midst of their exclusion and it turns out academic negligence is more culture and ideology than literal omission. This book, then, enters the academy at a time of desperation, a historical juncture where we need to take note of the research already under way in the minds, bodies, and spirits of our progeny; they are already and always have been budding social scientists in localities we often failed to recognize. I wonder as educators and scholars, what world will we help them discover? Conventional academic research is too often performed on the backs of class, gender, race, and age biases with such regularity that they go unnoticed: uncritical approaches to knowledge production that equate equal treatment across social groups with equality and young minds with ignorance. The authors in this book illustrate that research that brackets culture has never served to advance a monolithic, equal public education but instead particularly advantageous forms in a select number of locales that parade as ideal models, serving to mask the need to develop culturally relevant, theoretically complex understandings of the experiences of young human beings. Our young need to be reconceptualized as intellectuals in their own right, with knowledge claims that compete with adult understandings on the grounds of race, class, gender, sexual identity, and age, not simply as children and youth lacking the outlooks that adults possess.

Contrary to the purported success of standardized forms of research and assessment, the methods elaborated in this book have been a reaction to the failure of unidirectional research practices to give credence to students' and children's ways of knowing. The precocious research practices included here, with their dialogic complexity, can help inform the integration of a belief in the equal worth of humans with culturally relevant inquiry, imperative for developing understandings necessary for maintaining education for a public democracy, including examination of competing notions of what constitutes research practice and knowledge production. As Carl Grant (2003) described, research that claims to "help needs to be more broadly conceptually defined to include help that would change school policy and practice to better meet the needs and interests of students instead of assuring that students conform to the demands of the school" (p. 4). Within this context, this collection of writings offers a tentative description of experiences conducting research initiated with the voices of the cleverest of children and youth.

This book stands as evidence that research that honors the voices of young human beings gives rich meaning to the variations of social encounters while embracing an ethic of care that asserts conclusions must be drawn tentatively, giving credence to the right of the subject-as-of-yet-unknown to be heard. As a hermeneutical act of interpretation, rigorous research with children and youth is drawn into relation with the context under which the research is conducted and the processes of its interpretation, including the forces that form the very basis for human interaction. Foucault reminds us that researchers must account for power relations by resisting universal narratives and broad conceptions of justice while also criticizing hegemonic practices, searching out the opportunities for contestation, and contributing the most tentative of interpretations,

> I dream of the intellectual destroyer of evidence and universalities, the one who, in the inertias and constraints of the present, locates and marks the weak points, the openings, the lines of power, who incessantly displaces himself, doesn't know exactly where he is heading nor what he'll think tomorrow because he is too attentive to the present . . . (1989, p. 155)

Thus, we are reminded that precocious research practices have been *spinning off* counterhegemonic notions of youth and childhood from the start, from the young male slave, Anytus, who illustrated his command of mathematics to Plato to Dylan Klebold and Eric Harris, whose Columbine massacre acted as a reminder to educators that the measure of a high-quality education is not simply the ability to return a series of disembodied facts on a preformed test, but the development of communities of respect where differences are honored, knowledge is accompanied by discussions of its relation to power and privilege, and students are sanctioned to study and improve the conditions of their existence. Precocious research practices have proven that instrumental assessments might offer the pathways toward higher test scores while their uncaring nature leaves a wake of the most deadly outliers.

The most precocious research practices empower subjects who talk back, sometimes waiting until adulthood to speak about their youth, giving evidence to the conflicting relationship between the rigidity of formal assessments and the creative, open-endedness of youthful ways of knowing, that whereas the former often tries to stabilize knowledge, the latter often opens conventional knowledge to play and ongoing rearticulation. Children and youth have often highlighted the limitations of conventional research practices—the structured interview protocol and the preformed survey instrument—that take discourse as literal, highlighting the need to acknowledge the excesses of signification. That signifiers are limited in what they signify and a single word might have multiple meanings or, in reaction to a probing question, might simply be spoken for the enjoyment a child receives in the utterance gives credence to the trouble with prescribed research methods. The immoderate discourses introduced by these authors opens the reader to the flight of imagination, the youthful world of nonrational knowledge where inquiry practices are enacted in process. Too often in educational research, the playful discourse of the young, what Wittgenstein defined more broadly as the language games in which humans partake, is not embraced as evidence of what Kincheloe and Steinberg (1993) described as postformal thought, cognition that is situated in the particularities of context and time, shaped by power relationships, and open to alternative ways of rearticulating and dearticulating thought. Educational research methods have too often excoriated the playfulness of knowing, a search for exactitude that suppresses imagination and, as Greene (1995) put it,

> requires a refusal of what Foucault called "normalization," the power of which imposes homogeneity and allows people "to determine levels, to fix specialties, and to render the differences useful by fitting them one to another." To resist such tendencies is to become aware of the ways in which certain dominant social practices enclose us in molds, define us in accord with extrinsic demands, discourage us from going beyond ourselves and from acting on possibility. (p. 135)

Precocious methodologies shed a more critical light on research with children and youth that posit it is necessary to develop compensatory techniques for overcoming the naiveté and unpredictability of youthful subjects. Utilizing critical theory, the methodologies developed here question the creation of research subjects presumed unknowing before the investigation begins and asks how children's and youth's ways of thinking can be viewed not as a deficiency but as offering compelling insights that, in the transition to adulthood, are more often than not lost. Could it be, as we gain stature and influence, knowledge turns back on itself and the will to transgress diminishes—knowledge that once served to exceed convention operating as a form of resistance to changing thought, no longer a tool for embracing new ways of knowing? The authors in this book inquire, how can we get past frameworks where the authority invested in the investigator is one of omnipotence, of orchestrating research protocols and delicately pulling already formulated thought from the most innocent of minds? Can research with children and youth extend beyond assessment of the ability to conform? As the work of Bakhtin (1990) proposed, might future methodologies better reflect the tenets of dialogic interaction where all voices have something to offer in the process of knowledge creation?

It seems if this book offers any direction for research with children and youth, it is that knowledge has rarely been adequately represented in disciplinary bodies and children and youth have never been so tractable as to offer unchanging insights, that those who sense marginalization have often become experts at illusion, telling investigators what they want to hear but possibly little of what they might be thinking at any moment in time. In what might be interpreted as a form of resistance, precocious research practices recognize that young human beings on many occasions stand in opposition to investigators who utilize conventional approaches. Their rebellion can sometimes be evidenced in the provision of the most outrageous answers—strategic responses that align with what they think will draw the interest of the investigator or simply a resounding no. Sadly, in what might be understood as an obsession with large-scale empirical assessment, the marginalization of culture, context, and voice that might seem like a necessary sacrifice in unidirectional research becomes constitutive of the approach when children and youth face high-stakes testing on a daily basis. The logic necessary to move past standardized, technocratic forms of research and into interactive, dynamic, contextual inquiry is lost through uncritical forms of accountability and it is assumed that few other choices exist. The result is that the highly rigorous research practices discussed in this book must not only recoup existing approaches to the research and assessment of youth and children, but must exceed them with culturally relevant, dialogic practices that better help schools meet their needs. Within an era where young adults together take hundreds of thousands of high-stakes tests a year while many schools lack the resources to provide textbooks for every student, we can no longer assume that knowledge production will lead toward enlightened understanding.

So what are we to do with the contradiction between the two registers, of moral worth as a standard and culturally relevant methodologies as contextually specific? In one sense, the authors in this book overcome this false binary with writing that suggests complex, critically informed research practices have the ability to connect generalizations and particularities in ways that provide investigators with a far more textured understanding of the voices of children and youth (Raizen, 1989). Focusing on the context of research, the modernist belief in the equal moral worth of all persons can be used as a springboard into postmodernist attention to partiality and difference. When scholars tune in to the voices of children and youth, it is difficult to abstract ideas from the contexts in which they are learned and put to use, making it possible to develop practices grounded in postformal notions of cognition. Equally important, these ideas might be tentatively transferred and adapted through respectful deliberation as the context might warrant appropriate and necessary. Precociousness indicates an enacted nature, a symbiotic view of research as a foundation for participatory democratic education that integrates the belief that all people deserve high-quality, rigorous schooling with research and assessment that is culturally relevant; modes of learning that attend to questions of not just *if* it is learned but also *what* is learned and *how* it is put to use; and methodologies that emerge from various subcultures, informed by the dispossessed and made relevant through nuanced understandings of voice. Research with children and youth employs the will to speak one's thoughts to inspire movement toward crossroads, the measure of the particularities of place understood through dialogic interactions, the significance invented en route to a place that remains in part a mystery even when the dialogue ends.

Whether in a classroom or the home, the precocious methodologies presented in this book take the experiences of young human beings seriously, as researchers who study with children and youth work together to discern how they—the researcher and the researched—give meaning to their lives and the role that schooling might play in the process. Operating within integrated research methodologies, voice is given to issues of injustice. An investigator studies with a group of inner-city elementary school students regarding the forces that might bring them to devalue their bilingualism. In the process they study literature that connects home cultures, class differences, and present-day stereotypes to the current movement for English-only education and, through their knowledge production, they assert their bilingual voices through myriad channels, from bilingual readings to peer education programs that allow them to teach monolingual students a second language. As a team, investigators and students work together to uncover the benefits of bilingualism through an exploration of the lives of community members who are monolingual, building a repertoire of ideas for supporting the cross-cultural knowledge that comes from knowing two languages. Through integration, the most precocious research practices bring young human beings to self-actualize, students and investigators are not only learning new ways of conducting research, but also to read, write, and communicate. With their interest piqued and a sense that their lives are worthy of study, the researcher and the researched learn that assessment is not just conforming to the demands of schools, but sharing critical aspects of their identity and life experiences.

Soto and Swadener's book illuminates the synergy between two often competing conceptions of research, that the belief in equal moral worth can be considered in relation to culturally relevant research methodologies, and it can be done through research with children and youth, who, it seems through the work of the authors included here, offer the cleverest voices.

REFERENCES

Bakhtin, M. M. (1990). Authory and hero in aesthetic activity. In M. Holquist & V. Liapunov (Eds.), *Art and answerability: Early philosophical essays by M. M. Bakhtin* (V. Liapunov, Trans.) (pp. 4–456). Austin: University of Texas Press.

Cannella, G. S. (1997). *Deconstructing early childhood education: Social justice and revolution.* New York: Peter Lang.

Foucault, M. (1989). The end of the monarchy of sex. In S. Lotringer (Ed.), *Foucault live: Interviews, 1966–1984* (J. Johnson, Trans.). New York: Semiotext(e).

Grant, C. A. (2003). Oppression, privilege, and high-stakes testing. *Multicultural Perspectives, 6*(1), 3–11.

Greene, M. (1995). *Releasing the imagination.* San Francisco: Jossey-Bass.

Kincheloe, J., & Steinberg, S. (1993). A tentative description of post-formal thinking: The critical confrontation with cognitive theory. *Harvard Educational Review, 63*(3), 296–320.

Raizen, S. (1989). *Reforming education for work: A cognitive science perspective.* Berkeley, CA: NCRVE.

CONTRIBUTORS

ADLER, SUSAN MATOBA, is assistant professor in the Department of Curriculum and Instruction at the University of Illinois at Urbana-Champaign. She has been on the Early Childhood Education faculty at the University of Michigan (Ann Arbor and Flint), the University of Wisconsin (Madison and Platteville), and Oakland University in Michigan. Her research focuses on Asian-American families and she has written *Mothering, Education, and Ethnicity: The Transformation of Japanese American Children.*

BLAISE, MINDY, is a senior lecturer in New Learning at RMIT University, Australia. Before receiving her doctorate from Teachers College, Columbia University, she was an early childhood teacher. Mindy is interested in using alternative theoretical perspectives such as feminist poststructuralism in researching and teaching to make sense of the complexities of classroom life.

BRADBURRY, KELLY, is a literacy coach for Indianapolis Public Schools. She is a former fifth-grade teacher.

EDMISTON, BRIAN, is an associate professor of Teaching and Learning at Ohio State University. His research interests include action research in the uses of play, drama, and imagination in the classroom. He is coauthor of *Imagining to Learn: Inquiry, Ethics, and Integration through Drama* and is currently completing *Playing for Life: A Father and Son Imagining Ethical Selves.*

GENISHI, CELIA, is a professor of Education and coordinator of the Program in Early Childhood, the Department of Curriculum and Teaching, Teachers College, Columbia University. She is coauthor (with Anne Haas Dyson) of *Language Assessment in the Early Years*; (with Millie Almy) of *Ways of Studying Children*, editor of *Ways of Assessing Children and Curriculum*, and coeditor (with Anne Haas Dyson) of *The Need for Story: Cultural Diversity in Classroom and Community*. She is also the author of articles about children's language, classroom observation, and assessment. Her research interests include collaborative research with teachers on alternative assessments, childhood bilingualism, and language use in classrooms—all topics related to her overall interest in social justice.

GRAUE, ELIZABETH, is a professor in the Department of Curriculum and Instruction at the University of Wisconsin–Madison, where she teaches courses in early childhood education and research methods. Her work is currently focused on inclusive home–school relations, examining the perspectives held by parents, children, preservice teachers, and practicing teachers.

GUITIERREZ-GOMEZ, CATHY, teaches in the Early Childhood Multicultural Education program at the University of New Mexico in Albuquerque. Her research interests include young children and language and literacy development, multicultural teacher preparation, parent involvement, full-day kindergarten, and children's videos and their impact on children's developing perceptions. She has made numerous presentations at early childhood professional conferences, including NAEYC, NABE, ACEI, and Head Start.

HABASHI, JANETTE, is a Palestinian from the old city of Jerusalem. She was educated in Ramallah and earned a degree in Social Work from Bethlehem University in the West Bank in 1992. The British Council in Jerusalem awarded her a two-year fellowship to finish her master's degree in Counseling in Education. She started her doctoral program at Hebrew University, and then transferred to Kent State University in Ohio, where she completed her Ph.D. in 2003.

HATZINIKOLAOU, AGGELOS, is a doctoral student in Elementary Education at Aristotle University of Thessaloniki, Greece, who has worked as a teacher for seventeen years, ten of which were with children excluded from or at risk for failure at school, for example, Roma children either in their own settlements or in neighboring schools in underprivileged areas in Thessaloniki. The last two years he has taught prison inmates basic literacy and numeracy.

HAWKINS, MARGARET R., is an assistant professor in the Department of Curriculum and Instruction at the University of Wisconsin at Madison, where she directs the ESL and bilingual certification and graduate programs. Her professional career includes teaching and scholarship in the areas of literacies, sociolinguistics, and language teacher education. Current projects include collaborative research on the language and literacy development of young English learners in schools, and supporting/researching school-based initiatives on home–school relations.

HONG, MIN, is an assistant professor of Education at Teachers College, Columbia University. Previously, she was an early childhood teacher at The William T. Harris School, a public school, in New York City. Min is a National Board Certified Teacher. She is the author of numerous articles and books for early childhood teachers. Her research interests include English Language Learners, professional development for early childhood teachers, culturally responsive practice with parents, and early literacy instruction.

JIPSON, JANICE, is a professor of Interdisciplinary Studies at National Louis University. She received her B.S. in English, M.S. in School Psychology, and Ph.D. in Curriculum Studies–Early Childhood Education, all from the University of Wisconsin–Madison. Her recent publications include *Repositioning Feminism and Education: Perspectives on Educating for Social Change; Daredevil Research: Recreating Analytic Practice; Intersections: Feminisms/Early Childhoods; Questions of You and the Struggle for Collaborative Life;* and *Resistance and Representation: Rethinking Childhood Education.* Her current research focuses on Elizabeth Peabody.

JIPSON, JENNIFER, is an assistant professor at Sarah Lawrence College. She received her B.A. from Smith College and received her M.S. and Ph.D. in Developmental Psychology from the University of California–Santa Cruz. Following her doctoral work, Jennifer completed a postdoctoral fellowship in Developmental Psychology at the University of Michigan. Her research focuses on young children's cognitive and language development in the context of everyday family activity (e.g., parent–child interaction, visits to museums, and other informal learning environments).

KINCHELOE, JOE, is professor of education at the City University of New York Graduate Center and Brooklyn College where he serves as the Belle Zeller Chair of Public Policy and Administration. He is the author of numerous books and articles about pedagogy, research, education and social justice, issues of cognition and cultural context, and educational reform. His books include *Teachers as Researchers, Toil and Trouble, Getting Beyond the Facts: Teaching Social Studies/Social Sciences in the Twenty-First Century, Multiple Intelligences Reconsidered, The Sign of the Burger: McDonald's and the Culture of Power,* and *Changing Multiculturalism* (with Shirley Steinberg). His coedited works include *White Reign: Deploying Whiteness in America* and the Gustavus Myers Human Rights award winner, *Measured Lies: The Bell Curve Examined.*

LASTA, JULIANA, is a doctoral student at Teachers College, Columbia University. Born and raised in Argentina, she received her bachelor's degree in School Psychology. While in Argentina, she worked in a medical facility for economically disadvantaged children, providing assessment to over twenty schools in the hospital district in math and language arts, and conducted family therapy to promote social and learning abilities in children. She is currently a guest lecturer at several universities in Argentina and continues her studies in her two main interests: education and family therapy.

MARTÍNEZ-ROLDÁN, CARMEN, is an assistant professor at Arizona State University. She received and completed a two-year postdoctoral fellowship at the University of Iowa. She earned her Ph.D. in Language, Reading, and Culture from the University of Arizona and has a master's degree in Curriculum and Instruction and a second concentration on Administration and Supervision of Schools from the University of Puerto Rico and the Dominican Republic.

MEDINA, CARMEN, is an assistant professor in the Department of Language and Literacy Education at the University of British Columbia, Vancouver, where she teaches courses on elementary language literacy education. Her research examines students' responses to Latino/a children's literature, Latino/a literary theory, biliteracy, and drama in education.

MITAKIDOU, SOULA, is an assistant professor in the Department of Primary Education at Aristotle University in Thessaloniki, Greece. Her teaching experience covers a wide age range from preschool to graduate school students, and she has worked extensively with teachers in in-service workshops. Her recent publications and presentations focus on many aspects of diversity, including integrated instructional strategies and marginalized learners. She has also translated and published Greek folktales and co-authored children's books.

PEARSON, SUSAN, is an English as a Second Language teacher for Indianapolis public schools.

SOTO, LOURDES DIAZ, is a professor of Education at the Pennsylvania State University. She has taught and worked with families and children in Puerto Rico (Dorado Academy), Florida (Florida Atlantic University), New York City (Teachers College, Columbia University), and Pennsylvania (Lehigh University and Penn State). Her publications include *Language, Culture, and Power: Bilingual Families Struggle for Quality Education* and two edited volumes entitled *Making a Difference in the Lives of Bilingual/Bicultural Learners* and *The Politics of Early Childhood Education*. Scholarship and collegial opportunities have taken her to Costa Rica, Greece, Spain, Taiwan, Norway, and Uruguay. In addition, she has published numerous refereed articles and book chapters examining issues of social justice and equity.

SUN, YU-CHI, born and raised in Taiwan, is currently a Ph.D. candidate at The Pennsylvania State University. She has taught English as a foreign language to young students in the elementary, secondary, and junior college levels, as well as adult students in Taipei, Taiwan. She is currently completing her doctoral thesis, which has been chosen to receive the 2003 Pennsylvania Educational Research Association (PERA) Outstanding Research Award. Using narrative inquiry, she has been writing the experiences of three young Chinese immigrant daughters through their own perceptions of their schooling, family relationships, and self-identity.

SWADENER, BETH BLUE, is professor of Early Childhood Education and Policy Studies at Arizona State University and does research on social policy, professional development, language and culture issues, and early education in Sub-Saharan Africa. Her edited and coauthored books include *Reconceptualizing the Early Childhood Curriculum; Children and Families "At Promise": Deconstructing the Discourse of Risk; Semiotics of Dis/ability: Interrogating Categories of Difference; Does the Village Still Raise the Child?: A Collaborative Study in Changing Childrearing and Early Education in Kenya;* and *Decolonizing Research in Cross-Cultural Contexts: Critical Personal Narratives*. Beth is active in a number of peace, social justice, and child advocacy groups.

VANDEN WYNGAARD, MARGUERITE, is a third-generation professional musician and began her career in secondary choral education. After fourteen years in the secondary classroom, she earned a Ph.D. in Curriculum and Instruction and has begun to establish herself in understanding, practice, and curriculum alignment that support culturally relevant pedagogy. Currently, she is director of Achievement Initiatives at Washtenaw Intermediate School District, in Ann Arbor, Michigan, where she is a leader in professional development and continues to lead workshops in Unlearning Oppression as well as culturally relevant pedagogy.

RETHINKING CHILDHOOD

JOE L. KINCHELOE & JANICE A. JIPSON, *General Editors*

A revolution is occurring regarding the study of childhood. Traditional notions of child development are under attack, as are the methods by which children are studied. At the same time, the nature of childhood itself is changing as children gain access to information once reserved for adults only. Technological innovations, media, and electronic information have narrowed the distinction between adults and children, forcing educators to rethink the world of schooling in this new context.

This series of textbooks and monographs encourages scholarship in all of these areas, eliciting critical investigations in developmental psychology, early childhood education, multicultural education, and cultural studies of childhood.

Proposals and manuscripts may be sent to the general editors:

>Joe L. Kincheloe
>c/o Peter Lang Publishing, Inc.
>275 Seventh Avenue, 28th floor
>New York, New York 10001

To order other books in this series, please contact our Customer Service Department at:

>(800) 770-LANG (within the U.S.)
>(212) 647-7706 (outside the U.S.)
>(212) 647-7707 FAX

Or browse online by series at:
>www.peterlangusa.com